Even the demons submit

Occasional Papers, no. 25
Institute of Mennonite Studies

Occasional Papers are occasional publications of the Institute of Mennonite Studies at Associated Mennonite Biblical Seminary, Elkhart, Indiana. IMS was founded in 1958 to promote and create opportunities for research, conversation, and publication on topics and issues vital to Mennonite congregations and the Anabaptist faith tradition.

In the Occasional Papers series, IMS—sometimes in collaboration with other Mennonite publishers—publishes essays in the fields of Bible, history, theology, ethics, and pastoral ministry. The intent of the series is to foster discussion and to seek counsel, particularly from within the Mennonite theological community. Many essays are in finished form; some may be in a more germinal stage, released for purposes of testing and inviting critical response.

In accepting papers for publication, IMS gives priority to authors (faculty, students, alumni) from Mennonite seminaries, colleges, and universities.

Even the demons submit

Continuing Jesus' ministry of deliverance

Edited by Loren L. Johns and James R. Krabill

Institute of Mennonite Studies
Elkhart, Indiana

Co-published with Herald Press
Scottdale, Pennsylvania
Waterloo, Ontario

3003 Benham Avenue, Elkhart, Indiana 46517-1999
www.ambs.edu/IMS

Co-published with Herald Press
616 Walnut Avenue, Scottdale, Pennsylvania 15683
490 Dutton Drive, Unit C8, Waterloo, Ontario N2L 6H7
www.heraldpress.com

Printed in the United States of America
by Evangel Press, Nappanee, Indiana
Institute of Mennonite Studies ISBN 0-936273-40-2

Library of Congress Cataloging-in-Publication Data

Even the demons submit : continuing Jesus' ministry of deliverance / edited by Loren L. Johns and James R. Krabill.
p. cm. — (Occasional papers ; no. 25)
Some contributions are from a conference held in Apr. 2004.
Includes bibliographical references (p.) and indexes.
ISBN 0-936273-40-2 (alk. paper)
1. Exorcism—Congresses. 2. Demonology—Mennonites—Congresses. I. Johns, Loren L. II. Krabill, James R. III. Series: Occasional papers (Institute of Mennonite Studies (Elkhart, Ind.)) ; no. 25.
BV873.E8E84 2006
235'.4—dc22
2006015175

Book design by Mary E. Klassen.

Dedication

To Dean Hochstetler

"The seventy returned with joy, saying,
'Lord, in your name even the demons submit to us!'
He said to them,
'I watched Satan fall from heaven like a flash of lightning.
See, I have given you authority to tread on snakes and scorpions,
and over all the power of the enemy;
and nothing will hurt you.
Nevertheless, do not rejoice at this,
that the spirits submit to you,
but rejoice that your names are written in heaven.'"

Luke 10:17-20

Contents

Foreword

Mary H. Schertz

Before we begin reading the Bible, we bind the spirits, Bob Ekblad told us. It was a most unlikely setting for an exorcism. I was sitting in a posh hotel meeting room in Philadelphia, surrounded by professors and graduate students at the annual meeting of the Society of Biblical Literature. I had been drawn to this workshop by the author of *Reading the Bible with the Damned,*[1] because I had read a powerful article he had written about teaching the Bible in a prison in Washington State.[2] I had expected to hear him talk about doing Bible study. Instead, he told us we would be reading the Bible together. He would do with us a study that he had done earlier that week with the prisoners. He would use with us the same teaching strategies that he used with the inmates of Skagit County jail. So, before we started, we would ask Jesus to bind the spirits. We needed to name them, and then we would pray.

This roomful of proper academics began tentatively, a little nervously. But with Ekblad's gentle direction, we were soon moving into authentic naming of the demons dogging us in this particular setting—spirits of competition, envy, insecurity, pride, doubt. Then in a simple, almost matter-of-fact prayer of deliverance, our teacher asked Jesus to bind those spirits and to free our minds and hearts for this reading of the text. What followed was remarkable, remarkable in any setting, but near miraculous in the somewhat sterile atmosphere of a major academic convention. It was holy ground. In those simple exercises of listening hard to the word of God in scripture and in one another, healing happened. We became what we in fact were but had been keeping hidden: weary and needy pilgrims taking refreshment at this unlikely way station. There was grace.

---

1. Bob Ekblad, *Reading the Bible with the Damned* (Louisville, KY: Westminster John Knox Press, 2005).

2. "Jesus' Surprising Offer of Living Cocaine," in *Through the Eyes of Another: Intercultural Reading of the Bible,* ed. Hans de Wit et al. (Elkhart, IN: Institute of Mennonite Studies, 2004), 131–41.

For me, Bob Ekblad's simple act of asking Jesus to bind the spirits resonated strongly with the conference several years earlier that generated the essays in this volume. At that conference, as in the Philadelphia hotel, people with widely divergent ways of thinking gathered to learn how God is at work resisting evil. The Institute of Mennonite Studies consultation, "Hard Cases: Confronting the Spirit World," held at Associated Mennonite Biblical Seminary in April 2004, brought together pastors, scholars, people engaged in deliverance ministries, and not a few people who had experienced deliverance. There were two powerful impulses behind that conference. One was the integrity and charism of Dean Hochstetler, a pastor ordained for deliverance ministry by Indiana-Michigan Mennonite Conference, and the clear testimonies of the many people he has helped find their way back to God. The other was a profound sense of need on the part of some area pastors of congregations providing care for families overwhelmed by chaotic and demonic factors. These are the pastors and these are the congregations dealing—with great courage, deep compassion, and too few resources—with what Duane Beck describes as hard cases, situations in which a variety of illnesses, addictions, sins, and poverties "ravage people at an accelerating pace over several generations." The goal of the conference was to provide a setting for conversation about what deliverance ministries have to contribute to these congregational situations and, just as important, what congregations have to contribute to the ministry of deliverance.

The night we heard "Gwen's" story[3] was the moment when I finally understood, heart and head, that exorcism in the context of congregational compassion and accountability is one way God overcomes evil. One refrain in the story that Gwen told, with her pastor, Duane Beck, was "Nothing worked; everything helped." The healing that was in process in Gwen's life and in her family had many facets. Help had come from many directions—the children's schools, the local police force, social workers, the church, her pastors, and Dean Hochstetler. In that mix, there had been no single answer. There had been no easy answer. Healing continued to be a process, and much was still chaotic in her household. But in that mix, and in that still-messy process of coming back to God, Dean's ministry and the congregational support and follow-up to that ministry had played a vital role. Confronting the spirits and binding them marked a significant turning point.

3. See chapter 9 in this volume and Duane Beck's reflections in chapter 10.

Her teenagers, she told us, still said every night a prayer that Dean taught them.

As with all conferences, many words were spoken in the course of several days. But when Gwen and Duane finished speaking, words failed us. There was a silence and then, as one, the attending body rose in ovation. Smiles and tears and clapping hands said "Thanks be to God," in ways that we could not then put into words. We finished the evening by walking in silence to the chapel to sing the hymns of our tradition that speak explicitly about the demonic. Singing, we were reminded that if evil gathers force over the generations, so also does the power of God to resist that evil. We are not alone in the fight. Others have gone before, and others will come after us. We are the temporary stewards of these ministries.

Just as hard cases are complicated and messy, just as finding our way back to God is complicated and messy, so conversation about these matters is also complicated and messy. This book reflects that reality. Here you will find different pieces of the puzzle—not only different perspectives and points of view but also different kinds of material. Some essays are articulated with scholarly care. Others are reflections from a pastoral heart. There are stories and case studies. Some of what you will read here is intensely personal. Some of what you will read steps back to offer a larger perspective on the matter. Some of what you will read here is painful, and some of it is joyful. Our aim for the book is to reflect conversation and to promote conversation.

The diversity of the book is an attempt to honor the complexity of the issue. If you are looking for a simple how-to manual, this book is not for you. If you are looking for a single, easy answer, this book is not for you. But if you want to participate in conversation about the hard and holy work of partnering with God in the battle against evil, you will find much to ponder in this book. If you want to reflect on and care for the people around you who are struggling with hard cases, this book is for you. It is our hope that the varied voices represented in these pages will contribute to the church's discernment and faithful practice in this arena.

Acknowledgements

The editors and publishers extend our thanks to Dean Hochstetler, without whom the Hard Cases consultation and this book would never have happened. We also thank Harold Bauman and Duane Beck, who served with the Institute of Mennonite Studies staff and the editors to plan the consultation. And we thank all the presenters and writers who contributed to this volume, as well as Nelson Kraybill and Associated Mennonite Biblical Seminary, who have generously supported this project and the ongoing work of the IMS.

Much gratitude also goes to Barbara Nelson Gingerich, who managed the book project and edited it with her customary wise counsel and attention to detail. We are grateful, too, to Willard Swartley for his extraordinary effort in compiling a most useful bibliography, to Mary Klassen, whose sensitivity to good design is reflected in the appearance of the book, to Karen Ritchie for her fine copyediting services, and to James Nelson Gingerich, who contributed late night and early morning hours to format its pages.

Understanding the challenge

Chapter 1

Worldviews and why they matter

Paul G. Hiebert

To situate myself and provide a context for the following reflections, I should say that I am a member of the tribe of Anabaptists, of the clan of Mennonite Brethren, and that I grew up and did my college and seminary training within Mennonite circles. I have spent most of my adult life as a missiologist, having completed my seminary training at Mennonite Brethren Biblical Seminary, and later my anthropology degree at the University of Washington.

None of this, of course, makes treating the vast topic of worldviews any easier. In fact, the overwhelming task assigned to me here reminds me of a cartoon in the *Indian Times* a few years ago. The leading Indian cartoonist presented a scene in which a politician was addressing a large audience and began by announcing that "the subject on which I am about to address you is so controversial, I shall deny at the outset every remark I am about to make." With that disclaimer in mind, let us reflect a bit on the worldview question and why it is important to our understanding of the spiritual realities we encounter in our homes, neighborhoods, and faith communities.

A personal experience that changed my understanding

Years ago, I was preparing an article and could not seem to come up with a title for the piece. At the last minute, I decided to call it "The Flaw of the Excluded Middle."[1] In that now somewhat notorious publication, I describe my first years as a missionary in India. I recount how in preparation for that assignment—teaching Bible and other courses at the seminary and university—I had studied diligently, reading all the Hindu texts I could get my hands on. I was

1. "The Flaw of the Excluded Middle," chap. 12 in *Anthropological Reflections on Missiological Issues*, by Paul G. Hiebert (Grand Rapids, MI: Baker Books, 1994), 189–215. The article first appeared in *Missiology: An International Review* 10 (January 1982): 35–47. For an interpretation of this article's contribution to missiological studies, see "Flaw of the Excluded Middle," in *Evangelical Dictionary of World Missions*, ed. A. Scott Moreau (Grand Rapids, MI: Baker Books, 2000).

committed to finding a way of presenting the gospel winsomely to any Hindus I might meet.

When at last I had the opportunity to visit the villages of south India, accompanying my students on evangelistic trips, I seized the occasion to talk to the local people about Christ and Christian faith—about Christianity and Hindu philosophy and how the two compared and differed. To my great surprise, I soon discovered that the villagers had no idea what I was talking about. I found myself in the strange position of teaching Hindu people about Hinduism, in order to counter Hinduism! In many cases, it seemed, I actually knew more about Hinduism than they did! I thought, Now, this is nonsense. What is really going on here?

These experiences convinced me that I needed to live in an Indian village and study the religion of the common people. And so, for a two-year period while I worked on doctoral studies, that is exactly what I did.

What do ordinary people actually think and do? I wondered. I had studied philosophical Hinduism, assuming that most Hindus are philosophical Hindus. But they aren't. Most Hindus are ordinary folk Hindus. Just as most Muslims in today's world are folk Muslims. These practitioners have a veneer of orthodox beliefs, but just beneath the surface, most of them eke out everyday lives with little or no concern for ultimate questions. Those simply are not their issues. Their issues are diseases, success at work, and rounding up enough food each day to feed the family.

I began to study the practices in the village where I lived. Yes, I discovered, there were the well-known names of Krishna and Vishnu and Siva. And all the temples were there for worshiping Hinduism's highest divinities. But I also began to hear about Maisamma, Boscamma, Yellamma, Mudelamma, Ankalamma—and the names of four hundred or so smaller spirits that were running around everywhere and occupying a central place in people's minds and lives. None of these spirits, I would learn, are an official part of Hinduism, yet they were very much a part of life.

In village life, one might find the occasional person philosophizing about Hindu thought and practice. But I began to be aware that most people were busily practicing their daily folk religions—or animistic beliefs. Although a few people managed to integrate these in practicing their official religion, everyday life for most people focused almost exclusively on folk rites and beliefs. The result was that exorcisms, witchcraft, divination, and the evil eye were far more prominent features of the religion than were the official rituals carried out in the temple.

This observation eventually led me to a study of Indian Christians as well. There I discovered something remarkably similar—namely, that Christians went to church on Sunday, took baptism, and succeeded in articulating central Christian beliefs. But if you went to an ordinary house on an ordinary day and looked at what Christians were actually doing, they were also going to the diviner and the sorcerer for counsel and healing. Why? Because they had ended up with what we sometimes call split-level Christianity. As a result of our mission efforts, Hindus embraced the Christian message. As we brought hospitals, they began to show up at our institutions, seeking assistance. But the urgent daily questions asked at the middle level of people's lives, we were not answering. What we got, therefore, were Christians who went to church on Sunday, and when they were sick, they went to the hospital. But when a real crisis hit them or their families, they went off to see the shaman, the diviner, or a traditional healer who could address their need.

Why it is so important to study and understand worldview

I recently visited a village in India and noticed some big white crosses on the houses. I was impressed with this initiative and asked some of the local Christians about this form of public testimony. Oh, no, I was told, the crosses were not a testimony to the gospel. They were put up to protect the households against people who wished to do them harm or make them sick by looking at them with the evil eye. So all the Christians now use crosses to protect themselves, instead of using the charms and amulets they would have used before becoming Christians. This story reminds us that we cannot limit our understanding of what is going on to the level of formal Christianity. We must also come to grips theologically with—and provide answers to—people's beliefs and understandings at the level of folk religion. For this reason, it is important to address the issue of worldview early in the study of spiritual realities.

Worldviews exert their influence at the deepest level of a culture. All cultures have surface patterns of behavior—shaking hands, putting on clothes, sitting on chairs, for example. They create products—tables, airplanes, and houses. They develop belief systems—myths, creeds, and rituals. But behind and beneath all this, at the deepest level of a culture, one uncovers not only what people think *about*, but what they think *with*. Admittedly, it is hard to think about what we are thinking with, precisely because we are using it to think! But what one discovers, if one persists at this deepest exploration, is the logic, the assumptions, and the categories that make up a person's foundational worldview.

The modern secular worldview shapes our approach to spiritual realities

So what are the presuppositions we in the West bring to bear on the matter of spiritual realities? How has our worldview shaped the way we apprehend and approach this issue with which are increasingly faced?

Twenty or thirty years ago, this topic would not have been an issue on any major screen or conference agenda of the day. How did we get to that point from a time in the Middle Ages when spiritual matters would have been an issue in the life of the church? To be ordained, a priest had to "renounce the devil and all his ways." Exorcisms were a standard part of the rituals of the church. Deliverance ministries were a pastoral service the church was expected to offer to afflicted people in need.

The problem we face goes back to the period of the Enlightenment and the emergence of modern dualism. In this view, there is a natural world and a supernatural world. These two worlds are separate and distinct. Any intersection between them would be considered strange, highly unlikely, and enormously complex.

Key to the Greek worldview the West inherited is a sharp division between the spiritual or supernatural domain and the natural one. In the supernatural realm, according to this view, are beings such as God, demons, and angels. And in the natural domain are humans, animals, plants, and inanimate matter.

In many teaching contexts over the years, I have asked students to place in like categories a given list of items. Almost without thinking, participants in the exercise put together: *man, woman, girl*—human; *dog, cow, lion*—animal; *tree, bush, grass*—plant; *rocks, sand*—matter; *God, angels, demons*—supernatural. Perhaps 95 percent of seminarians perform as everyone else does, establishing similar categories and thus betraying their status as cardinal heretics, apparently ignorant or unaware of the biblical worldview, which puts things together quite differently.

This division of reality into natural and supernatural categories led in the West to a division between religion and science. This division is so common and assumed by now that we can hardly imagine things in any other way. A recent dissertation out of Cambridge has shown that the word *religion* emerged only around the seventeenth century. And it was defined by science at that time as "what science is not"! So defined, religion emerged as a product of the Enlightenment!

Most languages outside of the West do not have a word for religion. In the Western tradition, religion gradually became that which deals with matters of faith, while science developed as a discipline focusing on matters of experience and fact. Religion, in this view, has to do with otherworldly problems, and science has to do with this-worldly affairs.

Because science has to do with the natural order, if God wants to intervene in the earthly realm, God has to do a miracle—that is, God has to break the laws of nature. Thus, the natural order is what has become thought of as scientific knowledge or, as Lesslie Newbigin puts it, "public proof." Everyone who goes to school studies science—in

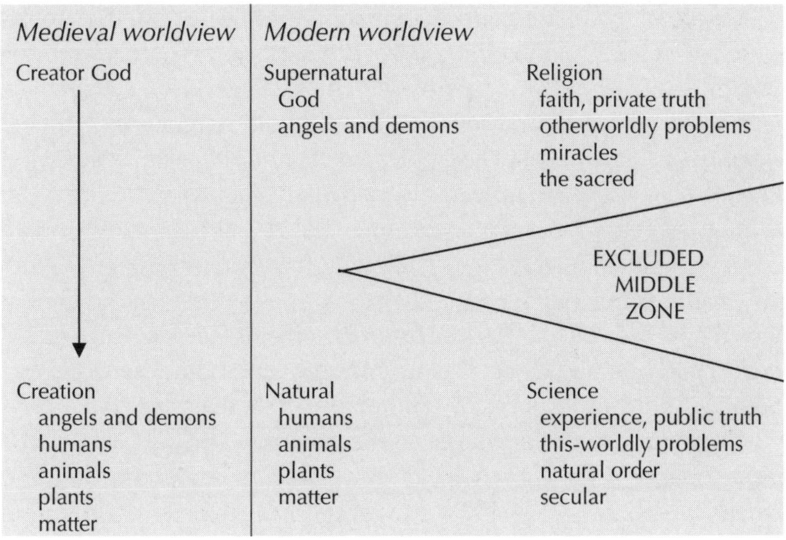

Fig. 1.1. The emergence of the modern worldview.

Christian and non-Christian institutions alike. But faith is a matter of private truth. One can teach it, if one chooses, in a Christian school, but it would be inappropriate to do so in a public secular university. To speak of truth, in the post-Enlightenment era, is to speak of science. Religion, on the other hand, is a matter of personal opinion and is relegated to the private sphere (see fig. 1.1).

Consequences for our understanding of spiritual realities

For eleven years, I taught at two major American universities. It was a given among most of my colleagues that God did not exist, that the modern world did not need to work with that "assumption" any longer.

Scientist Pierre-Simon Laplace is said to have observed, "We do not take angels and demons seriously." And I would dare to say that most Christians do not take them seriously either! How many Western Christians look for an angel when they step into a room? How many look for a demon? Yet my Indian friend Muggayya would always look around whenever he walked into a room to find out what spirits were there. It was a routine exercise.

Most Western Christians have embraced the modern scientific dichotomy between secular and sacred, natural and supernatural, science and religion, facts and faith, and between natural laws and miracles. Many follow their secular colleagues and neighbors in denying or at least questioning the reality of the supernatural and the possibility of what some refer to as "spiritual warfare." For secularists, such talk is superstition, the legacy of old religious beliefs that must be displaced by hard scientific facts and theories. If there is a battle being fought, it is the one we are waging here on earth between human systems, between different social structures, and between competing ideologies.

On the other hand, some Christians make sense of the dualist worldview they have inherited by embracing the view that if a battle is currently being waged, it is up in the heavens between God and Satan. There may be occasional fallout from that conflict that affects earth dwellers, but by and large, in their opinion, this battle is not one being fought at the earthly level in the here and now (see fig. 1.2).

Modern secular view	*Modern Christian view*
	Supernatural realm battle in the heavens between God and his angels, and Satan and his demons
Natural realm battle on earth between systems and individuals	Natural realm battle on earth between systems and individuals

Fig. 1.2. Modern views of spiritual warfare.

A cultural shift in the West regarding spiritual realities

For many years, the impact of this dualist worldview has shaped our perception of spiritual realities. It has led to a practical denial of any thing spiritual or supernatural in the natural realm that makes up most of our everyday lives. It has relegated God, as a supernatural being, to the heavens, and it has encouraged us to believe that any entry God might make into the natural realm has to be in the form of miracles that violate the natural laws of the material world. In consequence, humans see God present in the world only through miracles and not in the order of everyday living.

More seriously, we have learned to split reality into spiritual and natural realms rather than to view creation as an integrated whole. Liberal scholars have often denied spirit possession and have tried to explain such phenomena in biological or psychological terms. On the other hand, conservatives have often sought to explain spirit possession as radically distinct from and outside of any biological, psychological, or psychosocial considerations. Many current discussions in the West are still deeply shaped by this colossal divide.

A number of new developments in recent years indicate a shift in our thinking on these matters. First, in what is now being referred to as our postmodern world, we have begun to move away from the stark secularism of modernity that attempted to reduce everything to mere materiality. In its place, we are opening ourselves up to new worlds and alternative explanations of the reality around us.

Second, we are gaining an awareness that even in the modern worldview that lingers in our culture today, most of our entertainment depends on what Walter Wink has called "the myth of redemptive violence."[2] Even though in our rationalist, scientific worldview we have made every effort to rid ourselves of all things spiritual, much of popular culture—in particular the entertainment world and the sports industry—reflects the deep and intense "spiritual" nature of what is happening in these cultural expressions.

Third, more than 60 percent of the global faith family now resides in non-Western regions of the world. For most of these younger churches in Latin America, Africa, and Asia, the existence of spiritual realities is not debated. It is simply assumed and dealt with as a natural part of life. Western Christians may not always agree with the assessment and treatment of spiritual realities by churches in the South, but these churches take this realm seriously and will no doubt challenge the older churches to reexamine their attitudes toward things spiritual for many years to come.

Three emerging explanations of the spirit world

I believe that today in our post-postmodern world, as Huston Smith calls it, there are three principal worldviews that challenge the assumptions of modern science and vie for our attention in attempting to explain the spiritual reality of the world in which we live. These three approaches we will refer to as the tribal, the Indo-European, and the biblical worldviews.

The tribal worldview. Many younger churches today in Africa, Latin America, and parts of Asia come from what we might refer to as animistic backgrounds. By some estimates, more than 60 percent of the world's tribes believe in a high God. But in most of these cases, that God has departed from our world, leaving a huge gap between us as humans and this high God.

According to one West African tradition, for example, God created humans and took young men out to show them how to hunt. He taught these men always to carry their spears vertically so as not to poke the hunters walking ahead of them in the tall jungle grasses. But one young man said, "I don't care. I'm going to do what I want." So he held his spear at an angle out in front of him, and he poked God in the back. God said, "These people are hopeless." And so he left the world of humans and went away.

2. See Walter Wink, *Engaging the Powers: Discernment and Resistance in a World of Domination* (Minneapolis: Fortress Press, 1992).

According to another of many such stories, women who were pounding grain in a mortar lifted their pestles too high in the sky and hit God, sitting up there in the clouds. So God said, "These people are hopeless." And he went away, leaving us humans in a world full of all kinds of spirits, smaller gods, and powers.

In a tribal worldview, the earth and sky are inhabited by many different territorial spirits, shades, departed ancestors, animal spirits, witches, ghosts, and magical powers (see fig. 1.3). These forces are capricious, neither totally good (angels), nor totally bad (demons). They help those who placate them, and they harm those who oppose their wishes or neglect them or refuse to honor them.

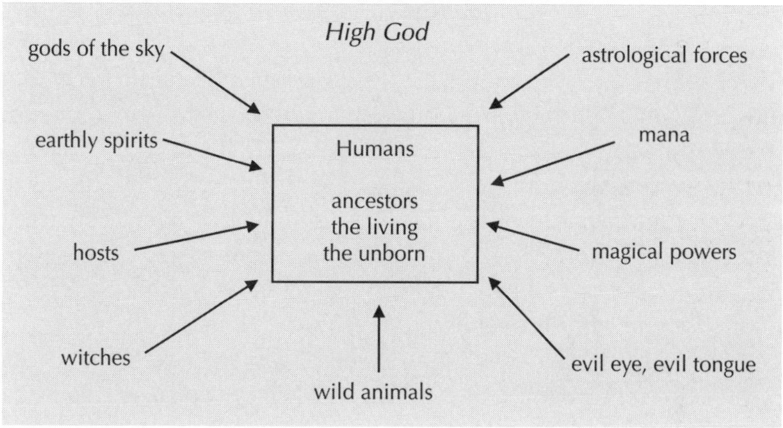

Fig. 1.3. The tribal worldview.

These territorial spirits are not heavenly spirits; they are earthbound. In the case of Indian villages, their power extends for only about ten miles. Such spirits have never been to heaven; they take part in the earth village, making life difficult for people who refuse to recognize their presence, and exercising power over everyday happenings and life experiences.

The supreme value for most people in such cultures is to enjoy good, long, and prosperous lives; to have many children; and to be remembered after they are gone. In contrast, evil is misfortune, sickness, untimely death, poverty, barrenness, and other such human problems. To achieve a full and prosperous life, people must placate the spirits and control the spiritual powers wishing to do them harm. Any and all methods may be used, one at a time or simultaneously, as long as they prove effective.

Because of the territorial nature of the tribal worldview, spiritual warfare is often perceived as a matter of our gods battling your gods, my magic battling your magic, and our shamans battling the world of spiritual forces. If we win the battle, it is because our gods are stronger. If we lose, it is because the enemy's gods are stronger.

Successful power encounters sometimes result in people following the victorious gods. This outcome is especially interesting where tribes and their gods are thought of in territorial terms, and where land plays an important role in people's view of the spiritual warfare taking place.

Those of us who have grown up in Western cultures are suspicious of animistic worldviews. We come barging into tribal cultures, saying, "Well, these things don't really exist, right?" In India, I sometimes found myself questioning what I was hearing and seeing. Early one morning, my friend Ayyanna burst into my room and woke me up, scared to death. "What's the matter, Ayyanna?" I asked.

"I was coming home from taking care of the sheep," he said. "My brother came out to replace me in keeping watch over the sheep, and I returned home in the middle of the night to get some sleep. As I came near the village, near Muggayya's cattle shed, a *rakshasa* jumped on me and threw me to the ground."

I had not yet learned what a rakshasa was, so I asked, "What's a rakshasa?" On hearing that a rakshasa is a large spirit with a huge head, bulging eyes, and protruding fangs, I thought to myself, "If that had jumped on me, I'd have been afraid too." At a deeper level, however, I was thinking, "Hmm, two o'clock in the morning, heavy curry dinner, half asleep, walks down the moonlit road, comes into the shadow of a tree, has palpitations, gets panicked, falls on the ground, finally recovers, and gets home." You see what I did with Ayyanna's story? I wrote it off as superstitious and nonsensical!

Soon after this happened, Muggayya, the owner of the cattle shed, came to see me, and I said, "Well, I suppose you've heard that a rakshasa attacked Ayyanna last night." Muggayya replied, with a perfectly straight face, "Was it down by my cattle shed?" I said, "Yes, but how did you know that?" He said, "Well, that's where one lives."

After this event, I talked to other villagers and discovered that half of them claimed to have seen the spirit. The other half had not seen it but clearly believed it existed. They were eager to show me the rakshasa, so we went down to the cattle shed and looked in the well where it was said to live, but the rakshasa was not at home that day, and I did not get to see it.

Does one need to see a rakshasa in order to believe it? Five hundred people in that village would testify to having seen it. No Western person has ever seen Hannibal or Julius Caesar, but we all believe in their existence, based on the testimony of others. Scientifically, it would appear that I need to accept the claims about the rakshasa, because of all the local evidence.

What do we do with such things? Our Western tendency is to reject them all. Yet ghosts and witches are a big issue in Africa now, as the problem of witchcraft reasserts itself and challenges the churches to respond. There are other forces as well: astrological forces, magic powers in divination, and forces that radiate something like supernatural electricity.

If a snake bites you in an Indian village, the clairvoyant will come and say a chant over you seven times for every stripe across the viper's back. Our Western response is: Does it ever work? Well, yes, sometimes you live, sometimes you die. But does it *really* work, we want to know?

To be fair, we also need to ask whether modern medicine works. Do we believe in it? Of course! But where do people take the most medicine? In the hospital. And where do many people die? In the hospital! Most people who die are taking a lot of medicine. A reasonable deduction is this: If you get sick, don't take medicine. Statistically, your chances of staying alive are better. Second, most people die lying down, so when you get sick and don't feel good, stand up. If you lie down, your chances of dying will only increase!

The elements we are discussing here as part of the tribal worldview are real life issues for many people around the world. In India one day, when I was visiting a village headman whom I had known for some time, I took a photograph of his little girl. A few days later, I went back to the village, and a little boy was in the headman's house. I asked, "Is this your nephew?"

"No," he said, "this is my son."

I said, "I have known you for a year or two and did not know that you had a son."

"Well," he said, "my first son died within weeks of his birth. Somebody must have had an evil eye. But we didn't know. My second son was born. He too died within weeks, so we knew it was a case of evil eye. But we had no idea who in the village was looking at our child, causing him to get sick and die because of their jealousy. So when my third son was born, we gave him a girl's name and dressed him as a girl. Nobody looks at girls, so he lived for three or four years. Now he is strong enough to be turned into a boy, so we cut his hair, changed his name, and turned the little girl into a boy." The headman had defeated the evil eye by raising his son as a daughter for the first three years of the child's life. The strategy and remedy the village leader had employed had worked.

In another instance, I learned that Muggayya (the owner of the cattle shed) had one day hitched oxen to a cart and headed out to the fields. All of a sudden, the oxen and cart ran off the road and into the bramble bushes. Muggayya returned home, explained the misfortune as an ox with indigestion, tied a new ox to the cart, and started out once again. Again the oxen ran off the road at exactly the same spot and plunged into the bramble bushes. Now this kind of thing is not likely to happen twice. So Muggayya "did a divine." Through this means, he discovered that his personal goddess-deity, Maisamma, who sits on the well at the roadside, had watched Muggayya's wife come one day to take a bath in the well. Now, Muggayya had just brought his wife a new sari, and Maisamma—a kind of second wife to Muggayya—was madly jealous. How to correct the problem was obvious: Muggayya had to buy a little sari for Maisamma, carefully tie it around her, tell her he was sorry, and repent of his oversight, before taking his ox and cart and heading back out to the field. When Muggayya had completed the prescribed ritual, the problems with the oxen in the bramble bushes came to an end.

In animistic cultures, the gospel is often seen as good news because it promises to deliver people from fear of the spirits that have plagued them, and it promises them a good life here on earth. Not surprisingly, if one promises a health-and-wealth gospel, it will attract people.

But this response raises a missiological question: Can one simply work within the religious phenomenology of a people? Can one contextualize the gospel into a tribal worldview, or does doing so entail selling out and making the worldview christo-pagan? Too often, I fear, people convert to the Christian faith at the higher belief level, but they receive little help in knowing how to deal with the spirits and the healing and divination they encounter routinely in village life.

The religious phenomenology of a people is what they believe to be true. We have no choice but to take it seriously, precisely because it is what they believe in. We Western missionaries may say that these spirits and other such things don't really exist. And local people will tell us, "Then don't come as missionaries, because you will be unable to deal with our reality."

Generally speaking, people do not jump quickly or easily from one worldview to another. The discipling process is a slow and gradual one. Such patience is the way God worked with Abraham and with the people of Israel throughout the Old Testament.

In this light, the conversation in many circles today about territorial spirits is a tricky one. My concern is the potential emergence of a kind of Christian animism. When we speak of territorial spirits needing to be cast out, there is the danger of becoming victims—our God is for us and on our side; their god is for them and on their side. In such a case, if we win, our God beats their god. If their god wins, he is stronger than our God. This competition is at the core of tribal religion.

What is unique about the Old Testament is the admission that when Israel defeats the Philistines, it is God who defeats the Philistines. But when the Philistines defeat Israel, never do the biblical writers say that the Philistine gods are victorious over the God of Israel. The revolutionary thing about the Old Testament is that defeat is an expression of our God's judgment. Evil things happening to us are not the result of another god's greater power; they manifest punishment by our own God. This way of interpreting events is perhaps the most radical biblical challenge to the tribal worldview regarding spiritual reality.

The Indo-European worldview. Understandings of spiritual realities held today in much of south Asia and the West are shaped by what is often called the Indo-European worldview. With the migration and spread of Indo-European peoples from inner Asia to Europe, Mesopotamia, and south Asia, this worldview in its various forms became the basis for the religions of Babylon, Sumer, Canaan, Greece, India, and Germany, to name a few.

Central to the Indo-European worldview is a cosmic dualism between good and evil and a cosmic battle for control of the universe, taking place in the heavens between the good gods and the evil gods. The good gods are seeking to establish a kingdom of righteousness and order, and the evil gods seek to establish an evil empire. The goal of the conflict is to win the battle—to take control and establish order, at any cost. The outcome of the battle is uncertain, because both sides are equally strong. And the battle is unending, because when either good or evil is defeated, it simply rises from the rubble to fight again.

The battle is about power, might, and violence, all of which are necessary to save good and order. The focus is on the battle itself, not on the outcome of peace or shalom. Morality in this framework is based on pragmatism (we are justified in doing whatever works) and fairness. That is, we can use whatever methods the enemy uses, which generally means that in the end, we become like the enemy.

Conflict and competition are intrinsic to the world and lead to evolution (biology), progress (civilization), development (economics), and prowess (sports and entertainment). Fundamental to this worldview is the belief that good and evil are two independent entities coexisting from eternity. Given this kind of dualism, good and evil are understood to come from two different and opposing superhuman agencies. When these agencies, the gods, carry on battles in the heavens, human beings and nature down on earth experience the resulting fallout (see fig. 1.4). "When the elephants fight," goes the proverb, "the mice get trampled."

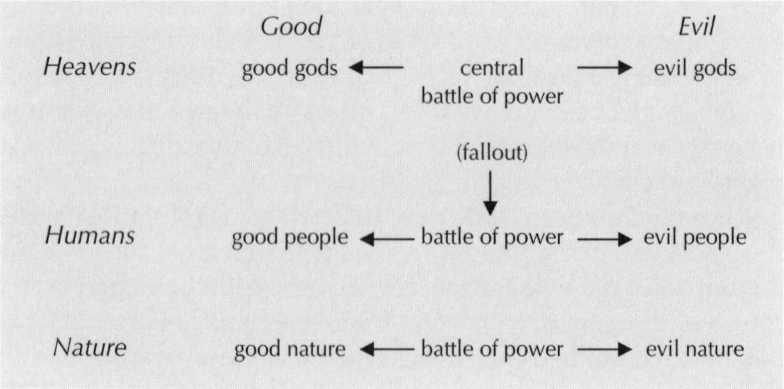

Fig. 1.4. The Indo-European worldview.

In the Indo-European worldview, human beings are puppets or pawns in the hands of the gods, and their earthly battles mirror what is happening in the heavenly realm. It is hardly a coincidence, notes David Bosch, that the game of chess was developed in Persia and reflects the fundamental Indo-European view of reality. As Omar Khayyám so aptly expresses it:

> 'Tis all a Chequer-board of Nights and Days
> Where Destiny with Men for Pieces plays:
> Hither and thither moves, and mates, and slays,
> And one by one back in the Closet lays.[3]

All of reality in this worldview is divided into two camps: God and Satan, angels and demons, good nations and evil ones, good humans and wicked ones. The good may be deceived or forced into doing evil things, but at heart they are good. The evil have no redeeming qualities and must be destroyed so that good may reign.

The line between the two camps is sharp. Such dualism is seen in the American tendency to categorize in opposites: good-bad, big-small, sweet-sour, success-failure, and truth-falsehood. Politically, our opponents must become our enemies. They must be branded as evil and we as good. Enemies are to be hated and destroyed. They must therefore be dehumanized and seen as other, as not-us. Francis Fukuyama, a policy planner in the U.S. State Department, perceived the end of the Cold War as "the end of history," leaving the world with no master plot, only "centuries of boredom" stretching ahead like a superhighway to nowhere. We need an enemy to give meaning to our lives.

Though Indo-European religions are for the most part dying out in the West, their underlying worldview still dominates much of American thought. It serves as a basis for our westerns, detective stories, murder mysteries, and science fiction. It is recounted in the adventures of superheroes such as Superman and Spiderman, and in most of our cartoons, such as Mickey Mouse, Donald Duck, and the epic showdowns between Popeye and Bluto. It is reenacted in Star Wars movies, dramatized in video games, and taught in the New Age movement. It is played out in football, basketball, and tennis. And it appears increasingly in certain types of Christian literature, such as the early books by Frank Perretti and the Left Behind series by Tim LaHaye and Jerry Jenkins.

The biblical worldview. The biblical images of spiritual realities depart radically from Indo-European ones at several key points and

3. From "The Rubáiyát"; translation by Edward Fitzgerald.

give us a different view of the cosmic spiritual warfare in which we are engaged.

According to the biblical testimony, good is eternal and evil is contingent. The Bible is clear: God and Satan, good and evil, are not two independent entities in coexistence from eternity. Rather, in the beginning was God, and God was good. Satan, sinners, and sin appear later in the biblical account.

Moreover, God's creation depends on God for continued existence. God did not, at some point in the past, create a universe that exists independent of God. Satan and sinners, like all creation, are dependent on God's sustaining power. Their very existence in their rebellion is testimony to God's mercy and love (see fig. 1.5 below).

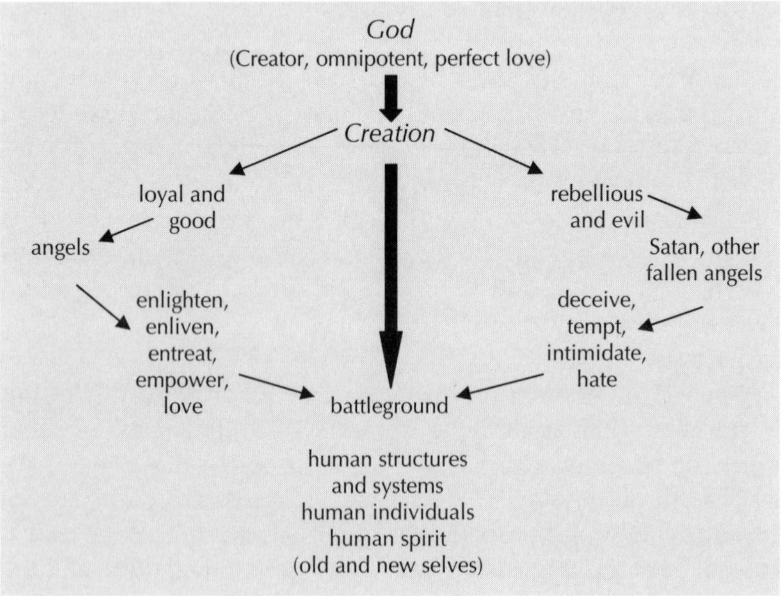

Fig. 1.5. The biblical worldview.

The central issue, therefore, is not one of brute power. God's omnipotence is never questioned in scripture. Even Satan and his hosts acknowledge it. The issue is holiness and evil, righteousness and sin. God is holy, light, love, and truth. Evil does not exist independently. It is a perversion of good. It is darkness, deceitfulness, and the source of death. It is broken relationships, idolatry and rebellion against God, alienation, and worship of the self.

At the heart of the gospel is shalom. Shalom begins with a right relationship with God, involving worship, holiness, and obedience. Prayer in Indo-European thought is a means to control the gods; in biblical thought, it is submission to God. In prayer we give God permission to use us and our resources to answer our prayers. It can therefore be costly.

Shalom also involves right relationships with humans. Right relationships are not characterized by hierarchy and exploitation, as in the Indo-European world, in which the strong lord it over the weak. Right relationships are expressed in love and care for one another as people created in the image of God, however broken or flawed we are. Shalom means to be for the other, rather than for oneself, and to commit oneself to the other, regardless of the other's response. Shalom gives priority to building community over completing tasks. This priority requires that we give up our Western need to control people and situations around us. It means we accept corporate decision making and accountability to the community.

If the central message of the Bible is not that a cosmic struggle between God and Satan will determine who will rule, what is it about? The battle between God and Satan rages on; that is clear. But that battle is for and within human hearts and societies; it is not a showdown to see which of them—God or Satan—is stronger. In this battle, humans are not passive victims of combat on a cosmic plane. We are the central actors and the locus of the action. We are the rebels, and ever since the temptation of Adam, self-worship has been the basis of our idolatry.

God's goal is to win the enemy over and bring peace, reconciliation, and shalom. Satan's goal is to keep people from turning to God. We must learn to see all fallen humans as us, not as other. At the deepest level, we are one humanity, called to love one another.

God's methods are the power of love, truth, peace, life, and light. Satan's methods are deceit, fear, violence, darkness, and death. We are called to love our enemies, not hate them, because they are us. We cannot use unrighteous methods in our struggle in the name of fairness, for then we fail and become like our enemies.

Power encounters, in the biblical view of things, may lead to greater opposition and persecution. The supreme power encounter is the cross on which Jesus defeated Satan. That the cross might be the ultimate victory makes no sense in Indo-European terms. Christ should have taken up the challenge of his tormentors and come down from the cross with his angelic hosts. He should have defeated Satan when he met him in the desert (1 Cor. 1:18-25). And yet the cross is not, in biblical terms, an apparent loss saved at the last moment by the resurrection. It is God's way of unmasking Satan's evil power and intent and of demonstrating God's own unconditional and unending love, even to the death, if need be (see fig. 1.6). If our understanding of spiritual warfare does not make sense of the cross, then it is wrong.

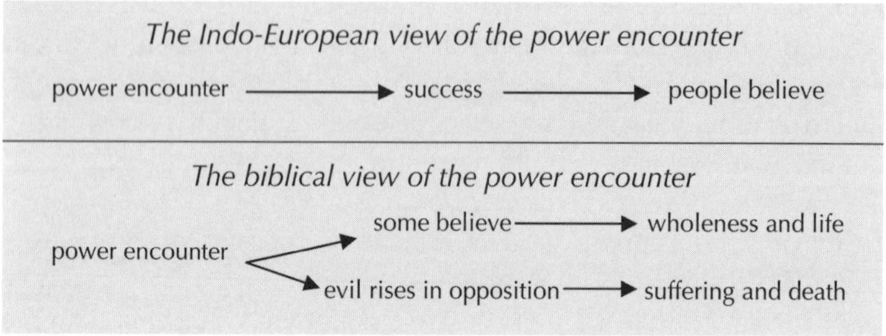

Fig. 1.6. Indo-European and biblical views of the power encounter.

As we develop a biblical approach to the question of spiritual reality, we must avoid two extremes: (1) denial of the reality of Satan and the spiritual battle within and around us in which we are engaged; and (2) undue fascination with and fear of Satan and his hosts. Our central focus must be on Christ, not on Satan. We should see God's angels at work more than we see demons. Our message is one of victory, hope, joy, and freedom, for we have the power of the Holy Spirit to overcome evil. The cosmic battle is over. We are messengers to declare to the world that Christ is indeed the Lord of everything in the heavens and on earth. For all authority has already been given to Jesus, the risen Lord (Matt. 28:18).

Indo-European	*Biblical*
battle between equals	rebellious creation
hate the enemy	love the enemy, hate the sin
use power and force	use love and truth
use the means the enemy uses	use only righteous means
inflict pain and suffering	bear pain and suffering
The way of the sword	**The way of the cross**

Fig. 1.7. Contrasting views of spiritual warfare.

Ultimately, the Indo-European and biblical worldviews represent contrasting understandings of spiritual warfare (see fig. 1.7).

Dealing with spiritual cases in today's world

In dealing with spirit realities today, whether in North America or in cross-cultural contexts around the world, we are wise to keep three things in mind.

Phenomenology. It is of utmost importance that we study and understand people's beliefs and practices about these matters. Some of what people do or believe may not be right or true, but it is nonetheless what they bring to the table.

For a full understanding of this or any aspect of the human reality, we must make full use of all the human sciences at our disposal: the physical-chemical, the biological, the psychological, the sociocultural, and the spiritual. Each of these constitutes a system of understandings and relationships. We are best served when we see the interrelatedness of these systems, taking what some have called a system of systems approach to the question (see fig. 1.8). It is often difficult to differentiate between root causes and symptoms in such instances, but disciplining ourselves to see the larger, interrelated connections in an individual's life gives us a much more accurate picture of the human reality we are facing.

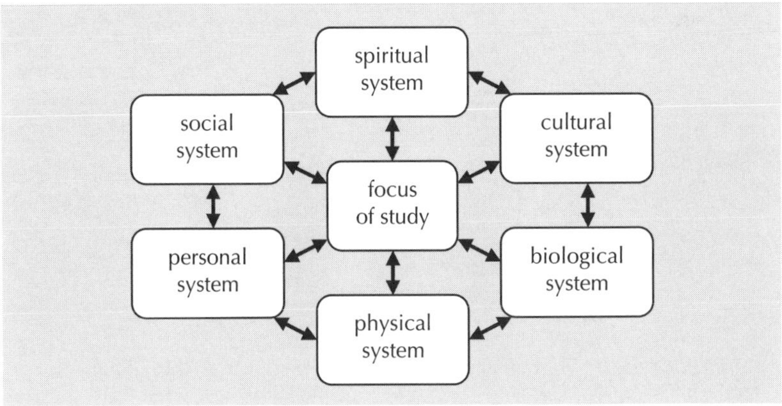

Fig. 1.8. A system of systems approach to the study of humans.

It is important at this early stage of assessment to refrain from making judgments, for they would almost certainly be premature. The outsider needs to understand a situation before judging it. The local people are the experts in such instances, and the outsider is the learner.

Ontology. Through Bible reading and prayer, it is possible to learn what God might be saying about a given situation. One can never go wrong if one tests the spirits in the light of scripture (see fig. 1.9). Helping local people read and understand scripture for themselves is an important, empowering part of the process. When an outsider dictates change in a person's life or community, that change is not likely to last, and the change agent becomes little more than a watchdog or policeman. But if an entire community makes a decision to change, then the mechanism is in place both to effect that change and to enforce it.

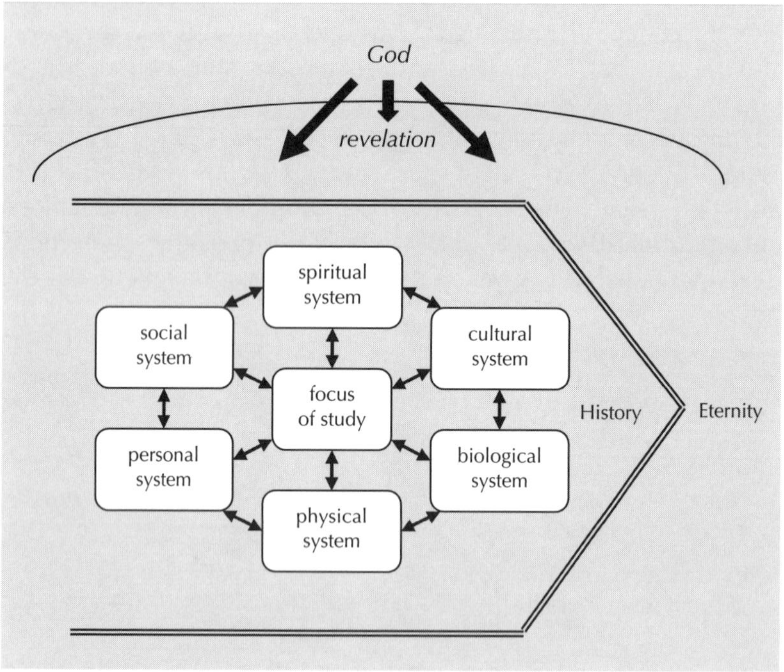

Fig. 1.9. A system of systems approach to testing the spirits in the light of scripture.

Missiology. Discipling is a long process of teaching, guiding, and modeling—of helping people move from where they are to where they ought to be. One should not expect people to jump from their existing world to a new one in a single leap. It is perhaps best to start with areas in which people already consciously struggle with their faith. Additional areas that might be addressed can then be suggested. It is essential to be humble, gentle, and kind throughout the process—never harsh, demanding, or condescending. Deep and lasting change is always a slow process, with renewed and repeated recommitment to the process on the part of the person all along the way.

As North Americans, we have plenty about which to be humble. Our own hidden myths profoundly affect the way we live our everyday lives: how we treat our spouses, organize our society, and fight our wars. We underestimate the extent to which enemies, battles, competition, self-interest, and greed are essential to our national and cultural understanding of reality. We ignore the fact that these values have their roots not in biblical but in ancient Indo-European beliefs and form the dominant religion of our society.

Our conversion from our pagan past is not yet complete. We need to read the gospel again, this time with an awareness of our own worldview and how it shapes our interpretation of the scriptures. In particular, we need to test current teachings about cosmic spiritual warfare to see whether they fit biblical teachings or reinforce a pagan religious worldview. Too often, they seem to reflect the fascination with warfare that dominates our society, rather than the love of holiness and shalom that characterizes the gospel. If we are not careful, we may become more involved in spiritual warfare and live less holy lives.

Chapter 2

Biblical faith confronts evil spiritual realities

Willard M. Swartley

To consider biblical faith with regard to evil spiritual realities requires a double focus. It calls us to examine how biblical faith evident in the scriptural canon confronts evil spiritual powers. Then we will consider how biblical faith as professed today leads us to confront evil spiritual realities. Along the way, we will also look briefly at the historical practice of the Christian church.[1]

Israel's confrontation of evil powers

According to scripture, Israel existed in a confrontation of opposing spiritual powers. During Israel's exodus from Egypt, the clash between the power of the Lord God of Israel and the power of Pharaoh's gods was dramatized through the plagues. As stated repeatedly in the plague narrative, the purpose clause is "that you may know that I am the Lord [Yahweh]" (see, for example, Exod. 10:2; 14:4, 18). The gods of Egypt—and specifically Pharaoh, whose power actualized that of the gods—will come to acknowledge that Yahweh is God alone. As one writer puts it, "The plagues expose and call to account the powers of darkness."[2]

1. I presented a version of this essay at the Conference on Deliverance Ministry, Eastern Mennonite Seminary, Harrisonburg, Virginia, 30 October 1989. It appeared as "Biblical Faith Confronting Opposing Spiritual Realities," *Direction* 29 (2000): 100–113. It has been adapted and is reprinted here by permission.

In an earlier essay on the biblical theology of deliverance ministry, I made the following statement (in reference to Paul's proclamation of the gospel as the power of God for salvation): "Evangelism is the primary form of power encounter and deliverance from the bondage of sin" (Thomas N. Finger and Willard M. Swartley, "Bondage and Deliverance: Biblical and Theological Perspectives," in *Essays on Spiritual Bondage and Deliverance,* Occasional Papers no. 11, ed. Willard M. Swartley [Elkhart, IN: Institute of Mennonite Studies, 1988], 22). I might well have added, "and deliverance from the bondage of evil spiritual realities."

2. Timothy James Kamp, "The Biblical Forms and Elements of Power Encounter" (master's thesis, Columbia Graduate School of Bible and Missions, 1985), 33.

Walter Wink shows that the notion of the powers has a multidimensional reality. They are both spiritual-psychic entities and sociopolitical entities.[3] In its appeal to the Exodus, Liberation Theology stresses the political-economic dimension and God's liberation of Israel from that oppression. This point is valid, but not if it is disconnected from the spiritual and religious issue at stake in the event. Israel's call from bondage and their establishment as a covenant people are first mighty demonstrations of Yahweh's power and right to covenant sovereignty as God over Israel.

Israel's liberation is at the same time their loyal subjection to God's rule. The first commandment marks life in the covenant: "You shall have no other gods before me" (Exod. 20:3). The second preserves the freedom of God to be God: "You shall not make for yourself an idol" (Exod. 20:4). That is, you shall not attempt to manage God through an image or a representation of the divine Yahweh power. The people are reminded of who they are as creatures, and the gods of the nations are exposed for what they are.

From this foundation, Israel's life and history continue. Joshua calls the people to a renewal of their covenant decision: Will you serve the gods of the nations, or will you choose to serve Yahweh, who delivered you from bondage? (Josh. 24:14-15). The command to drive out the nations around Israel is rooted in God's own holy war against false deities and the religious practices associated with them (Deut. 18:9-14).

Idolatry, the primary issue

Idolatry—allegiance to and worship of other powers and gods—is the fundamental issue of biblical faith. The story of David and Goliath puts the point unforgettably. Goliath marched up and down the Elah Valley, defying the God of Israel and claiming supremacy for the gods of the Philistines. Israel's warriors were terrified. Only the shepherd lad with a sling and five pebbles, armored by trust in God, was ready to take him on. Listen to David's piercing weapon against Goliath: "You come to me with sword and spear and javelin; but I come to

---

3. Walter Wink, *Engaging the Powers: Discernment and Resistance in a World of Domination* (Minneapolis: Fortress Press, 1992). See also his books *Naming the Powers: The Language of Power in the New Testament* (Philadelphia: Fortress Press, 1984); and *Unmasking the Powers: The Invisible Powers That Determine Human Existence* (Philadelphia: Fortress Press, 1986).

you in the name of the LORD of hosts, the God of the armies of Israel, whom you have defied. This very day the LORD will deliver you into my hand ... that all this assembly may know that the LORD does not save by sword and spear; for the battle is the LORD's and he will give you into our hand" (1 Sam. 17:45-47).

Elijah's contest with the prophets of Baal on Mount Carmel continues in dramatic style the theme of gods vs. the true God: "How long will you go limping with two different opinions? If the LORD is God, follow him; but if Baal, then follow him" (1 Kings 18:21). The end of the contest leads to the great outburst: "The LORD indeed is God; the LORD indeed is God" (1 Kings 18:39).

Israel's struggle with war and use of military might was an aspect of their submission to or rebellion against God's sovereignty. In the same way that God fought for Israel in the Exodus—when Israel had only to be still and trust God—so God wanted Israel to trust for divine victory to gain the land and to become secure politically. But Israel desired a human king like the nations around them. With a king came the armies and the idolatries of the surrounding countries.

As Psalm 106:36-37 puts it, "They served their idols, which became a snare to them. They sacrificed their sons and their daughters to the demons." Compare Deuteronomy 32:17: "They sacrificed to demons, not God, to deities they had never known." Because Israel went after the idols and forsook Yahweh, the Lord eventually consigned them to exile.

Yet some Israelites remained faithful to the Lord even amid the pressure of evil spiritual realities. The note of God's victory again sounded forth as Daniel and his friends were protected from the gods and the kings of the Babylonians. After Daniel survived the lion's den by God's arm of protection, King Darius was ready to own the Lord God's sovereignty. He issued a decree calling all people in his kingdom to "tremble and fear before the God of Daniel: For he is the living God, enduring forever. His kingdom shall never be destroyed, and his dominion has no end" (Dan. 6:26).

Israel's worship celebrates the triumph of God

Israel's worship centered on the triumph of God and the protection of God's people. Whether we look to the Song of the Sea in Exodus 15, the Psalms as Israel's hymnbook, or the praise oracles of the prophets, the focal point of all the great hymns of worship is "the LORD God reigns."

Isaiah 40–55 even dares to poke fun at the idols of the nations: "They hire a goldsmith, who makes [the gold and silver] into a god; then they fall down and worship!" (Isa. 46:6b). The kings of the great empires are doomed: King of Babylon, Day Star/Lucifer, is quickly fallen from the throne, cut down to the ground, brought down to Sheol, to the depths of the Pit; "maggots are the bed beneath you, and worms your covering" (Isa. 14:12, 14-15, 11).

The worship stream of the Bible declares that God triumphs over the evil spiritual realities, including human armies with sword and spear. The psalmist proclaims: "Great is the LORD, and greatly to be praised; he is to be revered above all gods. For all the gods of the peoples are idols, but the LORD made the heavens.... Say among the nations, 'The LORD is king!'" (Ps. 96:4-5, 10a; cf. Ps. 18:1-2).

Mark and Matthew: Jesus' kingdom plunders Satan

In Mark's Gospel, Jesus' proclamation of the kingdom of God in word and deed is the deathblow to the evil spiritual reality headed by Satan. About a third of Mark's Gospel contains exorcistic emphases, including one nature miracle in which the sea chaos is rebuked as though it were incited by demonic power (Mark 4:36-41). Mark's lead story of Jesus' ministry describes Jesus casting out a demon in the synagogue (Mark 1:23-28). Many similar stories are related.

Further, Jesus' ministry is defined in its essence as that of plundering Satan's ranks. As Matthew puts the key text, "If it is by the Spirit of God that I cast out demons, then the kingdom of God has come to you" (12:28). In *Jesus, a New Vision,* Marcus Borg presents Jesus and his mission as empowered by his Spirit-filled relation to God.[4] Jesus was a mediator of the world of Spirit-power into the material world. His exorcisms and miracles should be seen in that context.

Borg holds that it is impossible for us as moderns to grasp Jesus and his mission until we come to terms with our own culture. Enlightenment rationalism and empiricism have defined the limits of reality for us, effectively excluding the realm of Spirit. Jesus knew that Spirit was ultimate reality and he ministered on that basis, filled with deep compassion for those possessed by demons and suffering

4. Marcus J. Borg, *Jesus, a New Vision: Spirit, Culture, and the Life of Discipleship* (San Francisco: Harper & Row, 1987), esp. 39–75.

from illness. Only against this portrait of Spirit-power and intense compassion can we rightly glimpse the historical Jesus, the one his followers later described with a rich array of Christological titles.[5]

Luke: Jesus' mission destroys the evil powers

Luke's story of Jesus and the early church in Luke-Acts makes it abundantly clear that Jesus came to destroy the powers of evil that were oppressing humanity. Luke's story turns a wide furrow, showing how the gospel grows in the cradle of Judaism, how Jesus' ministry is empowered by prayer, how Jesus—anointed by the Spirit—proclaims in word and deed a gospel that "loosens the bonds of wickedness, undoes the bands of the coercing yoke, releases the oppressed into freedom, and breaks apart every unjust contract."[6]

Luke's gospel story is a story of peacemaking as well. In her book on Luke-Acts, *The Demise of the Devil,* Susan Garrett shows how Jesus' gospel mission is the downfall of Satan.[7] Many instances could be cited, but I will note one in Luke and several in Acts. In Luke 10:17-20, when the seventy return from their mission of proclaiming the peace gospel and are jubilant because even the demons were subject to them, Jesus exclaims, apparently reporting a visionary experience, "I watched Satan fall from heaven like a flash of lightning. See, I have given you authority to tread on snakes and scorpions, and over all the power of the enemy; and nothing will hurt you" (Luke 10:18-19).

Confrontation of demonic power lies, in fact, at the heart of the gospel story. As James Kallas puts it, "The arrival of the Kingdom is simultaneous with, dependent upon, and manifested in the routing of the demons. The Kingdom arrives in a limited localized area as the demon's rule is broken. The Kingdom will arrive on a worldwide basis when the worldwide rule of Satan is broken. The Kingdom's arrival is to be seen ... in the cleansing of the world which has fallen captive to and obeys the will of the God-opposed forces of the evil one."[8]

---

5. Ibid., 50.

6. Susan R. Garrett, *The Demise of the Devil: Magic and the Demonic in Luke's Writings* (Minneapolis: Fortress Press, 1989), 71–72.

7. Ibid.

8. James G. Kallas, *The Significance of the Synoptic Miracles* (Greenwich, CT: Seabury Press, 1961), 78. See also Kallas's *Jesus and the Power of Satan* (Philadelphia: Westminster Press, 1968; and *The Real Satan: From Biblical Times to the Present* (Minneapolis: Augsburg Publishing House, 1975).

Luke sums up Jesus' ministry as that of "preaching good news of peace, ... how he went about doing good and healing all that were oppressed by the devil, for God was with him" (Acts 10:36-38, RSV). Similarly, Luke sums up Paul's mission to the Gentiles as one of opening their eyes, "that they may turn from darkness to light and from the power of Satan to God, so that they may receive forgiveness of sins and a place among those who are sanctified" (Acts 26:18).

Binding the strong man[9]

Matthew, Mark, and Luke thus present Jesus' ministry as a clash with the powers of evil. In fact, one of the leading portraits of Jesus in the synoptic Gospels is as an exorcist. Jesus drove out demons and pushed back the forces of evil. Many scholars see this aspect of Jesus' presentation in the Gospels as authentic rather than as a theological overlay. Mark and Luke emphasize this dimension of Jesus' ministry more than Matthew does. Luke 10:1-20, the passage cited above, depicts the mission of the seventy as a proclamation of the gospel of peace and the downfall of Satan. Demons were subject to the authority of the disciples as they announced the coming of God's kingdom.

When Jesus appointed the twelve to be with him and to proclaim the gospel, he gave them "authority to cast out demons" (Mark 3:15). In Matthew's mission discourse, Jesus' granting the twelve this authority precedes his sending them out (Matthew 10).

Matthew 12:22-30 shows Jesus defending himself against the Pharisees' accusation (in Mark 3:21 his family is also upset) precisely on the issue of his authority and power to cast out demons (cf. Mark 3:20-27). The Matthew-Luke parallel puts it sharply: "If it is by the Spirit of God ['finger of God' in Luke 11:20] that I cast out demons, then the kingdom of God has come upon you" (Matt. 12:28).

In this so-called Beelzebul controversy, the Pharisees accuse Jesus of casting out demons by the power of Satan. Jesus answers with a riddle: How can Satan cast out Satan? Of this response, Augustine comments, "So let the Pharisees choose what they want. If Satan could not cast out Satan, they could find nothing to say against the Lord. But if Satan can cast out Satan, let them look out for themselves

---

9. This section is adapted from "Binding the Strong Man: Matthew 12:22-30," *The Mennonite* (18 November 2003), 16–17, and is used with permission. It includes notes not in the printed article.

all the more and let them abandon his kingdom because it cannot stand divided against itself."[10]

Jesus then makes a stunning claim: If his source of power is God's Spirit, then "the kingdom of God has come to you." Chrysostom sees in this response a note of conciliation, because Jesus says not only that the kingdom of God has come but also that it has come "to you." That is, "good things have come specifically to you, so why then do you feel so displeased that you are wonderfully blessed? Why do you make war against your own salvation?"[11]

Jesus' deeds of deliverance were a potential blessing to all. But Satan countered Jesus' ministry regularly, instigating criticism and opposition, to keep people from seeing Jesus' exorcisms as signs that the kingdom of God had come and that the Spirit of God was at work in Jesus Christ. As Richard Gardner comments, "If that is so, then God's reign is taking shape in and through Jesus' deeds, overcoming the forces of evil. And Jesus' critics are in the position of opposing God's rule!"[12]

Exorcisms, like Jesus' other mighty works, function in the Gospels to disclose who Jesus really is. This is the central point of the text. Jesus is not just another person or even just another prophet. He comes as God's Messiah to free not only Israel but all people from evil's power. He sets the captives free.

Victory over evil

Exorcisms in the Gospels are Christological disclosures. By whose power does Jesus cast out demons? Who is able to bind the strong man (Satan) and plunder his house? Jesus is who he claims to be, Messiah and Son of God. Throughout the Gospels, Jesus comes as divine warrior to overcome and defeat the powers of evil. Exorcisms and healings play a major role in his ministry, announcing the inbreaking of God's reign. Jesus' nonviolent, authoritative confrontation of the demons is consummated in his victory over evil through his death on the cross. In this struggle against evil, Jesus teaches his disciples not to fear but to believe and have faith. The New Testament word for

10. Augustine, Sermon 71.1, *Matthew 1–13*, ed. Manlio Simonetti; Ancient Christian Commentary on Scripture (ACCS), vol. 1a (Downers Grove, IL: InterVarsity Press, 2001), 246.

11. Chrysostom, The Gospel of Matthew, Homily 41.2, *Matthew 1–13*, ed. Simonetti, ACCS, 248.

12. Richard B. Gardner, *Matthew*, Believers Church Bible Commentary (Scottdale, PA: Herald Press, 1991), 201.

"believe" *(pisteuō)* matches the Old Testament's call to "have faith" *(batach)* in God's promise to fight for Israel.

Was authority to cast out demons peculiar to Jesus and the disciples, or was it also to be extended to later followers of Jesus? Matthew 12:22-30 and Mark 9:38-40 indicate that other people in the first century cast out demons. In Mark 9, they do so in Jesus' name, and Jesus says, "Whoever is not against us is for us." But in Matthew 12, where opponents ascribe his power to Satan, Jesus' counter-question in verse 27 prods the Pharisees not to be too quick in their judgment, for they will be judged accordingly. Finally, Jesus says, "Whoever is not with me is against me" (v. 30). The sayings are opposite, because the contexts are opposite. The bottom line is the same: There are two forces at work in the world. The key question is whether we are on Jesus' side or against him.

Exorcistic prayers and power

The narratives of Acts 8, 13, and 16, and the early centuries of church history clearly attest that the authority to exorcise in the name and power of Jesus was an essential and ongoing feature of the church's ministry. In the early centuries, baptismal candidates coming from a background of pagan idolatry underwent a lengthy period of catechism that included exorcistic prayers. Baptism was the climax of their decisive break with the powers of darkness. To this day, Syrian Orthodox baptismal rites retain strong exorcistic language, addressed directly against Satan.

In the modern West, this dimension of Jesus' ministry is problematic, because many Christians cannot grasp the reality of the spirit world. With the exception of those who practice deliverance ministries, a gap exists between our reality and the reality of our brothers and sisters in many parts of the two-thirds world.

Interpreters in our time offer four types of rational explanations. One type proposes that what was formerly thought to be demonic oppression is mental illness. Psychiatric treatment replaces exorcism. Second, social science explains demonization as the result of social ostracism and marginalization. Some social science commentaries explain Jesus' exorcisms as bold actions of inclusion that reintegrate outcasts into society. Third, in the last several decades, commentaries have regarded political ideology as symbolic of political oppression. In one view, for example, the Gadarene's "legion" of demons represents the Roman army legion. Fourth, René Girard sees Satan as representing the scandal and offense that arises from rivalry. For Girard, clever Satan does cast out Satan. He first generates the rivalry and division that heats into hatred, so that the community is about to explode or war threatens between two communities or nations. The crisis is averted (also Satan's work) by means of a selected, targeted scapegoat, whose death restores peace to the community—until Satan generates the next cycle of rivalry leading to violence. Jesus exposed this generative system of violence, and the Gospels reveal the truth. Jesus is not guilty; God sides with the scapegoated victim.

Although each of these explanations is fascinating, each is inadequate in expositing the text and its significance for the life of the church today. These analyses deal only with the symptoms or attendant circumstances of demonic oppression and thus represent only partial truth. Answers that are more complete are to be found in Tim Geddert's recent commentary on Mark 4 and in my book, *Mark: The Way for All Nations.*[13]

Acts: The power of the gospel mission

Most striking, however, is the way Luke accentuates the power of the gospel mission as victory over magic, sorcery, and demonic power in the evil spiritual realities of the Greco-Roman world. The four key stories are Philip's (and the apostles') encounter with Simon Magus in Samaria (Acts 8), Paul's encounter with Elymas the magician in Salamis, Cyprus (Acts 13), Paul's exorcism of a spirit of divination from a slave girl in Macedonia (Acts 16), and the gospel's confrontation of sorcery and magical arts in Ephesus (Acts 19).

In this last story, some Jewish exorcists tried using the name of Jesus to cast out demons from those demonized, but it did not work. They were not themselves believers in Jesus and thus were doing exorcism as a form of magic. Paul's confrontation with Demetrius, the silversmith, falls into the same category. It shows the gospel overcoming the powers of idolatry and the demons that inspire that idolatry.

These stories form the inclusio, the beginning and the end, of both the missionary spread of the gospel outside Jewish culture and the

13. See Tim Geddert, *Mark*, Believers Church Bible Commentary (Scottdale, PA: Herald Press, 2000), 53–54, 82–88, and esp. 237–39; and Willard M. Swartley, *Mark: The Way for All Nations* (Scottdale, PA: Herald Press, 1981), 103–104.

Pauline mission as a whole. Even the Macedonian mission begins and ends with such stories (Acts 16 and 19). Clearly, Luke wants to show that the gospel of Jesus Christ is in its essence the power of God to overcome magic, idolatry, sorcery, and every spirit reality that ruled and oppressed people in the Greco-Roman world.

In Luke's jubilee, the gospel of Jesus breaks every yoke of oppression, both in the spirit world and in the socioeconomic political structures that oppress humankind. In Paul's words to Elymas, the gospel dares to say to every evil spiritual reality, "You son of the devil, you enemy of all righteousness, full of all deceit and villainy, will you not stop making crooked the straight paths of the Lord?" (Acts 13:10).

Paul's theology of Christ's triumph

Pauline theology has at its center Jesus Christ's triumph over the powers in his death, resurrection, and exaltation to God's right hand. Paul holds with boldness the truth that the gospel frees humans from all spiritual political structures of oppression, as well as from bondage to sin. The gospel frees people from the spirit powers that lie behind pagan religions and philosophies, and behind the law as means for self-justification (Gal. 4:5, 8-9). Paul speaks of being redeemed from being under the law and from "the elemental spirits *[stoicheia]* of the universe" (Col. 2:8, 18-23). These structures and rituals were powers that dominated life and thus destroyed freedom. For the Jews, the power in question was the law—not the law itself, but the works of the law as a means of salvation. For the Greeks, the *stoicheia* consisted of astrological fate and fortune—powers that governed the cycles of nature and imparted secret knowledge—and other occult ways of ordering life.

From these texts, we gain a basic understanding of idolatry. Structures that provide order for existence turn into ultimate values—ends in themselves—and thus are elevated to powers over one's life, and finally are worshiped as gods. Romans 1 shows the same pattern: through sinful impulses, humans fail to see God's revelation in nature and therefore turn to idolatry, worshiping the creation and creatures instead of the Creator. Hence, "God gave them up"—repeated three times (Rom. 1:24, 26, 28)—to the course and consequences of their wickedness. Only the power of the liberating gospel can free humans from this chain of sin. Indeed, Jesus "gave himself for our sins to set us free from the present evil age" (Gal. 1:4).

Paul speaks specifically of Christ's triumph over principalities, powers, dominions, and thrones. Astoundingly, 1 Corinthians 15:24-27 claims that every authority, rule, and power has been put in subjection to Christ. When Jesus hands over the kingdom to the Father, they will be stripped of all power. We find further descriptions of Christ's triumph in other portions of Pauline scripture (Col. 1:15-16, 20; 2:10, 15; Eph. 1:19-23; 3:9-10; Rom. 8:35-39) and in other apostolic writings (1 Pet. 3:22; Rev. 18:2, 10). According to the New Testament, the powers were created to serve God, but their rebellious aspirations (as also in Isaiah 14; Ezekiel 28; Daniel 5–6) have made them adversaries to God.

These powers have a positive function within the world outside of Christ: as agents of God's wrath, they restrain evil (Rom. 13:4). But they can also readily become instruments of the demonic (recall the Old Testament link between the judgment of God and the demonic). Indeed, these powers crucified the Lord of Glory (1 Cor. 2:6-9).

Jesus' way of disarming the powers

Jesus' life ministry was a battle against the powers, and his death is the final defeat of Satan, the climactic holy war battle. William Brownlee notes that Jesus' "exorcisms are the inauguration of a holy war which reaches its climax in His death and resurrection wherein He decisively defeated the Devil and his hordes. In this capacity He is acting as the divine warrior."[14]

When we view Jesus as God's divine warrior to conquer evil, we see a major transformation of Old Testament holy war. Humans are no longer the enemy to be destroyed. Rather, Jesus commands, "Love your enemies and pray for those who persecute you" (Matt. 5:44), and "bless those who curse you, pray for those who abuse you" (Luke 6:28). With the ministry of Jesus, the fight of God and God's followers against evil is directed not against other people but against the spiritual powers that inspire human wickedness.

In Paul's most explicit description of Christ's triumph over the powers, he says that Christ "disarmed the rulers and authorities and

14. William Brownlee, "From Holy War to Holy Martyrdom," in *The Quest for the Kingdom of God*, ed. H. B. Huffmon, F. A. Spina, and A. R. W. Green (Winona Lake, IN: Eisenbrauns, 1983), 286.

made a public example of them" (Col. 2:15); that is, he exposed how they operated in the cross. Philip Bender regards the middle form of the verb *(apekdusamenos)* as significant: instead of directly attacking the authorities, Christ stripped himself of their power, thus eluding their grasp and creating a new community of power independent of these authorities.[15]

The writer of Ephesians sees the new Christian community, composed of previously hostile parties, as a demonstration of God's superiority over the principalities and so-called powers (Eph. 1:20-23; 3:9-10). The famous text in Ephesians 6:10-18 calls us to Christian warfare. In this battle, our weapons are not carnal or worldly but have divine power to destroy strongholds, every argument that sets itself up as a proud obstacle to the knowledge of God. By this means, we take every thought captive to Jesus Christ. Our weapons include truth, righteousness, the peace gospel, faith, salvation, and the Spirit-empowered Word of God (cf. Isa. 7:9b; 11:4-5; 49:2; 52:7; 59:17). Prayer is the important means by which we appropriate God's armor for our victorious living (Eph. 6:18).

Spiritual conflicts in the early church

Over the centuries, the church knew that spiritual warfare was its primary calling, although for much of its history it failed to use only the weapons of the Word and the Spirit. As Everett Ferguson writes about the early church's missionary success in the first three centuries, "The most notable mark of the early church was its ability to deal with the spirit world in the Roman Empire. ... I am persuaded that an important factor in the Christian success in the Roman world was the promise which [Christianity] made of deliverance from demons."[16] From the New Testament onward, the Christian mission was a mission of "driving out" demons. Martyrdom—and later, asceticism—engaged a "spiritual prize fight" with this enemy. The bishop's office was "to tread down Satan under his feet." Full membership in the Christian church, by baptism, was preceded by dramatic exorcisms. Once inside the Christian church, the Christian enjoyed the millennial sensations of a modern African antisorcery cult. The church was the commu-

15. Philip D. Bender, "The Holy War Trajectory in the Synoptic Gospels and the Pauline Writings" (master's thesis, Associated Mennonite Biblical Seminary, 1987).

16. Everett Ferguson, *Demonology of the Early Christian World* (New York: E. Mellen Press, 1984), 129.

nity for which Satan had been bound: his limitless powers had been bridled to permit the triumph of the gospel. More immediately, the practicing Christian gained immunity from sorcery.[17]

Ferguson further observes that the early church fathers regarded Jesus' death and resurrection as the defeat of Satan. For Irenaeus, "Christ's victory over the devil [is] the key motif in developing his doctrine of the atonement!" Also, "the preaching of the gospel is a means of defeating the demons."[18] It brings the victory of Christ to bear on oppression here and now, and it releases humans from Satan's tyranny. "By reason of the victory won in Christ, Christians could have confidence that they would prevail over the demons. By reason of [their] baptism, ... Christian[s] had been delivered from the power of demons and had been identified with Christ."[19]

Precisely on the point of baptism, the early church knew what we have forgotten. In many parts of the early Christian church, baptism was regarded as a person's exorcism.[20] People came to the gospel from paganism and were under the spell of the demons of the pagan religions. Hence, baptism was a rite of expelling the demon powers. Because catechumens were usually baptized on Easter morning, the six weeks of Lent provided the occasion to cleanse the new believer from every defilement of the old loyalty. Those to be baptized would go to the priest or minister every morning for these six weeks to be prayed over. These prayers focused on the power of the gospel to break every demonic influence from the past and to transfer the baptizand from the kingdom of darkness to the kingdom of light.

Worship and warfare

In *Celebrating the Faith: Evangelism through Worship,* Robert Webber describes these early church practices. The sign of the cross was used to indicate the sealing of the catechumen to Jesus Christ against all bondage to every spiritual power. Laying hands on the candidate may have been an exorcistic act, the mediation of divine power against all other power. The priest or minister also gave salt to the candidate,

---

17. Peter Brown, "Sorcery, Demons and the Rise of Christianity: From Late Antiquity into the Middle Ages," in *Religion and Society in the Age of Saint Augustine* (New York: Harper & Row, 1972), 136.

18. Ferguson, *Demonology of the Early Christian World,* 124.

19. Ibid., 125.

20. See Alan Kreider, *The Change of Conversion and the Origin of Christendom* (Harrisburg, PA: Trinity Press International, 1999), 17.

a sign of hospitality, welcoming the person into the covenant. A rite of breathing was also used; the candidate blew out every evil spirit and inhaled the Holy Spirit.[21]

As Webber summarizes,

> The period of purification and enlightenment, of spiritual journey preceding baptism, emphasizes not instruction, but spiritual recollection and readiness. It brings before the converting person the essence of what it means to be converted to Christ and equips the new convert with the weapons of spiritual warfare. It calls the convert into an ultimate rejection of Satan and all works of evil.... Rejecting Satan and accepting the tradition is absolutely essential to conversion.[22]

That baptism and exorcism were closely linked in the Eastern and Roman Catholic communions through the centuries is well attested. Henry Ansgar Kelly traces this history in *The Devil at Baptism*. According to his account, at baptism the priest asked the candidates, "Have you renounced Satan?" The candidates answered, "We have renounced him." In some rites, the candidates were then instructed to breathe out Satan and spit on him.

Another text speaks of breathing out anything of a nature contrary to the gospel. In some rites, long exorcistic prayers accompanied baptism; in them, words were addressed directly to the devil, commanding him to leave and never to return:

> Be rebuked and go out, unclean spirit. For I adjure you by him who walked upon the surface of the sea as if upon dry land, and rebuked the storm of winds, whose glance dries up abysses, and whose threat dissolves mountains. For he even now commands you through us. Be afraid, go out, and leave these creatures and do not return or hide in them or encounter any of them or work upon them or attack them either by night or by day or at the hour of noon. But go to your own Tartarus until the determined great day of judgment. Be afraid of God ... before whom

21. Robert E. Webber, *Celebrating Our Faith: Evangelism through Worship* (San Francisco: Harper & Row, 1986), 35–37.

22. Ibid., 82.

> angels tremble. ... Go out and depart from the sealed, newly chosen soldiers of Christ our God.[23]

If we are to be God's witnessing people, it is imperative that we know whom we serve and whom we have renounced. The matter of allegiance is all important.

God's people confronting the spirit world: The story continues

Through some brief examples, we consider now where biblical faith would lead believers today. Loren Entz, Mennonite missionary in Burkina Faso, tells the story of how Abou, a Muslim leader who became a Christian, claimed Christ's power in victory against the sorcery power of the village's elders:

> One night elders who were fetishers invited Abou in order to test him. Was the power of his Jesus greater than their fetish occult power? First they tried to poison him with food, but Abou found victory over that as he offered a prayer of thanks before he partook of the food. God showed himself to be Abou's right hand and he suffered no ill effects.
>
> Then the elders took him to their sacred grounds late that night. Abou was placed beside a huge gaping hole. The six elders sat on the other side of the hole. Fire escaped from the hole. A special whistling brought poisonous bees from the pit to do their evil work against Abou, but again with no success. Abou could not be stopped.
>
> They had one test left, a test which no one else had ever escaped. The old men whistled a second time and a huge snake about 18 inches in diameter emerged. It came toward Abou. It tried to push him into the pit, as countless others before him had been pushed in and disappeared. But the snake could only brush his leg. The snake itself fell into the pit. There was no doubt whose power was greater, God's power working through Abou or that of the fetishes through the village elders. The rest of the

23. Henry Ansgar Kelly, *The Devil at Baptism: Ritual, Theology, and Drama* (Ithaca: Cornell University Press, 1985), 164.

> night, Abou preached of Jesus to them, until daybreak, when he returned to Orodara.[24]

At a seminar in Lancaster, Pennsylvania, a woman who served in a mission in a Central American country told about how her life had been threatened by a witchdoctor who was about to hurl a huge weight on her. As the man advanced toward her, she and two other Christians, all in their own first (but different) languages, said, "In the name of Jesus, drop it!" The man collapsed and could do no harm. Afterward he acknowledged the power of Jesus over his witchcraft.

In a small New England town, a young woman who visited a Mennonite church needed to be exorcized to get free from covenant membership of sixteen years in a Satanist coven. The battle was heavy, but the Lord Jesus triumphed and she is free. To coven members who put curses on her because she would not come to the annual renewal ritual, she wrote a letter of confidence and joy, expressing her desire that they too would come to realize God's great power and love.[25]

In another case, less dramatic but no less significant, a seminary student called together a small group for a prayer and deliverance service. This service involved using a liturgy I had developed for such occasions. During group prayer, there was time for the oppressed person to name each known spirit of bondage and to cut free from it in the name of Jesus. After eight such uses of the liturgy, and naming footholds of bondage for each, the person felt full release and experienced a breakthrough in the healing process. Anointing with oil for healing followed, and then all who were present shared communion. Because we began with a time of worship (singing, prayer, and reading scripture), the event lasted half a day.

Some Christians may be asking: Are there really spirit realities? I do not ask that. Instead, I ask: How do we become a true people of God, clothed with the full armor of God, who have the courage to stand against every evil spiritual reality? And how can we make our worship services vibrant proclamations of the gospel of Jesus Christ, so that worship is evangelism, an evangelism that delivers people from darkness to light?

---

24. Loren Entz, "Challenges to Abou's Jesus," *Evangelical Missions Quarterly* 22, no. 1 (January 1986): 48–50.

25. Personal letter. For a fuller description, see pages 111–12 of this volume.

Conclusion

What can we learn from this biblical evidence that can inform ministry today? First, what appears to be demonized behavior may also be intertwined with psychological disorder, or it may not be. Second, discernment is needed for each situation. A clear test is how a person responds to scripture read authoritatively, or to praise of Jesus Christ. Third, love for the person must be strong, and resistance against the devil and his work must be equally strong. Fourth, no demon will ever leave on the basis of someone's human authority. Only in the name of Jesus Christ and by his power and the power of God Almighty are people freed from demonizing oppression. This liberation is possible because Jesus has bound the strong man. His house has been and will continue to be plundered by Jesus' followers as they minister in Jesus' name.

What can the church do? We ought to retain or put back into baptismal vows the question "Do you renounce Satan and all his works?" We need to put on the whole armor of God (Eph. 6:10-18), so that we can withstand the crafty tactics of Satan. And we must pray for one another and seek the Spirit's discernment and empowerment in our daily living and special ministries. Also, we ought to join those who, when freed from the devil's bondage, joyfully exclaim, "Praise the name of Jesus, praise the name of Jesus, praise the name of Jesus."

Chapter 3

Generational sin and demonic oppression

Lawrence E. Burkholder

Along with a significant segment of Christianity within the culture today, modern Western society is disputing the nature of reality. On one side of this theological watershed, one finds widespread acceptance of the neo-Gnostic message that people are inherently connected to God. From this perspective, atonement is primarily about uncovering our divinity.[1] This monistic worldview asserts that there is a seamless flow from God to all else; everything is connected to everything. In this paradigm, demons are a normal part of the higher invisible realms.

In contrast, covenant theology holds that creation is totally other than God. There is a basic distinction or dualism between God and creation—a dualism that understands God as subject and creation as object. This worldview presupposes boundaries that God established, which separate created realms from one another and from God. A key premise of this paper is that demons refuse God's creational limits, a point illustrated by the "chains of deepest darkness" texts in 2 Peter 2:4 and Jude 6. In these passages, fallen angels are said to have been imprisoned for breaching boundaries.

Our decision regarding reality's monistic or dualistic nature bears directly on the general problem of theodicy. It also controls the debate about the existence and operation of demons as agents of evil. I propose to show how four aspects of covenant theology help explain the functioning of generational demonic oppressions in people.

Covenant theology and creational boundaries

How might a Christian doctrine of creational boundaries guide us on the perplexing problem of ancestral spirits? How should therapists and pastors respond when someone says that ancestral human

1. Huston Smith, *Forgotten Truth: The Primordial Tradition* (New York: Harper & Row, 1976), 110.

spirits are oppressing them? Studies suggest that approximately 4–8 percent of the population of North America believe that they have communicated with the dead, have been controlled or possessed by a spirit of the dead, or have knowledge of past lives.[2] People hear voices, see spirits, perform automatic writing, and experience direct spirit control of their voices, including xenoglossy, which is the speaking of unlearned languages. Within Dissociative Identity Disorder (DID), one in five people with multiple personalities has an alter personality that claims to be that of a dead relative.[3]

In the face of such data, I suggest that we must hold to the boundaries. People go to Sheol in the Old Testament, or to Hades and paradise in the New Testament. There is no lingering in some hypothetical near-earth realm. Thus, when he was called up from Sheol by the Witch of Endor (1 Sam. 28:19), what did Samuel tell Saul? "Tomorrow you and your sons shall be with me." There will be no hanging around to tidy up unfinished business.[4]

The question of human spirit boundaries also applies to the mix of alter egos, demons, and other personality fragments that may be present in DID. Therapists report that in some cases, mysterious entities seem to fit none of the usual personality categories of core ego, alter parts, or demons. This observation has led some Christian therapists to speculate that external human spirits—dead or living—may be involved in the system.

Since 1987, Tom Hawkins of Virginia has worked with more than a thousand people with DID. Addressing the issue of human spirits, both living and ancestral, Hawkins says a mystery "part" can be any of four things. It could be a memory replay so vivid that it seems as

---

2. According to John Palmer, "A Community Mail Survey of Psychic Experiences," *Journal of the American Society for Psychical Research* 73 (1979): 232, in Charlottesville, VA, the number is 8 percent. The number in Winnipeg, MB, is around 4 percent, according to Colin A. Ross and Shaun Joshi, "Paranormal Experiences in the General Population," *Journal of Nervous and Mental Disease* 180 (1992): 358. Both studies were done by people attached to hospital psychiatric units.

3. Colin A. Ross, G. Ron Norton, and Kay Wozney, "Multiple Personality Disorder: An Analysis of 236 Cases," *Canadian Journal of Psychiatry* 34 (June 1989): 415.

4. In private conversation, James Krabill, a former mission worker in Ivory Coast, has noted that many African Christians hold that the death boundary in 1 Samuel 28 can be breached, but that scripture forbids one to do so. Space prohibits a full discussion here, but I believe that Satan's lying signs and wonders of 2 Thess. 2:9-11 fully account for ancestral spirit phenomena in Africa and other regions.

though another person's voice—that of a parent or an abuser—is playing like a tape inside one's head.

Or it could be a self-interjected perpetrator alter. In this case, the trauma victim creates an alter like the captor or tormentor, in order to think like the abuser and thus lessen the torment. If the tormentor should die, a victim or therapist without an adequate theology of creational boundaries might believe a human ancestral spirit to be present.

Third, the part might be a pre-alter with a familiar spirit. The alleged ancestral spirit is a human pre-alter fragment with an attached familiar demonic spirit, which can give the alter the identity of the demon's previous host. The human alter functions as a front end for a demonic presence.

Finally, the mystery part could be a demon with an encoded human blueprint. In this case, the familiar spirit uses as a template a personality blueprint of another human in whom it lived previously, which permits it to appear as a human alter in the current host human. The difference between these two cases is that in the latter instance, there is an external human personality pattern, and in the previous, there is an internally generated human alter.

Covenant theology and representational headship

A second aspect of covenant theology that bears on generational sin and demonization is the principle of the human as "representational head." Walter Brueggemann, among others, points to Old Testament enthronement texts in which the king is "raised from the dust" to be ruler.[5] In like manner, Adam and Eve were raised from the dust to be regents. In God's covenant with Adam and Eve to "tend the garden or die," *to tend* means "to guard": They were not to grant the serpent and chaos access to the garden. But they failed and instead sold humanity's birthright to the serpent. Therefore, with Adam and Eve as our representational heads, we as a race broke covenant with God and formed a covenant with Satan. This central spiritual transaction is the ultimate basis by which Satan's demons have access to humans.

When God made the Sinaitic covenant with Israel, Yahweh, as the superior party, stipulated consequences for the performance

5. Walter Brueggemann, "From Dust to Kingship," *Zeitschrift für die Alttestamentliche Wissenschaft* 84 (1972): 1–18.

and nonperformance of the various provisions. These stipulations are shaped by the basic Ancient Near Eastern blessing and curse formulae.[6] Exodus 20:5-6 gives the basic formula and is paralleled by Exodus 34:6-7 and Deuteronomy 5:9-10. Other texts that teach the formula with small variations are Numbers 14:18, Deuteronomy 7:9-10, and Jeremiah 32:18. All of these specify blessings to the thousandth generation and curses to the third and fourth generations, rhetorical time frames that emphasize God's greater desire to bless than to curse. Leviticus 26 summarizes stipulations in a progression: the promise of prosperity for obedience (vv. 3-13), a warning of curses following disobedience (vv. 14-39), and the provision for restoration (vv. 40–45). These conditions are repeated in greater detail in Deuteronomy 28–30; chapter 30 has a powerful statement of covenant curse reversal and restoration after repentance.

Scripture cites leaders who practiced representational headship in confessing their own and their ancestors' sins as a prelude to restoration by God. We see this spiritual process in the psalmist (106:6), in Jeremiah (3:25 and 14:20), Nehemiah (1:6-7), and Daniel (9:4-19).

It is one thing to function as representative head for one's family line, but how far may one push this principle? The following illustrations may cast some light on the question. In 2002, a member of my intercessory prayer support team asked me to lead in prayers of release for her niece, the wife of her nephew, in an American state. This woman had a history of ancestral sin, sexual abuse, and institutionalization. Another member of my team with the gift of prophecy was given messages that seemed to say we ought to go ahead, so we gathered a small group and prayed. My intercessor, the aunt, took on the role of confessor for the family. The results of these prayers remain unclear, but I think we did right in having the aunt act representationally for a family member unable to act for herself.

A second example shows a different side of the issue. When I was leading a person with DID to deal with certain idolatrous sins of the past, we decided that the core could act as head for several other alters who had also been involved in the particular occult activities. As we enumerated the parts to be included, one alter screamed internally,

---

6. Although Julius Wellhausen dated the hypothetical D document behind Deuteronomy to about 622 BCE, it reflects a vassal treaty structure known already in the Late Bronze Age (that is, about 1300 BCE). See R. K. Harrison, *Introduction to the Old Testament* (Grand Rapids, MI: Eerdmans, 1969), 649.

"Count me in!" In this instance, the spiritual oppressions that brought these issues to our attention subsequently disappeared.

Covenant theology and the generational transmission of sin

In this section, I will consider several practical theological aspects of generational curses and demonic oppressions. A number of issues present themselves.

How does the doctrine of multigenerational curse and blessing relate to theodicy, the problem of evil? In his commentary on Deuteronomy 28, Duane Christensen calls the obey/blessing and disobey/curse linkages "an oversimplification." He points to Job as an example of one who obeyed and suffered.[7] Theodicy—the problem of evil—introduces the big picture, which in this case leads us to ask, If God blesses obedience and curses disobedience in the covenant relationship, what does Satan do? Satan curses obedience to God and blesses disobedience! There are about 202 curse references in the Bible. God utters the curse 143 times,[8] leaving about 59 that are pronounced by Satan or Satan's human servants. Because covenant dynamics need to take into account the actions of personal agents at three vertices and not simply two, one therefore might refer to the covenant triangle.

Doesn't the Old Testament ultimately teach personal responsibility for sins? Ezekiel 18:2-4 is sometimes cited as teaching personal responsibility for sins: "It is only the person who sins that shall die"—a principle echoed in Jeremiah 31:29-30. Ezekiel develops the theme in some detail in chapter 18, considering various ethical permutations that might arise from righteous parents and offspring, and the reverse of each, before declaring again in verse 20, "A child shall not suffer for the iniquity of a parent." However, directly between the two assertions of personal accountability, verse 14 states a crucial caveat to the principle of personal accountability. It says that the consequences of the father's sins are not passed to the son if the son sees his father's sins and "does not do likewise." Thus, even with personal accountability, the ancestral connection is cut only when a

---

7. Duane L. Christensen, *Word Biblical Commentary* 6B: *Deuteronomy 21:10–34:12* (Nashville: Thomas Nelson, 2002), 673.

8. Ed Murphy, *The Handbook for Spiritual Warfare* (Nashville: Thomas Nelson, 1992), 442–43.

subsequent generation repents. Sanctification requires repentance for both personal and ancestral sin.

Aren't people who worry about generational sin really closet Mormons? The "Mormon question" was brought to my attention a few years ago when I presented a colloquium on the theology of deliverance healing at Conrad Grebel University College. The first audience response was from Tom Yoder Neufeld: "What keeps you from being an evangelical Anabaptist Mennonite Mormon exorcist?" He was really asking whether the doctrine of ancestral sin and demonic oppression is fundamentally different from the Mormon belief that the living are responsible for the salvation of the ancestral dead. This is a fair question that is easily answered. In dealing with ancestral sin, I am not trying to save my ancestors, but I am trying to deal with the guilt and consequences of their actions for my life. It is for my life that I seek cleansing as I engage in representational prayers of confession, renunciation, and restoration. My ancestors remain accountable before God for whatever sins they may have committed, just as the scriptures say we all are.

Doesn't Jesus reject generational sin? The classic text here is John 9:1-7, the account of Jesus healing the man born blind. The disciples' question is, "Who sinned—this man or his parents?" Jesus' reply was "neither," or, as Leon Morris puts it, "in this case."[9] Instead, "he was born blind so that God's works might be revealed in him." Theologically, this answer may be as problematic as the answer that points to generational sin, because it seems to attribute the man's blindness to God's actions. Is God taking one step backward in order to take two forward? Mennonite Anabaptists who adhere to an unrestricted Arminianism may be as uncomfortable with this answer as with an ancestral or personal explanation!

However, Matthew 23:32-36 presents a clear generational assessment of Jerusalem's coming destruction. Jesus says, "Fill up then, the measure of your ancestors" (v. 32), and "upon you may come all the righteous blood shed" from Abel to Zechariah (v. 35). The Pharisees will suffer from both their ancestors' and their own guilt.

Does not the New Testament say the law has been abolished in Jesus Christ? The curse is that the law created sin (Rom. 4:15), but obedience does not justify those whose sin is so defined. (Note that Paul, the apostle of justification through faith, writes in Philippians

9. Leon Morris, *The Gospel according to John* (Grand Rapids, MI: Eerdmans, 1971), 478.

3:6 that "as to righteousness under the law, [I was] blameless.") This double bind is the curse of the law, which Jesus abolished. Although his obedience removes us from the catch-22, the law still stands (Matt. 5:18).

Are not terms such as *generational sin* and *curse* just euphemisms for historical process? A single individual is a complex phenomenon. Each of us has our individual DNA, a brain, a will, a human spirit. In addition, we have intergenerational emotional scripts and personal emotional wounds. Christians also have the presence of the Holy Spirit. Unfortunately, we may also have a demonic familiar spirit. On the stage of life, we follow a general script, but each of us can also do improvisational theater within this framework.

The Holy Spirit helps the characters with their lines, but the familiar spirit character is dedicated to pulling the whole performance off course. The demonic performer causes characters to stumble over their lines. When our play is done and the next generation begins, new characters come on stage with a new set of wills, emotional transactions, and spirits. But the same demon will be there and will remain there until someone works with the Artistic Director to write the demon out of the script.[10]

What is the shelf life of multigenerational curses? The Mosaic code of blessings to the thousandth generation and curses to the fourth is rhetorical. My experience suggests that multigenerational curses usually do not last more than 300 years. Deuteronomy 23:2-3 specifies that those born of illicit sexual unions—as well as Ammonites and Moabites—are prohibited from the Lord's assembly to the tenth generation. If one were to apply this passage, using a forty-year generation, a literalistic hermeneutic would yield 400 years.

What kind of sin triggers a multigenerational curse? The kind of sin that triggers a multigenerational curse is sin that God anathematizes. In the Mosaic code, such sins include idolatry and murder but not something as minor as plowing with an ox and donkey yoked together (Deut. 22:10). Beware the diversionary straw men used by critics and skeptics of deliverance healing to muddy scripture's discrimination between mortal and venial sin, a distinction explicitly stated in 1 John 5:16-17.

10. Passage of time, according to the scriptural motif of third and fourth generations, will eventually send the demon offstage. However, the propensity for new familial sin to enter the scene will generate replacement familiar spirits.

How are multigenerational curses cut? In the Ancient Near East, Israel was unique in its doctrine of covenant curse reversals.[11] Commentators remind us that the psalter is a deliverance book.[12] In the Old Testament, the name of Yahweh was powerful in deliverance, as exemplified in Psalm 44:5, "Through your name we tread down our assailants." When the Old Testament principle is brought forward to the covenant of Jesus Christ, the process outlined in Leviticus 26 and Deuteronomy 28–30 continues: confession and repentance of the triggering sin(s), forgiveness of ancestors, and walking in truth. However, Yahweh's name is replaced with Jesus' name, as we see in the hymn in Philippians 2:9, which exalts Jesus' name above all names (citing Isa. 45:23).

Covenant theology and markers of generational demonic activity

Discernment of the spirits is an important spiritual gift often neglected, to the peril of the church today. An important part of such discernment is the ability to recognize patterns in the landscape of a person's family history. Though the following list of markers is not exhaustive, it will cover the main points of entry through which generational curses gain access in family lines.

Idolatry. If the family line has any history of idolatrous practices, ancestral curses will be present. Such idolatrous practices include water dousing; traditional folk healing, with charms and incantations (for example, use of Johann Georg Hohman's *The Long Lost Friend*); contemporary energy healing techniques, such as therapeutic touch, acupuncture, or homeopathy; "second sight"; or any "psi powers." People who worship such demonic nature gods are themselves setting in motion such curses on their descendants.

Gross or mortal sin. Gross or mortal sin includes such sins as murder, rape, incest, abuse of various kinds, self-curses, dedications and deals with Satan (especially those sealed with blood in witchcraft

11. Herbert Wolf, "The Transcendent Nature of Covenant Curse Reversals," in *Israel's Apostasy and Restoration*, ed. Avrahim Gilead (Grand Rapids, MI: Baker Books, 1988), 319–23.

12. Friday M. Mbon, "Deliverance in the Complaint Psalms: Religious Claim or Religious Experience?" *Studies in Biblical Theology* 12, no. 1 (April 1982): 9. Mbon is referring to Sigmund Mowinkel's comments on the Hebrew term *awen*, "sorcery," which he understood to include supernatural beings, demons, or evil spirits.

and coven rituals). It also includes such habitual sins of the flesh as religious legalism, sexual addictions, and alcoholism.

Recurring physical illness. Deuteronomy 28:18 speaks of a curse that causes infertility and reproductive problems: "Cursed shall be the fruit of your womb, the fruit of your ground, the increase of your cattle and the issue of your flock." Charles Kraft illustrates this curse with a case of women in three consecutive generations who had hysterectomies at virtually the same age.[13] The coincidence alerted the ministering team to look for a familiar spirit, which they subsequently found.

Recurring mental illness. Also in Deuteronomy 28, we read, "The LORD will afflict you with madness, blindness, and confusion of mind" (v. 28). "[You will be] driven mad by the sight" (v. 34) and "[you will have a] trembling heart, failing eyes, and a languishing spirit" (v. 65). As part of the covenant curses triggered by disobedience, these phrases may relate to recurring mental illness.

Recurring mental illness is an Achilles heel for mainstream medicine, in part because it raises the specter of eugenics. In 1927, the U.S. Supreme Court upheld laws encouraging compulsory sterilization of people who were mentally ill, because science had "proven that mental illness is genetic." As Justice Oliver Wendell Holmes said, "Three generations of imbeciles is enough."[14] The outcome is well known: the Americans who were sterilized were heavily overrepresented by single-parent southern black women on welfare.[15] Many biological psychiatrists today still believe that the ultimate causes of mental illness will be found in our genetic makeup. The field has spent a century of intensive research trying to prove it, but as recently as 2003, Wolfgang Maier reported that research on "genome-wide scans in schizophrenia, bipolar disorder, alcoholism, [and] late-onset Alzheimer's disease" shows that (1) no single gene causes these or contributes most to their occurrence; (2) multiple susceptibility

---

13. Charles Kraft, *Defeating Dark Angels* (Ann Arbor, MI: Servant Publications, 1992), 74–75.

14. Miriam Reed, "Sterilization, Eugenics, and Margaret Sanger," http://www-personal.umd.umich.edu/~ppennock/doc-eugenics.htm.

15. Alvin Pam, "Biological Psychiatry: Science or Pseudoscience?" in Colin A. Ross and Alvin Pam, *Pseudoscience in Biological Psychiatry: Blaming the Body* (New York: John Wiley & Sons, Inc., 1995), 12.

genes are at work, but contribute only modest effects; (3) there is environmental influence on all psychiatric disorders.[16]

Two principles seem to follow from these observations. First, mental disturbances usually signal soul distress, in the same way that a toothache signals tooth decay. Second, the personality "stage" can be quite crowded, depending on the amount and degree of triggering emotional and sin trauma. Soul distress provides fruitful grazing ground for demons that both create and exacerbate anxiety, panic, mania, melancholia, epilepsy, and schizophrenia. As a result, more than one ancestral demonic character is often at work.

Familiar spirits counterfeit and manipulate our emotional woundedness, a point I observed in working with a depressed person who had seen psychiatrists and general practitioners for years. I was called after a suicide attempt. A family member said that I was the first person who had actually been helpful, because I was the first helper to trace the depression and attached demons four generations back. An ancestor had been standing on a high barn beam with a rope on his neck when God stopped him. He had been born with a disfigurement, which his parents turned into a curse by shutting him away in a back room whenever company came.

When recurring mental illness alerts us to possible multigenerational demonic involvement, we should look for three types of confirmation. First, check for ancestral initiating trauma—life events with the potential to breach ego walls. Such trauma can be organic, psychological, or spiritual. The Colin Ross trauma model for mental illness has the potential to change the etiological paradigm employed by psychiatry. Ross asserts that family and twin studies controlled for abusive families or parents show high statistical significance for DID and posttraumatic stress disorder. "In the absence of severe trauma, cases [of DID] would not occur no matter what the fostering pattern."[17]

Second, identify all paranormal phenomena. A genogram of Carl Jung is most illuminating in this respect.[18] Over the course of 300 years, the Jung ancestral lines exhibited a wide range of paranormal activities, such as mediumship, mood disorders, visions, and psi

---

16. Wolfgang Maier, "Psychiatric Genetics," in *Psychiatric Genetics: Methods and Reviews*, ed. Marion Leboyer and Frank Bellivier (Totawa, NJ: Humana Press, 2003), 4–7.

17. Colin A. Ross, "Conclusion: A Trauma Model," in *Pseudoscience in Biological Psychiatry*, 270.

18. Lawrence E. Burkholder, "Who Am I?" (unpublished notes, April 2004).

powers. Jung's own rejection of orthodox Christian faith may have contributed to this situation. Jung's biographers refer to a "psychosis" that he suffered from 1911 to 1919. However, we may well wonder whether it actually consisted of demonic manifestations resulting from recurring patterns of idolatrous worship, spiritualism, and paranormal phenomena in the Jung family line.

Third, look for voices and visions with anti-Christian content. Whether these come via schizophrenia or epilepsy, hallucinogens, sensory manipulations, channeling, false religion, or any of several other access doorways, a common thread is the avoidance, disavowal, or misrepresentation of Jesus' atonement. Such voices and visions must be put to the test indicated in 1 John 4:1-3. Much discernment may be needed, because of the factors discussed above. The helper must identify the nature of the voice or source, whether memory, perpetrator interject, human alter, or familiar spirit. From a psychological perspective, Ross notes that more than 40 percent of those with DID had previously been diagnosed as schizophrenic,[19] probably because of the voices. He observes that the presence of internal voices arguing and commenting implies DID, which biological psychiatrists may miss because of their pro-genetic paradigm bias.

In a short but provocative sentence, Dan G. McCartney writes, "Jesus did what Adam should have done; he cast the serpent out of the garden."[20] Thus, the stage of our lives is no less than the Garden of Eden itself, and deliverance healing is a part of reclaiming paradise. In Jesus Christ, we have been given the awesome opportunity to take back the garden from the serpent and to reclaim our birthright. Can one imagine a greater calling for Christian healers?

---

19. Ross, Norton, and Wozney, "Multiple Personality Disorder," 415.

20. Dan G. McCartney, "*Ecce Homo*: The Coming of the Kingdom as the Restoration of Human Vicegerency," *Westminster Theological Journal* 56 (Fall 1994): 10.

Chapter 4

Suffering, sin, and the generous grace of God

A response to Lawrence E. Burkholder

Heidi Siemens-Rhodes

Lawrence Burkholder's essay is rooted in theological inquiry and personal and pastoral experience. As a seminary student and someone who has never personally observed the face of individual demonic oppression—or the paranormal in any form—I am tempted to sit down directly and let the voice of experience stand as is. This is a temptation I will resist, with the Spirit's help.

I hear in Burkholder's presentation a call for holistic treatment of the "hard cases." Hard cases are always beyond the scope of any one healing entity or method. Cases of severe distress undoubtedly will have physical, mental, emotional, and spiritual aspects, and perhaps others. Just as "the individual" can be an unhelpful concept in addressing hard cases—family and environment, along with other factors, must come into play—so is there no individual healer, except the Creator God, who works through all those who surround a hurting person with help. This indeed may be the most Anabaptist of all the aspects we are discussing.

Perhaps the least Anabaptist aspect of Burkholder's essay is the idea that certain "mortal" sins are triggers for a multigenerational curse. It is true that a hierarchical distinction is made between mortal and other sins in 1 John 5, as in the broader church tradition. But as Anabaptists, we hold Jesus to be our model—Jesus who said, "You hypocrite, first take the log out of your own eye, and then you will see clearly to take the speck out of your neighbor's eye" (Matt. 7:5). And, "You have heard that it was said to those of ancient times, 'You shall not murder'; and 'whoever murders shall be liable to judgment.' But I say to you that if you are angry with a brother or sister, you will be liable to judgment; and if you insult a brother or sister, you will be liable to the council; and if you say, 'You fool,' you will be liable to the hell of fire" (Matt. 5:21-22).

Jesus also said, "Let anyone among you who is without sin be the first to throw a stone" (John 8:7). We are all sinners, saved by grace, which we can all claim through repentance. When there is no repentance, when sinful patterns become deeply a part of who we are, repentance becomes a less and less feasible option. But it is always an option. There is no mention of a hierarchy of sins in the 1995 *Confession of Faith in a Mennonite Perspective.*[1] I question whether certain types of sin can or should be singled out as entrance points for the demonic.

Our spiritual connections to previous generations are deep and formative. Without a doubt, we are fundamentally affected by the choices our parents and their parents made. I find it more difficult to accept the claim that familial spirits and curses are to blame when we see patterns of behavior—especially abuse—that plague several generations. We certainly do learn sins within the context of the family, and I do not doubt that this learned behavior pleases Satan and the forces of evil. But I wonder whether the distinction between what one might call *generational learned behavior* and *generational transmitted demonic presence* is an important one.

I am intrigued by Burkholder's image of the stage of a person's life, occupied by the various parts of who we are, including—for a Christian—the Holy Spirit as guide. In this image, a familiar spirit has taken up residence on this stage and will remain there until the individual, or a subsequent generation, repudiates it. But does this familiar spirit pass from only one person in each generation to one of his or her physical offspring? On the face of it, this may seem a ridiculously meticulous question. I ask it because if the familiar spirit is not a discrete entity, but can spread itself to more than one child or over more than one living person in different generations, how is it different from the more widely acknowledged concept of sin itself? That is, how is the sin of anger different from the familiar spirit named Anger? How can we conceptualize the "stage" of a person who is not plagued by a familiar spirit? Who or what instigates the cycle of temptation and sin and repentance on the stage of someone not afflicted by the demonic?

Another question relates to the theological basis of generational sin in the Old Testament blessing and curse formulas. The first clause, which promises blessing to the thousandth generation, is much

1. *Confession of Faith in a Mennonite Perspective* (Scottdale, PA: Herald Press, 1995).

stronger than the second, the curse, which is passed on to three or four subsequent generations. If we take the latter so literally and seriously, shouldn't we emphasize the former all the more? Who among us has no godly person in the last 1,000 generations of his or her family tree? I ask this not to be flippant, but simply to highlight the negative slant inherent in searching one's pedigree for a sinful ancestor when one is troubled. We are affected by the sins we witness and those visited on us in our family systems, but as Burkholder states, using Ezekiel 18:14, "the consequences of the father's sins are not passed to the son if the son sees his father's sins and 'does not do likewise.'" Repentance and renewal are the birthright and the responsibility of every generation.

Personal suffering is not necessarily a consequence of our sins or those of any other person. We certainly do suffer the consequences of our sins in an ultimate sense. But as the biblical wisdom literature tells us, it is also true that gross sinners sometimes prosper, and the saints suffer through no fault of their own. We should be careful when we seek to specify the cause of the trouble in a hard case. We must, rather, remember the multifaceted nature of humans as relational, historical, physical, and spiritual beings.

With Burkholder, I hope that we as helpers of those who are troubled will remember that Christ's life, death, and resurrection broke the powers of sin and death. As a result, we as Christ's followers have been given power to contend with evil. May we all rely heavily on the Holy Spirit's guidance in using that power to cast out evil—first from within our own selves, and then in the lives of those who may come to us seeking deliverance.

Chapter 5

The systemic spirit of the family

Reframing intergenerational sin in a therapeutic culture

Ronald E. Hammer

As a pastoral counselor who does marriage and family counseling, I view the concept of intergenerational sin and its effects on a particular client from two distinct but related vantage points. One is a psychofamilial perspective, in which the transgenerational family projection processes reflect a highly undifferentiated client—in most cases the identified patient in the family of origin. The second is a biblical and theological perspective, in which the image of God in a member of the body of Christ seems drastically unrealized and disconnected from shalom as found in the community of faith. I believe God has created this person in the image of God and desires that we endeavor together to realize the fullness of that image through the work of Christ and the sanctification of the Holy Spirit.

Those who focus on the demonic and on deliverance ministry sometimes miss the significant ways a community surrounds people and provides hope and help. They focus more on a particular cultural framework as normative, and juxtapose their approach with that of mainstream medicine, as if theirs were a separate—supernatural—healing science. I would rather examine the similarities between deliverance ministry and a family systems therapeutic approach, and emphasize a faith connected more to the spiritual power of love than to the power of supernatural intervention—even if that supernatural is God.

Bowenian family therapy

Bowenian family therapy identifies eight basic processes, including family projection and multigenerational transmission.[1] The family

1. C. Margaret Hall, *The Bowen Family Theory and Its Uses* (Northvale, NJ: J. Aronson, 1991).

projection process describes the ways the emotional immaturity present in any family is transmitted to the most dependent child, especially when one or both parents display this immaturity. For example, an unfulfilled mother who feels lack of care and respect from the father may involve herself in the life of the youngest child, born soon after the death of her own mother. She projects an extreme directedness to this child, examining and criticizing every step the child makes. The child will feel the same inadequacies and lack of fulfillment the mother feels, and will manifest these feelings in repeated failures. The father's emotional immaturity does not allow him to connect with this child, so he becomes an absent father, further reinforcing the projection.

When these failures in the marriage relationship are transmitted multigenerationally, each subsequent generation tends to become less mature, without understanding the dynamics at work. When this phenomenon is operative with multiple family projections, and is carried on for three or four generations, the mental and emotional distress can become severe. The stress will produce poor health and unbearable relational dynamics. This family system explanation resonates with deliverance ministry's exploration of dysfunctional patterns of coping in demonized individuals, such as abuse, occult experimentation, and abandonment. It provides a reasonable, but not less spiritual, explanation of the "punishing children for the iniquity of parents" passage in Deuteronomy 5:9. The use of genograms to map the family system may be of great benefit to the deliverance minister.[2]

The therapeutic response from a Bowenian perspective invites the client to identify these dysfunctional projections and begin to work at resolving the brokenness. Resolution comes with understanding the methods this particular system uses, such as triangling, family rules, myths, or secrets. Therapy will also examine how the client has been coerced by parents or other members of the family of origin into adopting a pseudo-self. The client may even go to the parents or siblings to confront the situation, thereby gaining freedom from its coercive power. This freedom allows a more real self—a differentiated self—to operate genuinely and authentically within the family system. I compare this therapy with the naming of the demons, which

2. Monica McGoldrick, Randy Gerson, and Sylvia Shellenberger, *Genograms: Assessment and Intervention* (New York: W. W. Norton, 1999).

often have dysfunctional names (Anger, Unforgiveness, Infirmity) that describe more a quality or an action than a person. Next comes a confrontation of the power these demons have, and confession as a means of releasing the demonized person from their coercive control. The person loses the false, demonic representation of his identity and is free to manifest abundant, true life.

The therapist functions as a partner in the journey of discovery. She provide a safe relationship and some ability to see patterns and processes in the client's family of origin. The therapist offers a structure the client must believe will be beneficial, if it is to be effective. Often the therapist must gently but consistently assure the client, on faith alone, that resolution is possible. For instance, a conversation with a long lost aunt may bring some resolution. The client may not understand it, and may even resist it, but afterward will come back with a new self-understanding that allows for more differentiation. If the entire family enters therapy, the potential for more holistic functioning becomes even greater. In my work with families, I often encourage them to find good social support systems that will stand with them through the process.

The commitment of deliverance ministers, and the rest of the community, to stay in relationship with the demonized person through difficult realizations and manifestations seems to work in a similar fashion. The minister helps people see things they perhaps could not see on their own and encourages them to trust—have faith in—the blood of Christ, the work of the Holy Spirit, and the power of the Word of God.

Where true spiritual power lies

Christ calls us to be discerning communities willing to enter a person's journey. Such engagement is the place of real spiritual power. There Christ most powerfully confronts evil in the world. I no longer call such confrontations supernatural, but they are no less miraculous and no more void of Christian spirituality. Different cultural viewpoints and belief systems exist within the context of our Christian faith. One is not necessarily more spiritual than another; one does not necessarily resolve some problems but not others.

Some have suggested that we in the West have lost touch with spiritual warfare and have exchanged it for something less than what scripture describes. I do not accept that assertion if it is based on the fact that our culture rejects demonology as a viable framework for describing disease and mental illness. I know several people who were not helped by deliverance ministry but found healing in counseling. I do not think their problems were mental rather than spiritual. Personhood is far too complex for such a simplistic distinction.

A person's belief system and culture are constantly influenced by experiences and relationships. This interaction is one of the miraculous parts of our faith in Christ as examplar. He met people from different cultures in their own contexts. We meet people missionally in their cultural contexts. Consider the story of the woman at the well in John or that of the rich young ruler in Luke. Look at the story in Luke 7 of the Roman soldier with his military culture. He exhibited such great faith! And consider how the rich Hebrew culture exhibited in the New Testament used belief in spirits as an explanation of all physical and mental illness. As a cross-cultural counselor, I make every attempt to engage clients in a way that fits their worldview and culture.

This observation leads me to a comparison between deliverance ministry and family systems theory. When therapists rely on techniques and tricks as the means of healing, they lose the power that comes from faithful and genuine care for a client. It's just magic. When counselors try to develop a systematic, step-by-step method for working with clients, they lose the real healing environment—that space where people feel loved, respected, and consistently connected to someone who works to understand them and empower them to embrace the image of God in themselves.

Irving Yalom, pioneer of existential psychotherapy, tells the story of a client who seemed stuck for a long time. Session after session of frustrated resistance occurred. The same issues were rehashed over and over. Then, seemingly out of nowhere, the client changed in one session. The client seemed to finally connect on a deeper level, had a significant cathartic session, and left a renewed person. Yalom, curious about what had happened, brought up this encounter in the next session and inquired about what had precipitated this wonderful change. The client replied, "I don't know, but you moved your hand up and down several times in the session. Every time you moved your hand up and down, everything seemed to make sense."[3]

---

3. Irving Yalom, plenary address, 1st Annual Conference on Personal Meaning, International Network on Personal Meaning (Vancouver, BC, August 2000).

Deliverance sometimes seems to be an attempt to use magic to cast out demons. Mapping territorial demons, saying special words, prescribing a course of action, or offering certain prayers that cannot be resisted: all are based on some amalgamation of biblical stories that represent some supernatural spell.[4] The fact that Jesus once asked the spirits to name themselves does not mean that doing so should become a standard practice in deliverance. The fact that some Bible verses say our authority comes in the name of Jesus does not mean that this phrase has some magical power over demons. I am not saying that those words and techniques are without merit. However, I am troubled that deliverance ministry seems to emphasize such techniques more than it stresses the power of love and faithful caring. The latter seems more consistent with a scriptural way of healing.

In each exorcism story in the Gospels, Jesus seems to use a different technique. Each demonized person seems to have a unique manifestation. If the biblical exorcisms are the model for deliverance ministry today, I would expect that deliverance would work as it did with Jesus. That is, the results would be immediate, and those who were freed would experience no recidivism. However, the cases presented in this book—like most cases of demonic possession—take extended periods of time and repeated work to bring a person to healing.

Community and the recovery of the image of God

In contemplating the successful resolution of such "hard cases," I propose that the faithful caring of the community and the community's sincere belief have provided an environment in which people have felt loved, respected, and consistently connected to others who have worked to understand them and empower them to embrace the image of God within. They went through most of the same processes that family therapy has defined in a way that is more culturally understandable in the West.

Another concern I have about deliverance in our Western culture is that it contributes to the family systems process known as scapegoating. People scapegoat when they blame one member of

---

4. Charles H. Kraft, *Christianity with Power: Your Worldview and Your Experience of the Supernatural* (Ann Arbor, MI: Vine Books, 1989); see also C. Peter Wagner, *Engaging the Enemy: How to Fight and Defeat Territorial Spirits* (Ventura, CA: Gospel Light Publications, 1995).

the family system for the problems the family is experiencing.[5] The scapegoat is portrayed as the cause of the anxiety within the family: if the scapegoat could be straightened out, the family would be fine. Treating the scapegoat as the problem only intensifies the enmeshment of the family, even when the shift of focus temporarily relieves the family's anxiety.

In my counseling, I continue to hear people blaming Satan or demons for their problems and see them feeling trapped in their situation. The devil is an easy scapegoat for more readily explainable interpersonal or intrapsychic problems. My college roommate woke up suddenly from an afternoon nap and realized he was late for class; the first words out of his mouth were "Satan! You reset my clock!" The practice of deliverance in a culture that does not frequently identify the workings of demonic phenomena seems to produce misanthropic behaviors which are then blamed on an attack by Satan. Those who express clear projection of their problems in terms of an attack of Satan (or his many minions) I often refer to a deliverance minister who can educate them and perhaps work within their worldview better than I can. Sometimes they return when they realize that they have been scapegoated. However, I worry that the deliverance minister will further entrench the issues by characterizing some relief as the casting out of a demon. I worry that a sense of supernatural freedom from bondage will be followed by the return of the same issues.

Family therapy comes with its own mythology: the family system seems to have its own homeostatic personality that carries across generations. We give it power and a will, put boundaries on it, and engage it or disengage it. We can explain some of its power in relational terms, but Bowen still calls it the most basic structure of humanity. For the most part, psychotherapy's effectiveness does not measure up to the myth that our society creates around it. But it is our modality of choice for emotional and psychological healing, and we Christians should be the best practitioners of it. We have the real connection that allows people to realize their greatest potential. We have the Holy Spirit within us to work in this cultural context with discernment and with agape love. I hope that my clients experience more depth in their own self-discovery because of my faith, not because I bring some new trick into the therapy room—as theophostic counseling

5. Virginia Satir, *The New Peoplemaking* (Mountain View, CA: Science and Behavior Books, 1988).

would promote, with magical, deep healing prayers[6]—but because I am connected to God. With that connection I bring the capacity to connect with the client in a God-filled way.

A case of deliverance

Julie originally came in with her parents but later called to seek individual counseling. She was a twenty-four-year-old graduate student who was living with her parents and her brother. She had an identical twin sister across the state, with whom she had a symbiotic connectedness not uncommon between identical twins. Julie presented the issue of her relationship with her brother, which was increasingly disturbing for the whole family. Her thoughts came out in a sometimes confused fashion, which she often apologized for in the first few months of our work together. She related stories about how both her father and her brother abused her physically as she grew up. At one point, her father left the family, but her parents reconciled, and the whole family moved across the country to join him.

As we discussed her relationship with her brother and his possible bipolar disorder (later diagnosed after hospitalization), Julie often had almost uncontrollable physical impulses to protect and cover herself. As we talked about the violent history of her household, she became increasingly agitated and emotional. I recognized some post-traumatic stress, as well as defense and coping mechanisms that had left Julie relatively detached from herself. She reported self-mutilation in the form of severe scratching of her arms, a sign of her desire to gain some real identity. The sessions soon focused more on her own internal issues than on the ongoing saga of her brother's mental illness and its impact on her.

Initially, we worked on responses to her brother that helped her maintain better personal boundaries. We also worked at stabilizing the relationships with her family, especially with her twin sister. This progress created some space to work on the internal struggle Julie had been experiencing for years. We discussed her view of God, which was moving from a fundamentalist evangelical view to a more liberal feminist understanding. This change was producing an internal struggle, as she tried to make sense of a God who had not protected her or her family.

---

6. Edward M. Smith, *Healing Life's Deepest Hurts: Let the Light of Christ Dispel the Darkness in Your Soul* (Ventura, CA: Regal Books, 2002).

Her relationships with men, including her relationship with her present boyfriend, had led to conversations and actions that Julie described as inconsistent with her values and desires. She felt coerced and was frustrated about the bad choices she had made in those relationships and about actions that reflected a passion she did not feel for the other person. She wanted to stop. She felt that her personal boundaries had been invaded, but she felt trapped in what was rapidly becoming yet another abusive relationship. She was living one more chapter in a story of relationships that ended because of abuse, a story that began in her childhood relationships with her father and brother.

She initially externalized the problems, attributing them to situations in her life and to her faults. Her repeated apologies for anything negative reinforced a deep indwelling of or possession by a spirit of abuse. When we used the word *abuse* and connected it to her self-image, which reinforced the abuse, it became a name that she later described as another self. Julie was beginning to engage some internal personal power that she used to bring more truth into the present relationship with her male friend. She ended actions that she did not choose, and she honestly conveyed her lack of romantic feelings. The family felt the pressure of her new differentiation and began to try to push her back into unhealthy patterns. However, she has continued to maintain this differentiation, and the system is beginning to respond in a more healthy fashion. Her male friend responded well to her disclosures and her boundaries, reinforcing her power to be in a relationship characterized by mutuality and respect.

One could describe Julie's behaviors and viewpoints as a spiritual bondage. The family history and intergenerational issues suggest some kind of generational oppression. While not as bound as the Gerasene man inhabited by unclean spirits (Mark 5:1-20), she did suffer from uncontrollable self-abuse and conflictual relationships that are sometimes labeled as demonic. From a mental health perspective, Julie would be diagnosed with mild borderline personality disorder, along with some trauma-related adjustment disorders.

I had approximately forty sessions with Julie. I consider her prognosis excellent for better interpersonal relationships and for more understanding of herself as made in the image of God, as a powerful and fulfilled person. She continues to recognize her previous reactive ways, which were driven by lack of ego strength and the manipulation of the family system. Her ability to stand as an empowered, differentiated person and to maintain healthy family relationships gives hope not only for Julie but also for the family. She continues to have conflicts both internally and interpersonally, but she is recognizing earlier and earlier her own choices in them. This realization has allowed her to make more respectful choices for herself and in how she relates to others.

Nonbelieving psychotherapists help people understand themselves better and change dysfunctional behaviors. They use most of the same techniques that psychotherapists who claim faith in Christ use. Shamans and other deliverance healers free people from negative forces in their lives. They use many of the techniques that Christian deliverance healers rely on.

Success is not to be conceived narrowly as help in addressing the problems people face; it also means connecting them with a community that can introduce them to the God who created them in the divine image. Have they come into a deeper connection with a life-giving community where they can experience abundant life for themselves and know something of the reign of God? If so, we see a glimpse of the power that was at work when Jesus healed and cast out demons. We see the very revelation of Christ, the one who holds life, coming forth powerfully in the world.

An Anabaptist view

This conviction of the power of the kingdom comes from my Anabaptist beliefs. Alvin Dueck, Anabaptist psychologist, considers the reign of God a primary model for psychotherapy.[7] The character of the therapist as shaped by the kingdom community plays a significant role in the therapeutic process. An Anabaptist understanding of the power of the community in establishing a justice that reflects God's reign shapes the therapist beyond the religious trappings of our faith. Psychotherapy can be either a competing religion or a cultural understanding that submits to the reign of God. Dueck discusses the cultural differences that sometimes get confused with different techniques and practices. If one tries to impose an ideological premise of a particular Christian culture as normative across cultures, one mistakes those premises as the reign of God. The reign of God comes

7. Alvin C. Dueck, *From Jerusalem to Athens: Ethical Perspectives on Culture, Religion, and Psychotherapy* (Grand Rapids, MI: Baker Books, 1995).

from a common ethic formed in the community that relates to Christ as the example of this ethic.

Dueck lists some characteristics of this ethic: peace, justice, compassion, service, and faithfulness.[8] All of these characterize the Anabaptist faith. He sees the church as deciding how these qualities or virtues are practiced in any given day. The ethic of caring community, relational connectedness, and freedom from oppressive systems stands as the healing ethic behind both deliverance ministries and psychotherapy. We can carry these elements into any cultural perspective. The power of the community to discern and interpret scripture resonates with the Anabaptist perspective. If one regards as timeless and universal a dogma that proceeds from a particular culture and time, the gospel gets trapped in a particular method and worldview. When the community continues to challenge and rethink dogma, it may sometimes be in error but will always find correctives.

Deliverance ministry and supernatural explanations of intergenerational sin seem to remain locked in an anachronistic cultural dogma. Today, Western culture as a whole seems to have turned to therapy as its mode of deliverance. Certain pockets of the Christian community still embrace a more supernatural healing process as more God-centered, and as long as they reflect the ethics Dueck recognizes, Anabaptists should support them as we would missionally support other important cultural viewpoints.

Conclusion

I enjoy working collaboratively with the deliverance ministry in my church. We often make referrals to each other and discuss our clients with one another. We disagree about the theological implications of what actually happens in deliverance and counseling, but we realize that both ministries, counseling and deliverance, bring people through difficult situations. For me as a practical theologian, this result is what matters. Does the praxis work, without coercion or oppression? Does the praxis help people discover who they are, as created in God's image? Is the praxis listening to the clients and to their belief system, attempting to work within it, or is it debunking their understanding of evil in the world? Does the praxis try to

8. Ibid., 71.

manipulate a vulnerable person, using suggestion or the arrogant swagger I sometimes see in deliverance ministers?

Our collaboration as counselors and deliverance ministers helps keep all of us honest and appropriate. From either approach, we make sure that we do not overstep boundaries or presume to think that we understand exactly how people change or are delivered. When people come to see me and want to engage in the spiritual battle in a sincere, faithful way, I refer them to our deliverance ministry. The deliverance ministers often call me to consult about issues they do not understand, and they refer many people to the counselors in our counseling ministry. I am concerned when they think they can cure someone with a severe personality disorder or schizophrenic psychoses that manifest themselves in spiritual ways. As long as these ministers provide faithful and consistent care and involve the community in that care, they will help and not harm. Because of our culture today, the counseling ministry dwarfs the deliverance ministry in size and scope, but the best I can hope for in the counseling ministry is that we too do no harm and that we help everyone we can. As David Augsburger, Anabaptist pastoral counselor and theologian, writes:

> The power of healing is owned by community. It is community which can guarantee justice where one has been oppressed or exploited. It is community which goes beyond the mistreatment or misuse of its member families or persons to affirm the worth and dignity of every member. It is community which recognizes those who have the gift of evoking healing, which confers authority to intervene in the pain of those who suffer. It is community which must receive, support, and integrate the ill back into healthful roles and relationships. Healing and health are rooted in the networks of persons that validate and invigorate personhood.[9]

---

9. David W. Augsburger, *Pastoral Counseling across Cultures* (Philadelphia: Westminster John Knox Press, 1995), 365.

Chapter 6

Beyond denigration to a holistic understanding of deliverance ministries

A response to Ronald E. Hammer

Wesley Bontreger

I want to begin by noting a major point of agreement with Ronald Hammer: both of us affirm the faithful workers whose care and sacrifical love make a difference in the lives of wounded people.

Hammer's "The Systemic Spirit of the Family: Reframing Intergenerational Sin in a Therapeutic Culture" is an interesting study in exclusion and embrace. Although Hammer makes room for deliverance ministry, he presents a clear bias toward a family systems therapeutic approach over what he labels—somewhat disparagingly—"magical power" or a "supernatural healing process." He notes similarities in the treatment modalities and the goal of emotional and relationship health. But he does not address whether the initial source of the dysfunction or the dysfunction's specific patterns could indicate which therapeutic approach is likely to be more helpful.

Two questions are relevant here: First, do family systems therapists recognize demonization as a reality to be treated? And second, if the presence of demonic affliction or possession is the source of the dysfunction, shouldn't the nature of the affliction determine which approach will be more useful to the individual? If the answer is affirmative on both counts, then it seems illogical to suggest that a deliverance ministry approach is necessarily less redemptive or more reductionistic than a family systems approach.

Hammer notes similarities in treatment methods: the therapist maps out a genogram of the family system and the deliverance minister details patterns of sin dysfunction. I agree with his statement that a family systems approach is "not less spiritual" than a deliverance ministry one. Both use a multigenerational perspective and explore patterns of dysfunction, with the goal of helping an individual to an authentic and differentiated self. Both seek to empower freedom from dysfunction, so the person can experience a genuine faith and Christ-centered balance forming their identity in relation to God and others.

If the challenge for deliverance ministry therapists is to avoid seeing a demon behind every dysfunction, the challenge for psychodynamic therapists is to avoid embracing a Western cultural model that ignores or dismisses all supernatural reality. Countless cases can be cited, on both sides, of people who were or were not helped by the other approach. This circumstance would indicate that both approaches can be useful if effective discernment and diagnosis are implemented. Perhaps what we need is better integration, better collaboration between therapists of both intervention models in the church community.

Hammer cites the biblical example of the woman at the well yet misses the opportunity to explore the key biblical issue in pastoral intervention: the relationship between sin and dysfunction in a person's life. From a deliverance ministry perspective, the existence of such a connection constitutes a crucial criterion in determining the most effective approach in specific cases. This sin-dysfunction link is an area of potential integration between therapy and deliverance that needs further assessment and the development of models that could serve well in hard cases.

Although I agree with Hammer that a psychodynamic approach through counseling is no less scriptural than a deliverance model, it does seem evident, contrary to Hammer's assertion, that Western culture has lost touch with spiritual warfare and has denigrated it as reflecting an archaic, unenlightened view of phenomena now understood solely in medical and scientific terms. As long as therapists and pastors adhere exclusively to this health-disease model, they will be limited, perhaps even culture bound, in their ability to help people who are afflicted by demonization. A mentality, even within the church, that describes the deliverance ministry approach as using "tricks" and "magic" has left many pastors and leaders with little ability to help in hard cases, except to refer people to secular therapists and counselors.

I concur with Hammer's assessment that scapegoating is a modern cultural tendency, but it is unfair to conclude that deliverance ministry intervention will necessarily entrench or prolong dysfunctional patterns. Therapeutic modes such as reframing, genograms, Western worldview education, and interpersonal and intrapsychic reorientation are helpful but also have left many clients and parishioners without significant improvement after years of counseling. This lack of success in many cases may indicate the problem with subjecting spiritual phenomena to the criteria, definitions, or agendas of a Western worldview rather than to the truth of biblical principles.

Finally, I affirm Hammer's caution about manipulation, dependence on formulas, and irresponsible use of techniques. But the misuse of methods or modes of helping is no less prevalent in psychodynamic practice than in a deliverance approach. I applaud the model used in his church, in which counselors of both approaches collaborate to provide healing for troubled individuals and families. The church and faith community need more of these models. This collaboration has implications for more integrative teaching, preparation, and training for pastors and counselors in our seminaries. A healthy tension of theology and practice in variant intervention modes will better prepare leaders in the church to address the hard cases they will encounter. When more of this integration emerges, we will better meet a key challenge that Hammer appropriately points out, the task of helping hurting people be restored to true identity in the image of God and fully assimilated into a faith community of healthy relationships.

The challenge

Chapter 7

Case study: Mrs. E

Dean Hochstetler

Mrs. E is a stay-at-home mother with three children. Her husband is a businessman. Several people have worked with Mrs. E, including a pharmacist, a layperson from Mrs. E's congregation who has been part of a monthly class on spiritual warfare, Mrs. E's husband, and me.

When Mrs. E came to me, she recited a long litany of problems: "People and events suck me dry, and I have nothing left for my family. I am in high gear until I collapse. I have both short- and long-term memory loss. Severe pains move around in my body, especially on the left side. I feel deaf and dumb. I wear hearing aids, because of the calcification of my inner ear from surgery. My left eye twitches. I worry a lot. I feel abandoned and detached from my husband and parents. I am hyperactive in the extreme but also depressed. My sleep is disordered. I am short of breath. At times my vocal cords do not function. I have a lot of unhealed hurt and pain. Some doctors have thought that I might have multiple sclerosis."

Probing questions

In response to this sobering list, I asked Mrs. E several questions, knowing that about 75 percent of such problems have their origin in the emotional or spiritual areas of life, or in both.

"Do you have any unconfessed sin? If any other person or persons were involved in your sins, name them."

In response, Mrs. E said, "I am angry and bitter because I cannot live up to the expectations of my husband and his mother. I need to confess self-pity, abusiveness, bitterness, anger, and control of others. I had six sexual partners before marriage." The contracts implicitly struck in these affairs were subsequently addressed as sin and broken in Jesus' name, except for her contract with her last sexual partner, who became her husband.

She went on. "I have pondered suicide. I have had two miscarriages." The two babies were named by Mrs. E and her husband, who committed their spirits to God, who gave them.

I then asked, "What has been your personal involvement in the occult? What has been the involvement of your family?"

Mrs. E answered, "We used powwow healers.[1] We used acupuncture. My family used water witching.[2] My family also used a pendulum to determine the sex of unborn children and other things. We used magnets to purify the water in the house. We used shoe magnets.[3]

"One time my family brought in a practitioner who strung a wire from his computer to the client and one to the practitioner. Another wire went to a plate with vitamins, minerals, and herbs on it. The practitioner pushed on the client's fingernails, which produced blips on the computer. This allowed her to diagnose the ailment and prescribe the 'proper things' to use from the plate or tray.[4]

"We also used copper bar therapy and applied kinesiology.[5] We used injections from a homeopathic physician in Indianapolis.[6] We also used horoscopes and watched séances on television." (Although the husband's list and his family system structure were similar to those of Mrs. E, he was not afflicted as she was.)

I then asked Mrs. E to describe the family system of her family of origin, and to tell me what she knew of her ancestry.

She replied, "I grew up in a dysfunctional Amish family. My mother and father were unfaithful to each other. Mother was involved with a neighbor. Both sides of my family were in many instances involved in illicit sexual practices."

I then asked, "What is your medical history?"

Mrs. E responded, "I have sought help with my problems for ten years. I have migraine headaches. My mind is in a constant fog and

---

1. *Brauche* is the Pennsylvania Dutch word; in some places it is called "to try for." In another area of the United States, it is known as "measuring the soul."

2. Also known as "smelling."

3. A fetish.

4. All of this is age-old sorcery, a form of Taoism, as is acupuncture. This form of sorcery seems to become more efficacious when it involves a computer!

5. Muscle testing to determine medicine, herbs, and minerals that the person "needs." This too is a form of fortunetelling (see Deut. 18:9-15).

6. Samuel Hohnemann, a German physician, was the originator of homeopathy (also called naturopathy). He was a psychic and an occultist. For more information on the practice of homeopathy, see Jane D. Gumprecht, *New Age Health Care: Holy or Holistic?* (Orange, CA: Promise Publishing Co.), esp. chap. 10.

is dull constantly. I have had two psychiatrists, five psychologists, three general practitioners, five neurologists, and seven otolaryngologists. Dr. Swain, a physician from Indianapolis, is a specialist in both gynecology and gastroenterology. He said, 'Your internal organs are like those of an 80-year-old and a 300-pound-woman.' I went to the following clinics: Mayo Clinic in Rochester, Minnesota; Boron Clinic in Michigan; Indiana University; one in Denver, Colorado; the Complementary and Alternative Medicine Clinic at the University of Iowa; and a clinic in Salt Lake City, Utah. Three doctors thought I might have multiple sclerosis. No one gave me any help. In 1996, a doctor found pre-cancer cells. None are detected now. My medical records are extensive; they amount to a document four inches thick."

After several sessions with us, Mrs. E had a hospital stay for inflammation around the heart.

Diagnosis

Having had considerable experience over the years with these kinds of problems, I became convinced that the real problem was demonic invasion and control. On an emotional pain scale of 0 to 10 (with 0 as none and 10 as extreme), she reported, "My pain is 10." Her physical pain was similar.

Some people think Christians cannot be demonized. The Bible is relatively silent on this subject. However, my experience—and the experiences of many who work in this field—suggests that Christians can be demonically afflicted. Demonization does not fall out of the sky on someone. Contributing causes must be present; usually personal (approximately 18 percent) or ancestral (approximately 80 percent). Severe physical or emotional trauma accounts for an additional 2 percent or so.

Deliverance ministry and recovery

The deliverance phase in Mrs. E's case covered a three-month span with eight major sessions. Some were lengthy. Two people provided consistent pastoral care for Mrs. E. This kind of care is absolutely essential.[7]

---

7. Severely demonized people often experience severe emotional challenges. They need help to arrive at a sound biblical faith position regarding who Jesus is and regarding their relationship to him and to his finished work on the cross. They need help to rebuild their emotional structure.

The following account presents major landmarks in the journey to recovery on which Mrs. E continues.

First, Mrs. E confessed all known personal sin (see 1 John 1:9). She had found salvation in Jesus five years earlier in a Christian church and became involved in Bible studies. (Eighty-five percent of troubled people have resentment against someone living or dead; we addressed this in Mrs. E's case.)

Second, we put all of Mrs. E's ancestral sins under the blood of Jesus and broke the curses. (See Deut. 5:9; Gal. 3:13; Deuteronomy 27–28; Dan. 9:3-18; and Leviticus 18, 20, and 26. Jesus addresses this issue in Matthew 23 and Mark 9:21. See also 1 Pet. 1:18-19.)

Third, Mrs. E confessed all her occult involvements, one by one. In order to break the generational curses as well as those attached to personal involvements with dark powers, she also confessed involvements in the occult by members of her family system.

Fourth, I affirmed to Mrs. E in her presence that she is forgiven (see John 20:23; Matt. 12:29; 16:19).

The demonic structure

Demons are notorious liars (see John 8:44). Because Christians have received delegated authority (Luke 10:17-19) and are seated with Christ above the demonic realm (see Eph. 1:1–2:7), the demons can be bound to tell the truth before the living God. They seldom lie then, because they have great fear of the judgment after the return of Christ.

The demons were ordered in Jesus' name to reveal their presence or manifest themselves by pictures or messages to the mind (which Mrs. E needed to report to us), verbally (using her voice; such voices are often different from the person's own voice), or through body manifestations. All three of these factors came into focus. Most of the demon's voices were similar to Mrs. E's; some were different. The demons were cut off from Satan and isolated to Mrs. E personally. Jesus has won the victory over the demonic realm on the cross, and his resurrection is proof thereof. We apply that victory.

Because Mrs. E and her husband did not know better and medical science was not offering them hope or help, they resorted to alternative "therapies." Some of these brought more demonic forces to plague her. Some of these are sorcery (Deut. 18:9-15).

Demonic entities[8]

We identified several demonic entities that were affecting Mrs. E:

1. Allah #1 and eleven helpers entered through powwowing and unbelief in family. These included deafness, dumbness, pain in Mrs. E's left side, chest pain, and anxiety.
2. Nova was the spirit of witchcraft and had five helpers.
3. Jonah was the spirit of acupuncture and had four helpers.
4. Lowen was the spirit of unbelief and of witchcraft. It cited acupuncture and magnets as types of witchcraft.
5. Allah #2 entered with five helpers, through unbelief. It manifested itself through pain in the left side, stomach pain, chest pain, and anxiety.
6. Somue was a spirit of acupuncture with eight helpers. These also caused the pains of #4 above. This group was also attached to the shoe magnets.
7. Anger was present, along with three of the symptoms of multiple sclerosis. (There is a medical MS and a demonic look-alike. Mrs. E's symptoms were of the latter variety.) Anger was also in charge of MS and stomach pains.
8. Unforgiveness.
9. Pride.

Demons frequently have strange names. Sometimes the names are the same as the functions they perform, and they can be the names of human emotions. It is therefore important to differentiate between human emotions and demonic afflictions. Luke 8:26-39 illustrates this point. There is some overlap between the two, as the passage shows.

---

8. Demons are not corporations or political powers, as Walter Wink suggests in his "powers" trilogy (see the bibliography). They may be behind or influence some people who run these human entities. Ephesians 6:12 mentions "the spiritual forces of evil in the heavenly places," but corporations and political entities are not in heavenly realms. Nevertheless, under the influence of the spiritual forces of evil, the people who run these human structures often do evil things. Enron and WorldCom are examples.

March 11, 2003, was a decisive day. Most of the demons and their helpers were cast out in Jesus' name. Several were belligerent and refused to leave. They said, "We have been in this family line a long time." We ordered the demons to kneel and confess the victory of Jesus over them. They did. (The demons used Mrs. E's body to do so.) We ordered the demons to look at the cross of Jesus in Jerusalem. They replied, "We can't see it." We ordered them in Jesus' name, "We command your eyes to be opened." They replied, "We see it." We told them to look at Jesus' blood, and they fled. Mrs. E's head was on the floor at this point. As she was released from these wicked spirits, she began to sing about the blood of Jesus.

We spent time reading and talking about scripture passages dealing with Jesus and his blood: Isaiah 53 and 61, John 19:34, and Romans 6. We talked about Ephesians 1:1–2:7, on authority and being seated with Jesus at God's right hand. Mrs. E grasped the value of Jesus' blood to remove her guilt (see Heb. 9:11-14 and 10:19-22). We asked for lists from Mrs. E and her husband, outlining how they affirm each other, and another list of what needs help. First Corinthians 7 (issues of sexual morality) needed to be addressed with Mrs. E and her husband. These and other problems were addressed at a later date.

By April 1, 2003, Mrs. E was much improved. She saw her position in Christ and her identity with Jesus. She began to understand the value of the blood. Her anxiety had lessened, but it was still present. Assurance of salvation came.

We took a theophostic approach to her pain. She saw Jesus hold her in his arms and heal her. She saw a vision of light and felt a suction sensation that seemed to pull the darkness out of the top of her head. (This image refers to emotional issues.) Her mind brightened, and it ceased to be cloudy. Her abdominal pains were now gone, and she was not hot anymore.

Some days later, the inflammation around her heart recurred. Mrs. E's physician could now diagnose the problem and treat it successfully. She maintained frequent contact with one of the people providing pastoral care. Psalm 51 took on a new meaning for Mrs. E, as did Ephesians 6:10-18, on the Christian's armor.

On May 22, 2003, Mrs. E had a migraine headache. Her mind had some cloudiness. Her arm and chest hurt. We addressed the demons again, and more surfaced. I suspected a spirit of infirmity (see Luke

13:13). The discernment was correct. We discovered that Infirmity was indeed present, along with three helpers:

10. Aba controlled the left side.
11. Deaf and Dumb affected mind control and stupidity.
12. Pain invaded her head, arm, and chest.

These helpers threatened to go into Mrs. E's husband and their children because "he doesn't believe"; "he can't believe." It was an attempt at deception. Mrs. E used her own authority in Jesus against these spirits, ordering them to go to the abyss, roots and all. Infirmity replied, "I'll go halfway." We took up commands against Infirmity and informed it about what 1 Corinthians 11 says regarding headship. Mrs. E's husband is her immediate head under Christ. He assumed that role and commanded Infirmity to go to the abyss. The fog then lifted from her mind. The pains left, and she was "clear as a bell."

Conclusion

We sent Mrs. E to a Christian psychologist to see what he would say about how she had progressed through the deliverance process and hospital stay. She saw him three times, and he dismissed her, saying, "You don't need my help any more."[9]

After we had worked on corrections and additions to a rough draft of this case study, Mrs. E said, "This is my past history. I am forgiven. It is under the blood of Jesus. My guilt is gone. The curses are broken. If what happened to me will help someone else, I want to be a party to that help. I want to sign this paper, and when it is presented to a sizable audience, I want to be there. Moreover, I give permission to use my medical records and this case study for teaching purposes."

Epilogue: Reflections

Matthew 15:21-25 recounts the story of a Canaanite woman whose daughter was demonized. The woman said to Jesus, "Lord, help me."

---

9. Many churches in the West say they teach and practice all things, but church teaching about occult practices and their consequences is rare and gives little attention to the realm of the spirit world. In contrast, the Bible addresses this realm a lot. It is implicit in Jesus' command to teach, obey, and observe all he commanded, and to free the captives whom Satan has bound (Matt. 28:18-20). Our hope is that this case study will help lead us. A spouse's love or assurance of salvation cannot be proven scientifically; it lies in a different realm. The demonic realm is not provable by scientific investigation either but rather biblically and experientially.

Is demonization a present reality, a historical reality, or fiction? The Bible affirms it as a reality and so does contemporary experience—provided that our eyes and mind can see it. Modern Western worldviews prevent most Christians from seeing its reality.

Matthew 9:20-22, Mark 5:25-26, and Luke 8:43-44 tell us about a woman who sought the help of many physicians in order to relieve her hemorrhaging—in vain. Current medical practice in all probability could help someone with her affliction. We affirm the validity of the medical profession. It has its rightful place. We often need to avail ourselves of physicians' services. But demonic problems are seldom addressed by physicians or even considered as a possible etiology of someone's problems.

After our next-to-last session with Mrs. E, her doctors were able to diagnose and treat her physical problems. They said a bulged disc between two vertebrae in her neck was responsible for her rib cage inflammation and associated pain.

The dramatic case of Mrs. E affirms what the Gospels teach. Jesus restored Mrs. E as surely as he healed the Canaanite woman's daughter. John 8:31-36 tells us that Jesus said, "You will know the truth, and the truth will make you free." Luke 4:18 emphasizes that Jesus applied Isaiah 61 to himself. He says that he came to release the captives and free the oppressed. According to 1 John 3:8, he came to destroy Satan's works.

This case study is not primarily about the method one uses, although I have addressed that issue. It was written to encourage North American Christians to understand that events like those recorded in the New Testament are still happening today. Jesus is victorious over the demonic world through the cross. The 2,000 years that have passed since Jesus' ministry have changed nothing about Jesus' victory. Jesus' name continues to have authority. We are to use it to overcome all the "power of the enemy" (Luke 10:17-18). Hebrews 13:8 says, "Jesus is the same yesterday, today, and forever." Human nature has not changed either.

This case study was written to bring glory to God, to praise the Lord Jesus Christ, and to emulate his finished work on the cross. At no point do we work toward victory; victory over sin, death, and Satan has already been won on the cross. We needed only apply the victory to this situation.

Chapter 8

Case study: Mr. Q

Dean Hochstetler

Mr. Q is married. He and his wife have one child and are embers of a Mennonite church in northern Indiana. Several years ago, Mr. Q was having severe problems and could not find a way to cope.

A Sunday school class discussion and a sermon brought things to a head for him. Mr. Q sought help from the pastor, who counseled him. On January 15, 2001, the pastor called and told me about this thirty-year-old man. The pastor said, "We need help and we need it now." The pastor, Mr. Q, his wife, and another member of the church came to my house that evening.

Mr. Q's story

I listened to his story. Mr. Q's father had abandoned his family when Mr. Q was one year old. Mr. Q reported a "horrible childhood" with a stepfather. His pain level had been great and was still great. His biological father had been rejected and belittled by his own father (Mr. Q's grandfather), who had declared him hopeless, useless, and worthless. Mr. Q received the same treatment in his childhood home.

Mr. Q's stepfather was verbally and physically abusive to Mr. Q's mother. The father of Mr. Q's mother had often been drunk. As a result, Mr. Q's mother was raised by her stepfather. Mr. Q's ancestry was filled with occult practices. At age twenty-six, Mr. Q passed out once while making margaritas. What caused this episode is not known, although I wonder whether it may have been a demonic trance.

Both Mr. Q and his wife were raised in "the church." They met in a bar but decided to get out of the bar life. Mr. Q had confessed his sins in a blanket statement but had not been specific about them. He had had fourteen sexual partners before marriage but had specifically confessed none of these relationships.

That night in our home, Mr. Q confessed each one as a sin and broke the emotional contracts he had made with each person. He verbally sent the part he had of each person back and retrieved the part of himself the other person had, bringing it back to himself.

To heal the pain, I used a modified theophostic approach, which gets the counselor out of the way and puts Jesus in charge of telling the truth to the person about their pain. Jesus is the healer of pain. Just as Jesus honored the faith of four men who carried a paralytic to him for healing (Mark 2:1-12), so Jesus honors our faith when we bring people to him to be freed. Mr. Q's pain melted away.

Addressing the evil spirits

Later, we asked Mr. and Mrs. Q's permission to address any wicked spirits that may have been attached to him. They agreed. In addressing the evil spirits, I used the following method. First, I told Mr. Q, "I am not speaking to you, even though I am looking right at you and speaking at you. I am addressing the wicked spirit world." Second, I said, "Nothing may happen." That is, there may be no evil spirits present, though I suspected that there were, because of the level of family brokenness. Third, I said, "I will be watching for any bodily manifestations." Next, I said, "The spirits may put messages or pictures into your mind. If so, report them immediately." Fifth, I said, "They may become verbal and use your mouth." Finally, I noted, "It is possible that the evil spirits will take control of your bodily manifestations, put messages or pictures into your mind, *and* use your mouth."

I verbally tied the demon spirits to the chair in which Mr. Q was sitting, commanded in Jesus' name that they do no violence, and called them to manifest themselves. Mr. Q became very uncomfortable in thirty seconds. (Not all cases are like this one.) His face began to distort horribly. Although Mr. Q has a tenor voice, a deep bass voice began to speak, saying, "I am death and I have millions of helpers." This voice seemed to be more than an octave below the lowest note on a piano. I had never heard anything like it! The voices declared that they would never leave, but they did so in Jesus' name and were sent to the abyss. We found no more.

Mr. and Mrs. Q returned for another session on January 18. We sought to discover whether there were any more evil spirits. There were none. Mr. Q said, "From the evening of January 15 on, I have been at peace." I have checked with him four times since the event. He has made remarkable progress spiritually. His pastoral care is adequate.

I instructed Mr. Q and his wife to exercise authority in Jesus' name against any spirits that might afflict their child because of the child's ancestral history. Whether Mr. Q's "death spirits" were ancestral or personal, I do not know. I did not try to find out from the demons. They were told that any answer they gave would need to stand in the judgment before the living Lord Jesus Christ.

Soon after that evening in my home on January 15, 2001, Mr. Q underwent dramatic change. He went from being "dead wood" in the church to being a vibrant Christian. The marks of rebellion that had been in him disappeared. Now he teaches a Sunday school class. He and his wife are youth sponsors in his church.

Today Mr. Q is happy to confess that Jesus Christ is victor. Jesus demonstrated this victory to his disciples when he walked this earth. He commanded the demons to leave people and instructed the disciples to do the same. In Matthew 28:18-20, he tells his followers to teach new disciples "to obey everything that I have commanded you." This case study is one facet of the "everything" to which Christ referred. And it demonstrates that demonization is just as real now as it was 2,000 years ago.

Chapter 9

Case study: Gwen

As told to Duane Beck

Gwen is a divorced mother with three children: two daughters, ages eighteen and fifteen, and a thirteen-year-old son. Gwen was five days old when she and her sister were placed in foster care. Gwen's biological family had significant dysfunction, with suicide, alcohol addiction, and incest in their history. When Gwen was pregnant with her first child, her biological mother, in a drunken state, said to Gwen, "You will never be a better mother than me." Because of addictions, Gwen was not able to care for her first child and gave him up for adoption.

When Gwen was an infant, she and her sister were adopted into a conservative, legalistic Christian family that attended church regularly: "Sunday morning, Sunday evening, Wednesday evening, and any time the church was open," Gwen commented sarcastically. Her sister remembers that the sexual abuse began at bath time. Their adoptive father began to force sexual intercourse on both girls, beginning in early puberty. Gwen's adoptive father was addicted to nonprescription drugs and evidenced sexual addiction. The adoptive mother was passively complicit in the sexual abuse. When confronted about her acquiescence, she would blame Gwen for seducing her father.

Gwen ran away from her adoptive home at age sixteen. A pastor from another church told her parents that she could not come back home. She got involved with various men. "I was like a magnet. I attracted people who treated me horribly." Gwen turned to alcohol and drugs to "mask her pain." When her children were ages three, five, and eight, they were placed in a foster home for a year because of Gwen's negligence, a result of her alcohol abuse.

Later, Gwen remarried and was able to get the children back. Her new husband, who was twenty years older than Gwen, sexually abused her older daughter. Gwen and the children finally left home. The husband overdosed. Their house burnt down.

Gwen met a local pastor when he visited her husband in intensive care. She later commented, "That was the first time I had prayed in two years." That "chance" connection through a pastoral visit and prayer gave Gwen courage to seek spiritual help and to make contact with a church. "I didn't think I would ever darken a church door again," Gwen later commented. Months later, her husband committed suicide, just four days before he was to be sentenced for child sexual abuse.

The hard case

Gwen and her two younger children have bipolar disorder. Gwen also has schizophrenia and dementia. She has trouble with her balance. Her son has been diagnosed with schizophrenia. Gwen and her three children have used inpatient services at Oaklawn Psychiatric Hospital (Goshen, IN) many times. They have all participated in outpatient therapy at Oaklawn. Each member of the family has also experienced sexual abuse.

Growing up in a religiously abusive family, Gwen had experienced significant religious trauma. Her younger son had been traumatized by an ongoing memory of foster parents threatening him: "The devil will come out of the floor register to get you if you keep acting up!" Their present house had a pentagram on the basement wall, painted by a previous occupant.

All three children have had difficulty in school. The two younger children have been in Emotionally Handicapped (EH) classes. Gwen's son was expelled from school for fighting and for traumatizing peers and staff. He was then homeschooled with a teacher provided by the school system. After participating in Oaklawn's long-term residential treatment for eighteen months, Gwen's son has been home for almost a year. He has participated in an alternative school for emotionally disturbed students.

In addition to these physical, emotional, and spiritual needs, the family has dealt with financial crises, which at times have led to poor financial decisions. Family income places them at the poverty level.

Collaboration

No one social service agency, church, or community institution, and no single psychological, spiritual, or social service treatment modality has been entirely successful in bringing healing to Gwen and her family. Nevertheless, all of the groups involved have been helpful.

Agencies working with this family have been or continue to be their local church, Oaklawn (and other mental health centers), their local school, a community wraparound program, the welfare system, the police, and the juvenile probation system.

Dean Hochstetler, a Mennonite deliverance minister, helped Gwen in three sessions through the ministry of prayer and exorcism. Her pastor and another church member have on several occasions ministered to family members with binding prayers or exorcism. The church has drawn small groups together for times of special prayer.

Gwen has needed therapy and medication. Exorcism has dealt with past sins and helped break the power of spiritual confusion and demonic influences from family and church. Hospital care has provided opportunity to stabilize her life. School conferences have worked at proper educational instruction and behavior control for her children. Prayers for healing and for binding evil influences have made some difference. Pastoral and congregational care have provided crisis intervention and the practical help needed to empower and sustain the family during crises and in daily living. A church member has served as a financial advisor for everyday financial issues. Recently Gwen confronted her adoptive parents about the childhood sexual abuse. An Oaklawn therapist led the session in collaboration with Gwen's pastors and the pastors of her parents' church.

Oaklawn has worked with Gwen's church and with her children's schools. Case conferences have sometimes been set up at the initiative of one of the agencies or the church. Gwen's pastor has found it beneficial to be part of collaborative efforts in which all of the helping groups together develop plans for strengthening the family. The pastor can add the church perspective on the family situation and serve as advocate for Gwen and her children in the difficulties they confront. The schools, mental health agencies, the county wraparound program, law enforcement officers, court officials, and probation personnel all appreciate the support of Gwen's pastor and congregation and welcome the opportunity for collaboration.

With the exception of Oaklawn, most agencies do not think of collaborating with pastors and congregations. In such instances, it is helpful for the church to initiate collaboration with these groups. Gwen herself has been part of the collaborative process through her tenacious desire to get resources for her children.

Today Gwen and her children are more hopeful and stable than they were five years ago. Two children have made commitments to Christ and have been baptized. The two older girls are teaching Sunday school. But difficulties continue. The family still needs care, collaboration, and prayer. Despite recent physical setbacks, dementia, and ongoing discord among the teenage children, Gwen has hope.

Recently someone asked her how she keeps going. "Why do you keep hanging in there?" Gwen replied, "Yes, it is often chaotic at home. But none of my children is pregnant. None of them drinks, smokes, or does drugs. And all three are doing well at school." That is something for which one can be grateful! And Gwen will quickly add, "The support, guidance, and acceptance of the church carry me when I have no hope."

Gwen has been reframing her suffering to see it as redemptive. She is aware of the suffering Christ with her. Gwen's perspective is that almost everything that has happened to her has threatened her ability to parent. Dealing courageously with suffering, and understanding her suffering in relation to Christ, will mean that the power of the generational, cultural, and personal sins is broken and that her children will not have to deal with the sins of the past at the same intensity. Suffering love is redemptive.

"In this church I have found a different God than the one I knew as a child. God is no longer a judgmental God that I fear and want to keep at a distance, but a God who loves me and wants to be with me."

Responding to the challenge

Chapter 10

Trusting Jesus when quick fixes elude us

A Belmont Mennonite Church story

Duane Beck

Abuse and abandonment, mental illness and addictions, poverty and poor education, sinful living: these sometimes ravage people at an accelerating pace over several generations. Hard cases are often a result of all these factors, combined in one person's experience.

The accumulation of personal, generational, and social sin is real, and real hard. How does one congregation provide sustained and sustaining support for a family that experiences chaos much of the time? At Belmont Mennonite Church (Elkhart, IN), we wish we could embody Psalm 23, restoring souls, leading in paths of righteousness, and walking with Gwen's family in the valley of shadows.[1] But that is God's work. We are learning that our work is to allow Jesus to shepherd all of us as members of his body. We are together in this flock. "Of one another" is the frequent New Testament description of church reality. To say that our number includes hard cases does not imply that some in the church are worse than others; we all have a common need for restoration, guidance, and the protective presence of the Holy Spirit. Some of the flock that Jesus shepherds have simply had a more turbulent life.

The first challenge that confronts a congregation with hard cases is, of course, that we are in over our heads. We cannot fix these complex problems. One temptation is to ignore or reject troubled people, because we do not know how to help "hard cases." A second temptation is to try harder. So we burn up much energy with one family, have little energy left for others, and waste away as a congregation. A third option is to walk together as brothers and sisters on the path of Jesus. We learn from one another and lean on one another long enough for Christ to make us a new creation.

1. See Gwen's story (chapter 9 in this volume).

The second challenge is congregational balance. Unsolvable, ongoing family crises not only drain energy but also shift congregational and pastoral priorities toward the urgent, away from the important. Worship, faith formation, and community life receive only leftover time and energy. Congregational life and vitality are ignored. The wellspring of life dries up. Living water does not flow. Again we are called into the framework of what is possible. What is possible is to walk together as brothers and sisters, interceding for one another, holding onto one another, and giving God time to transform us through Jesus Christ.

The third congregational challenge is similar to the second. What are the priorities and paradigms, the identity and purpose of the church? Do we concentrate congregational priorities on the hard cases or on the healthy core? Is the congregation a beautiful bowl holding colorful, fresh organic fruit ready to feed a hungry world? Or is it a porous sieve, in which the church gets stained and polluted by the messes in the world? We are not sure. A strong case can be made for each. Perhaps these contrasts are as necessary to congregational life as inhaling and exhaling are to a person. Maybe our life depends on holding them in tension.

There is another level to consider, a level deeper than polarities, deeper than debates about identity and purpose. It is the inner spiritual shaping of people and congregations to hold hard cases in their hearts.

The Beatitudes invite transformation into Christ-likeness. They can help shape our responses to people for whom the accumulation of personal, generational, and social sin has been both real and real hard. The essence of the Beatitudes (Matt. 5:3-10) is the blessing of God. Yes, God does bless us with and through the challenges of hard cases.

Blessed are the poor in spirit. Humility is essential for ministry in hard cases. The complexity and magnitude of human need is bigger than we are. Our training and life experience are inadequate. We simply do not have the personal and spiritual resources to save people; we are poor in spirit. The temptation when we are overwhelmed is to avoid and retreat. Or to blame ourselves for being too weak in spiritual power, for having too little faith, or even for not being Christian enough. A second temptation is to stand off and blame the person we are so faithfully serving for being irresponsible, undisciplined, and sinful. Success can be an even bigger temptation. If something works, we work it to death.

Watch out! Hard cases hardly go away! There may be relief and even healing. We can celebrate steps toward transformation, but the complexity of internal and external issues is deeper than one hope-filled step. Finally, the poor in spirit remember that God's kingdom is bigger than we are. Our prayer is "I trust you, God." God works in many ways, through unlikely people and unimaginable coalitions. We offer a sacrifice of thanksgiving. And the poor in spirit are blessed to inherit the kingdom of heaven.

Blessed are those who mourn. Listen. Love. Empathize. Mourn. We have listened to Gwen's story. It feels like a rocket-propelled grenade has exploded, and the church is left holding the fragments of broken lives—broken lives for at least three generations of biological and adoptive families. "There, but for the grace of God, go I." Love. Marvel at the strength simply to survive. Glimpse the grace of God shining through at unimaginable moments. Mourn the loss of love for God over the generations. Mourn the loss of love within crucial, formative familial relationships. Mourning is a basic attitude for ministers of reconciliation who seek to recover lost love. And those who mourn are blessed with comfort.

Blessed are the meek. A gentle trust listens for God's will and focuses one's energy to do it. "God, I pray only for the knowledge of your will and the power to carry it out" is the eleventh step of the twelve-step spiritual programs that are so helpful for hard cases. Another prayer is basic to all involved in the hard cases: "God grant me the *serenity* to accept the things I cannot change, the *courage* to change the things I can, and the *wisdom* to know the difference."

Those who are meek trust that the power of God that raised Jesus from the dead is also at work among us. The meek are more like cups waiting to be filled than can openers forcing open a drink. But the meek are street smart, wise as serpents and harmless as doves. The meek walk in the belief that "God, who is rich in mercy, out of the great love with which he loved us even when we were dead through our trespasses, made us alive together with Christ" (Eph. 2:4-5). And the meek inherit the earth.

Blessed are those who hunger and thirst for righteousness. Blessed are the merciful. These two gifts of God's blessing hold the tension of righteousness and mercy, holiness and forgiveness, justice and peace.

It is this tension that makes salvation work. We have hunger pangs for people to live in right relationship with God. When survival instincts take over and people fall back into self-destructive habits, we weep, shake our heads, and wonder why. We support righteous living. It is life-giving. We confront honestly and clearly, while holding people in love, seeking to be full of mercy toward them as we believe Jesus is full of mercy with us. We counsel financially in order to help them develop new habits of self-care.

Righteousness demands justice work. We become advocates in legal and financial systems that are often impersonal and uncaring. We help confront people who have abused these systems. We pull together people who work in the bureaucratic maze of social systems to join forces in walking with these hard cases. God has many friends in the city. Salvation and healing are the thrust of the fourth and fifth Beatitudes. Yes, being involved in hard cases leaves us hungry and thirsty to be filled and to be transformed into vessels that are mercy-filled.

Blessed are the pure in heart. The pure in heart are not quick to judge. In fact, in the mirror of hard cases, the pure in heart can see themselves—their own weaknesses, temptations, and self-centered tendencies. A financial adviser confronting ill-advised expenditures can be sensitive to her own self-centered purchases. We "all have sinned and fall short of the glory of God" (Rom. 3:23). To see ourselves as God sees us is the gift of the pure in heart. Loved and enjoyed. And the promise that they will see God is already fulfilled in the faces of those whose lives have been marked by hard relationships.

Blessed are the peacemakers. Peacemaking is at the heart of relating with hard cases. Shalom-making. A holistic approach to God's shalom-making includes counseling, advocating, praying, financial advising, organizing case conferences among helping organizations, and linking people with community resources. To paraphrase the proverb, it takes a village to restore a family.

Blessed are the persecuted. Evil is overtly and subtly present in hard cases. It works overtime to keep its tenacious hold on hard cases and would like nothing more than to get footholds in the congregation. As followers of Jesus, we believe that suffering love is redemptive. But it is hard. Yes, we can laugh when people laugh, multiplying joy, and we can weep when people weep, dividing sorrow. But what are we called to do when our brothers and sisters' lives are chaotic and out of control? Are we called to absorb anger? We pray. We pray for spiritual armor. We pray to bind and cast out the forces of evil. We pray in thanksgiving when the risen Lord Jesus intervenes. And we are blessed with the kingdom of heaven. This blessing launches us back to the beginning, the first Beatitude, in which the poor in spirit also inherit the kingdom of heaven. And the cycle of blessings and the cycle of transforming attitudes begin all over again.

We are upheld by the tenacity of God's grace and power through our risen Lord, Jesus Christ, who is present through the Holy Spirit. It is a tremendous privilege to be part of God's kingdom, and it is an honor to be entrusted with the responsibility to carry this treasure of Jesus Christ in these earthen vessels.

One of the heart songs of a person in our congregation whose life has been real hard is:

> Lord, listen to your children praying,
> Lord, send your Spirit in this place.
> Lord, listen to your children praying,
> send us love, send us power, send us grace.[2]

Hard cases have soft hearts.

---

2. By Ken Medema. © 1973 Hope Publishing Co., Carol Stream, IL 60188. All rights reserved. Used by permission.

Chapter 11

Congregation-based deliverance ministry

A Yellow Creek Mennonite Church story

Wesley Bontreger

When Dean and Edna Hochstetler came to Yellow Creek Mennonite Church in the early 1990s, many in our congregation were already acquainted with them and with Dean's well-established deliverance ministry. Dean had spoken to our high school youth group a couple years earlier. His address had a significant impact on the youth and sponsors and brought some awareness of deliverance ministry issues.

Our conversation about the Hochstetlers' becoming members at Yellow Creek identified three areas for discussion about Dean's ministry: theological clarity; Dean's unwavering commitment to the church and its ministries; and expectations about and desire for clear communication, accountability, and support.

Dean and Edna were taken in as members on July 19, 1992. Dean's initial ministry involvement included a significant teaching role, as Sunday school classes invited him to speak on the subject of deliverance ministry. Dean also began to get referrals of "hard cases" from leaders and other members. These referrals led to opportunities for in-depth teaching on spiritual bondage, worldview issues, and steps to freedom in Christ. In the mid-1990s, Dean began to hold classes for a group of members, which were open to anyone with interest in this subject. Dean also began to involve a few members in intervention and prayer support sessions with hard cases.

In 1997, the congregation reorganized its ministries and constitution, and developed a new vision for calling people to identify and use their gifts in ministry. We encouraged the emergence of new ministries through the concept of ministry teams. Out of this effort, we formed a new deliverance ministry team under the nurture commission of the congregation. Dean leads this team, which includes other key people whom Dean has trained and who were already involved in the ministry. This team meets monthly for prayer, planning, and consultation about people with whom members are working.

In recent years, many Sunday school classes have chosen related subjects for study and discussion. Although Dean has reduced his caseload and involvement, he continues to teach and serve as a consultant to other team members who are assigned hard cases or are teaching classes on this ministry. We have established a sequence of introductory and advanced training classes. The team is currently developing a process for identifying individuals with the necessary gifts and calling to pursue an active role in this ministry.

The development of this ministry has had a positive impact on the congregation. It has also raised some issues, which continue to be matters of discernment. One of the most prevalent has been overcoming some members' fears and uncertainties about deliverance ministry and teaching on it.

Early in this journey, some tension arose with members who were not open to or were skeptical of the concepts and biblical interpretation about coming to freedom in Christ. A challenge for us as leaders has been to strike a balance as we seek to validate and support this ministry while also being clear that deliverance ministry is not the only healing channel of grace or pastoral care for individuals. As is the case with any other ministry in the church, this area is not to be made an idol of nor is it to be promoted as more significant than other ministries.

Another area of challenge is the need to resolve misunderstandings and hurts that some people have reported in response to deliverance concepts. We have worked to improve sensitivity in teaching on matters that are personal and close to the life situations of members.

Whether in teaching or counseling, deliverance ministry needs to be gentle, hopeful, at times confrontational, but always carried out in love and backed with biblical integrity. Integrating this ministry into the life of the congregation requires that we give priority to maintaining communication between the deliverance ministry team and pastors and elders.

A major challenge is to assimilate individuals who were not previously part of the church into the life of the congregation after they have engaged in a deliverance process. The amount of time and commitment needed to walk with people in follow-up care is significant and vital to establishing relational bonds in the community of faith. We use a variety of means to do this through other ministries. For instance, we may assign a Stephen Minister,[1] give financial support for ongoing counseling, provide pastoral care, or activate our prayer team.

One change we are making is to involve pastoral leadership more in the teaching and training process. We are learning that it is important for those in deliverance ministry to have a greater awareness of broader congregational pastoral care issues, so we are strengthening the connections between this ministry and the vision of our leadership.

In summary, we continue to explore ways to enhance the effectiveness of this ministry as a means of discipling believers. We want to strengthen their biblical knowledge and their commitment to grow in the grace and victory of Jesus Christ. And we want to bring healing and hope to others as we share the calling of God to live in faithfulness to Christ. While we are still finding God's way, we want to recognize the powerful impact Dean and this ministry have had on many individuals and on the whole congregation over the last ten years. We praise God for the sense of awakening to this uncommon and underemphasized area of ministry.

1. Stephen Ministry is a one-to-one caregiving approach that uses trained lay members to support people through difficult times.

Chapter 12

In pursuit of truth and the healing touch of Jesus

My story

Dean Hochstetler, with Harold Bauman

My mother was the spiritual leader in our home. I was eight years old when she assigned me the task of memorizing the parable of the sower (Luke 8:5-7). I read on in the chapter, through the account of the Gerasene demoniac (Luke 8:26-39). I asked Mother, "What are demons?" She replied, "They existed during the time of Jesus and were evil spirits, but they are not reality today." I thought it was a strange answer, but it was what she had been taught by the church.

As I got older, I observed the practices of the local community. Miracles occurred. Powwowing[1] healings took place. People who used divining rods found well sites and field tiles. Horoscopes were used to order work schedules. I raised questions about the power behind these entities and was told by practitioners, "It works! Therefore, it is of God."

I was thirty-three years old when I realized I was living on the borrowed faith I had acquired from my parents: I did not have a personal relationship with Jesus. As a result of the preaching of an evangelist from south India, I found salvation. With it came the urge to work in the field of occult practices and demonization. For the next eight years, I studied, read the biblical accounts, asked questions, and made observations. My wife, Edna, and I had some hair-raising experiences

---

1. "Magic," otherwise known as *Brauche* (Pennsylvania Dutch, from the German *Bräuche,* "customs"). According to Samuel L. Yoder, who has written the article on Brauche in Global Anabaptist Mennonite Encyclopedia Online (GAMEO), "all authentic Amish powwowers agree that the art of *Brauche* is a gift of God and not self-induced" (http://www.gameo.org/). I maintain that powwowing is an evil practice, that its power derives from Satan, and that Christians must avoid it. Although I disagree with his conclusions, David W. Kriebel provides some perspective in his article, "Powwowing: A Persistent American Esoteric Tradition" (http://www.esoteric.msu.edu/VolumeIV/Powwow.htm).

in the course of studying this realm, experiences designed by Satan to stop my progress. The account of them is too lengthy for this essay.

Influential writings and people

I was influenced by the writings of N. Daniel of Madras, India, and by Kurt Koch, a West German theologian and medical psychologist. Koch had worked extensively in the field of occultism and its consequences for forty years.

Koch's doctoral thesis, *Christian Counseling and Occultism,*[2] and his books *Occult ABC*[3] and *The Lure of the Occult*[4] enhanced my understanding of demonic influences. His book *Occult Bondage and Deliverance*[5] contributed to my comprehension. The second half of this book was written by Koch's friend Alfred Lechler, a German Christian psychiatrist who understood occultism and demonization.

Koch told me that he and Lechler researched the connection of occultism with mental illness and emotional problems. They had studied 20,000 case histories over a period of fifteen years. They concluded that 55 percent of those who are mentally ill and emotionally disturbed had the occult factor in their own life or in their ancestry.[6]

The works of Watchman Nee, especially *The Normal Christian Life,*[7] changed my thinking still more. I studied the recorded works of Johann Christoph Blumhardt, a German Protestant pastor of Möttlingen, Germany. I secured the writings of Jessie Penn-Lewis, who wrote *War on the Saints,*[8] and John Nevius, author of *Demon Possession,*[9] published in 1897, which he wrote from his forty years' experience

---

2. Kurt E. Koch, *Christian Counseling and Occultism: The Christian Counseling of Persons Who Are Psychically Vexed or Ailing because of Involvement in Occultism* (Grand Rapids, MI: Kregel Publications, 1965).

3. Kurt E. Koch, *Occult ABC* ([Germany]: Literature Mission Aglasterhausen, 1980); distributed by Grand Rapids International Publications.

4. Kurt E. Koch, *The Lure of the Occult: 193 Case Studies of Occult Enslavement and Deliverance* (Grand Rapids, MI: Kregel Publications, 1971).

5. Kurt E. Koch, *Occult Bondage and Deliverance: Advice for Counselling the Sick, the Troubled, and the Occultly Oppressed* (Grand Rapids, MI: Kregel Publications, 1986).

6. This statement is not in print but was related to me by Koch in personal conversation in 1972.

7. Watchman Nee, *The Normal Christian Life* (London: Witness and Testimony Publishers, 1953).

8. Jessie Penn-Lewis, *War on the Saints: A Text Book for Believers on the Work of Deceiving Spirits among the Children of God* (Leicester: Overcomer Office, 1912).

9. John Livingston Nevius, *Demon Possession* (Grand Rapids, MI: Kregel Publications, 1968).

in China. New Testament professor Willard Swartley introduced me to the writings of Lutheran theologian James Kallas. His two most important works are *The Meaning of the Synoptic Miracles*[10] and *The Satanward View,*[11] an exposition of Paul's writings in which Kallas argues that the church is to continue all the work Jesus began (see Matt. 28:18-20).

Neil Anderson's writings, such as *The Bondage Breaker,*[12] advanced my understanding of people problems and their cure. *The Authority of the Believer* by J. A. MacMillan[13] is in my judgment worth its weight in gold, as is Paul Billheimer's *Destined for the Throne.*[14] Reginald Woolley's work on *Exorcism and the Healing of the Sick*[15] shows that church records demonstrate that healing prayer and exorcism were vital in the early church for the first three centuries. Those whom God had gifted for the task did the work. He says that in the fourth century, the church began to manipulate the realm of those "gifted" for the task. By the sixth century, the work was reserved for those ordained to priesthood and to designated sacraments.

I also became acquainted with people who had spent years observing the victory of Jesus over Satan's powers. C. Fred Dickason, chair of Moody Bible Institute's theology department; Gerald McGraw, who had a similar position at Toccoa Falls Bible College; and Ernest Rockstad and Mark Bubeck, both Baptist pastors, all contributed much to my understanding of the demonic realm. My contacts with Victor Matthews, professor at a Baptist Seminary (now at Southwest Missouri State University), helped me greatly. Later, Arlie Watson, psychologist and Baptist pastor from Salisbury, Maryland, contributed much to my understanding of Dissociative Identity Disorder (DID) and the demonization that frequently accompanies it. The only Mennonite besides Willard Swartley who gave me any help with

---

10. James G. Kallas, *The Significance of the Synoptic Miracles* (Greenwich, CT: Seabury Press, 1961).

11. James G. Kallas, *The Satanward View: A Study in Pauline Theology* (Philadelphia: Westminster Press, 1966).

12. Neil T. Anderson, *The Bondage Breaker* (Eugene, OR: Harvest House Publishers, 1993).

13. John A. MacMillan, *The Authority of the Believer* (Camp Hill, PA: Christian Publications, 1997).

14. Paul E. Billheimer, *Destined for the Throne* (Minneapolis, MN: Bethany House, 1996).

15. Reginald Maxwell Woolley, *Exorcism and the Healing of the Sick* (London: SPCK, 1932).

understanding the demonic realm was Donald Jacobs, missionary and anthropologist.

I met Timothy Warner in 1985. He taught missions theology and a course in "power encounter" at Trinity Evangelical Divinity School, Deerfield, Illinois. I was a resource person for that course for five years, which was taught at the doctoral level and attended by students from all over the world. Our dialogue on the subject continues to this day. In 1996, Warner preached from Mark 3:13-15 at my ordination. His book *Spiritual Warfare*[16] provides a basic understanding of the demonic realm and the victory of Jesus over these spirits.

Travels, observations, and learnings

In 1970, I contacted Kurt Koch. In 1972, we made a five-week trip together from Trinidad to Panama and various island countries in between. His discernment was keen, and I learned a lot from him. My travels have taken me to forty-two countries. I found the same demonic issues everywhere I went. They just had different faces. Nevertheless, it is important to avoid the tendency of some people to see demons behind every bush.

Commissioned to write, speak, and work

On returning from the Caribbean trip with Koch, I decided to write an article, "Christ's Works Versus the Devil's Counterfeits," for *Gospel Herald*, the official Mennonite periodical at the time. The editor, John Drescher, said to me, "You write the article and I will publish it." He put it in the May 1972 issue.

As I was praying one day in June 1972, I heard the voice of the Lord saying, "In September, I will send you on the road." I wondered about this message, because I felt I was neither a public figure nor an eloquent speaker.

About a month later, at work one day, I became ill. I finally sat down under a tree, in agony. Edna was gone, and the children were in school. My sister, Mary Ellen Kaufman, who was a nurse, came by and said to me, "You need to go to the doctor, and I am going along." When my family doctor and I discussed my symptoms, he said, "You have a bleeding ulcer." I disagreed, but he sent me for tests. They showed nothing amiss. I returned home, still in pain. Slowly, I real-

16. Timothy M. Warner, *Spiritual Warfare: Victory over the Powers of this Dark World* (Wheaton, IL: Crossway Books, 1991).

ized it was a satanic attack. I rebuked it in Jesus' name, and within an hour I was well!

A letter came in the mail the following day from leaders of a church in Pigeon, Michigan, who had read the article I had written in *Gospel Herald*. Their request was that I speak to them about these "dark" issues and the victory of Jesus over them. They asked, "Would you please come the weekend of September 9?" I agreed to go, and I have been busy speaking, teaching, and demonstrating the victory of Jesus over Satan and his host ever since.

I have learned that most pastors cannot define occult practices (see Deut. 18:9-14; Isa. 47:9-15) in terms that a congregation can understand. Moreover, they have never preached to their congregations on the dangers of these practices. I learned that people involved in occult practices do not have freedom in Christ.

Most people, including most church leaders, view demonization as the Bible's outdated way of speaking about mental illness. Moreover, many church leaders have taught that the principalities and powers of Ephesians 6:12 are corporations and political parties. The text, however, speaks of powers "in the heavenly places," which implies that the spiritual realm of evil motivates the *people* who are at the helm of the earthly organizations. Experience began to teach me that the biblical texts about the demonic realm speak to a reality that is much the same today as it was then. I do not mean to deny the reality of mental illness. These two realities can be present simultaneously.

Most Mennonite educators were initially opposed to the idea that the demonic realm is a reality in our society. John C. Wenger, a prominent and respected leader in the Mennonite Church, was a notable exception. He had no experience with the demonic realm, but he affirmed my work with it. To his eternal credit, he said, "I will pray that your courage does not fail you." He prayed for me for thirty years, until dementia prevented him from doing so. Howard Charles, long-time professor of New Testament at Associated Mennonite Biblical Seminary (AMBS) in Elkhart, Indiana, said to me, "Base your theology on God's Word. If, however, your experience and that of others is consistent and your theology says something else, then reexamine it; you have missed something." Willard Swartley, also on the AMBS faculty, was affirmative.

Criticism from church leaders was intense during this period. One even accused me of practicing medicine without a license!

Investigation and affirmation

A turning point came in 1978. Church leaders began to listen when a local pastor and his wife came asking for help. She had been in and out of mental hospitals and psychiatric care for years but had experienced no improvement. She had an Amish ancestry, and her early life contained much powwow healing, which is widespread in Amish circles. I pointed out what I thought the real problem was: ancestral demonic bondage. She became angry and walked out. Later, she returned, and we continued our conversation. I asked the couple to come back that Thursday evening. When they returned, she became so angry that she walked out for good. Her husband and I continued the discussion.

Six weeks later at the funeral home, her husband said, "I want to tell you a few things. Three days after we left your house the second time, we realized that what you said was true. We began to address the occult ancestral sin issue and brought it to the cross and blood of Jesus. The improvement in my wife was so great that she did not return to her psychiatrist. He called her six weeks later and said, 'You have not been coming in. Unless you do, you will be back in the hospital as before.' He put fear into her. She went to see him, returned home, and killed herself on August 18, 1978."

From the funeral home, Edna and I went to see J. C. Wenger. He referred us to Marlin Miller, then president of Associated Mennonite Biblical Seminary in Elkhart, Indiana. That was the beginning of an accountability committee, established to ascertain if what I was saying and doing was valid. I appreciate this committee and am still responsible to it.

Basic people problems and their care

The overwhelming problem of troubled people is sin and guilt. In my own observations and those of many other practitioners who work in the realm of occult bondage and deliverance, at least 85 percent of troubled people resent someone living or dead. These resentments *can* open a person to demonic affliction. Occult practices can also open the door. At least 80 percent of demonization comes via the family system, especially in dysfunctional families. It is thus crucial to break generational curses (see Deuteronomy 28; Dan. 9:3-18; and Matt. 23:29-39). Believers have authority because of their union with Christ (Romans 6; Eph. 1:1–2:7; 3:10). I have more problems convincing some people that their problem is sin and guilt and not demonic than I do in helping demonized persons. Demonization also occurs for reasons not listed here.

Most people in North America and western Europe—including Christians—have a faulty worldview. As modern people, they see reality in terms of what is rational, material, and scientifically provable. The Bible speaks of three spiritual realms: (1) in the highest realm are God, Jesus, and redeemed people (Eph. 2:6); (2) in the middle realm are good angels who are the saints' servants (Heb. 1:14) and evil angels who war against God, Jesus, and the saints; and (3) in the lower realm are unredeemed people and things. The spirit realm has rank, or hierarchy, and there is much interaction. Many missiologists are now saying these things about worldview.

Stories of demonization

I have experienced many strange phenomena caused by evil spirits. One man had the capability to produce demonically inspired speech way below the lowest note on a piano.[17] I have encountered ghost phenomena in buildings; doors were opened and shut by unseen hands, and pens wrote by themselves. Some buildings have been set on fire many times by wicked spirits. In *Demon Possession,* John Nevius calls these "fire demons."[18] In one case, a sick person sitting or standing next to a powwow healer had his illness transferred to the healer, with the result that the sick person was freed of the ailment. The healer had no ability to read scripture or pray. Pains erupted and moved about in his body with no medical explanation.

Ghost phenomena appeared without explanation soon after a husband and wife began to study the New Testament together. They were unable to get their spiritual life together. This man's healing abilities, which he thought were of God, were of such magnitude that morning sickness and birth pains appeared in the husband rather than in his pregnant wife.

In all these cases, applying the victory of Jesus cured the people involved. Many cases are far less spectacular. The case of Mrs. E involves various issues besides demonization.[19] The list could go on and on.

---

17. See the case study of Mr. Q in this volume.
18. Nevius, *Demon Possession,* 341.
19. See the case study of Mrs. E in this volume.

Mental illness and physical ailments are real, and the medical profession can be of great help. Demonization can also produce ailments that look like medical problems but are not. Jesus differentiated people problems and so should we (see Matt. 4:23-24). I have attempted to do so. The apostle Paul listed spiritual gifts. We need them all for the good of the church, Christ's body, which does what is of lasting value here on earth. If the church does not do Christ's work, it does not get done. God seldom bypasses the church, which represents Jesus in this world.

Steps to freedom and victory in Jesus for the oppressed person

"If the Son makes you free, you will be free indeed" (John 8:36). Discerning how to offer help to a troubled person can be difficult. In what follows, I suggest an outline of areas to be addressed in such discernment. This outline is not exhaustive with regard either to the elements or to the exact sequence of their use. It is not a complete outline for assessing the needs or procedures for restoring an afflicted person. Absolute honesty with God and one's counselor is necessary. We cannot deceive God! Confession of all known sin is a prerequisite. The person needs to make itemized lists. The counselor should pay heed to the following items when working with a client.

First, clients must confess all sins of pride and rebellion against God or any other authority, as well as resentment, hatred, and bitterness against anyone, living or dead.

Second, clients need to list their sexual partners outside of marriage. Then break the soul ties, the contracts outside of marriage (see Gen. 2:24; 1 Cor. 6:15-17; and Mark 10:7).

Third, provide a sample list of occult involvements and their meaning for people (Deut. 18:9-14 and Isa. 47:9-15). *Occult* refers to dark, secret, and hidden practices aided by the demonic spirit world. Occultism has a plethora of forms and is increasing at an alarming rate. Examples are water divining (smelling), pendulum use, magic healings (powwow), iris diagnosis, applied kinesiology, therapeutic touch, acupuncture, the use of crystals, Satan worship, and Ouija boards. These and more are still among us! The New Age agenda has added many items to this list. It is age-old sorcery in different clothes. People often do not understand the things in which they are involved. The counselor needs to inform clients what occult practices consist of and explain their consequences meaningfully (see Deut. 5:9; 2 Cor. 11:14; and 1 Pet. 5:8). A questionnaire can bring to light forms of the occult current to our society (see Appendix 1D below).

Fourth, ancestral sins, inherited curses, and burdens need to be brought to the cross. My experience shows that about 80 percent of demonization is ancestrally rooted. Some counselors believe the percentage is higher. People can often be burdened by the consequences and curses of their ancestors' evil deeds.

Fifth, clients must forgive everyone who has ever harmed them or caused them to suffer (see Matt. 18:15-22). Matthew 18 says that the person who refuses to forgive will be punished: "In anger his master turned him over to the jailers to be tortured, until he should pay back all he owed" (NIV). My experience teaches me that the word *jailers* here likely refers to demons who torment Christians who refuse to forgive their brothers or sisters.

Sixth, clients need to admit and confess deception and worship of false gods. Such worship could include worship of oneself!

Seventh, pronounce absolution (John 20:23). This act is tremendously helpful to our emotional welfare. People who have confessed sin need to hear that they are forgiven. It is important for those who have confessed sin to hear what the Bible says about it. Refer to the following passages, which clients need to understand: Exodus 12:13-14; John 19:35; Romans 5:9; 1 John 1:9; and Hebrews 9:11-14; 10:19-25. The Hebrews passages deal with a guilty conscience and how the blood of Jesus removes it. Romans 8:37-39 needs to be understood to handle Satan's accusations about one's past sin.

Eighth, check for the presence of demonic entities that are rooted in sin personally or ancestrally. There may be a need to bind or loose them (Matt. 12:29; 16:19; 18:18). This step comes last, unless you are impeded by demons as the work of freedom is progressing. If the client is a believer in Jesus and has a demon problem, all legal grounds (the garbage of life) for the evil presence must be broken before the demons can be removed in the name of Jesus. No such duality exists with unbelievers, because the person belongs to Satan. Demons need to be cast or crowded out, if they are attached to the person.

Ninth, some demons are exceedingly tenacious, and casting them out requires much time. Stay at it until it is done. Release does not necessarily happen all in one session. Even Jesus did not have instantaneous success in all cases (Luke 8:29). And not all troubled people are demonized. It is therefore important to check to see if attachments are present (see 1 John 4).[20] Confession of all known sin and guilt and an understanding of the full value of the cross of Jesus (John 19:30-35)—the value of the blood and broken body of Jesus—often forces the wicked spirits to leave. Emotional pain needs healing. The most important thing that a helping person can do is get the person to the healer, who is Jesus. Allow Jesus to do the healing. (A theophostic approach to healing may also be valuable in some cases.)

Tenth, renounce Satan, his host, his works, and his ways in the person's life, and consciously transfer the person from Satan's darkness to the kingdom of the Lord Jesus Christ and his light. This was standard practice at baptisms for the first three hundred years of church history. The church has neglected this practice for far too long. This process is a far better approach than one in which the pastor simply asks questions to which the baptismal candidate responds. Full commitment of one's life to Jesus turns that person from darkness to light (Acts 26:18).

Finally, pastoral care is essential until sound faith in Jesus is established (Luke 8:35). Severely demonized people are emotionally shattered, and their emotional structure needs to be rebuilt. Solid faith in the Lord Jesus is vital to maintaining victory. Help in other areas of life may also be needed. The helper does not have to be a pastor but can be a competent caregiver. Daily care may be necessary for a while. Biblical truth must be established in the person's life. The value of the cross of Jesus, his shed blood, death, burial, resurrection, ascension, and seat above the principalities and powers (demonic world) must be grasped. Help the person appropriate authority in Christ. Teach the Pauline concept of living and operating "in him" until it is understood and claimed. Take note of the many times "in him" appears in Romans 6 and Ephesians 1:1–2:7. Revelation 12:9-11 is still true: the devil is overcome by the blood of the Lamb and the word of our testimony.

Again, the above outline of areas to be addressed with a troubled person does not detail all the interventions that may be used or the sequence of their use. It is not a complete paper on method. I am indebted to the contributions of others working in deliverance

---

20. *Attachments* here refers to human emotions, such as anger, hatred, bitterness, or rage. Demons can have these names and qualities as well.

ministry, and I continue to learn from them. This is a field of work that has no experts!

Conclusion

Hebrews 13:8 affirms that "Jesus Christ is the same yesterday and today and forever." I have come to the conclusion that these words are true. Jesus' victory over demonic powers evident in the synoptic Gospels and in the teaching of Paul remains effective today. Demons are as real as the holy angels who are the saints' servants (Heb. 1:14).

Criticism of my work has receded markedly in the past fifteen years. I receive many phone calls from people asking for help with problems. These include not only troubled people but also medical doctors, psychologists, therapists, and church leaders who need help to understand and differentiate what they are observing in their clients and parishioners.

Along with Western society as a whole, Mennonites are becoming more and more aware and accepting of the concept of the spirit world. Three classes at Yellow Creek Mennonite Church now meet two hours a month for teaching in this area, one at an introductory level, one at an intermediate level, and one at an advanced level. Those who attend represent a wide scope of denominations. We have been thorough in teaching and demonstrating these principles with hands-on work. Some attendees are now competent to address these people problems and are doing so.

This important task needs to be carried on by the next generation; hence the need for training. Although society is becoming more secular, satanic activity is increasing at an alarming rate. People are in search of what gives them power. If the church does not demonstrate its sources of power, satanic forces will. The good news is that the truth about who Jesus is and what he did and does is still the effective cure for most deep-seated problems.

Chapter 13

Reflections on deliverance ministry

My story

Willard M. Swartley

The key influences contributing to my openness to ministry in the area of deliverance, which many scholars judiciously eschew, have been at least three. For more than thirty years I co-taught semiannually a course on war and peace in the Bible, which gave attention to the centrality of God's fight against evil in both Testaments, though with significant transformation in emphasis in the New Testament. Second, my New Testament specialty has been the synoptic Gospels, in which Jesus' exorcism of demons plays a crucial role, evidencing the coming of the kingdom of God.[1]

Third, in 1984 I was asked by Indiana-Michigan Mennonite Conference to serve as a biblical and theological consultant on Dean Hochstetler's Responsibility Committee, which was appointed by the conference. I replaced Marlin Miller, who had resigned because of the demands of his role as president of Associated Mennonite Biblical Seminary (AMBS). I served for about eight years, although I still receive reports of the committee meetings in which members reflect on specific cases in Dean's ministry.

Given the space constraints of this essay, my comments will focus on two brief points. In North America's current postmodern climate, the entertainment media serve up a standard diet of good guys versus bad guys drama. The spirit world often constitutes a key component in these stories. In some, satanic representation is present. We live in a culture and world where the good versus evil (Satan) ethos is ubiquitous.

Can the deliverance minister and the psychotherapist work with the same reality but with different languages and methods? Our cul-

1. See the Swartley entries in the bibliography for exposition of these first two factors.

tural disposition shapes the approach we prefer, which is then more likely to succeed in bringing resolution and healing.

When AMBS hosted a conference on bondage and deliverance in 1987, the tone and the issues were different from the issues that surface now.[2] Then, our culture was dominated by modernism. Many participants were skeptical about any claims to cast out demons. The question of whether demons exist surfaced continuously in the debate. No one focused on hard cases, because the key question was whether there is any such thing as spiritual bondage and deliverance.

Today, things look different. What has happened in the intervening years? We no longer live only in a culture oriented with a scientific, modern worldview. We live in a culture that has popularized the fight with the demonic; it appears in seemingly innocent forms in movies, television, and computer games. Still, grappling with the demonic (even in popular culture) is difficult for us. Our ordered, rational world screens out this potentiality.

Some years ago, I talked with Walter Wink over lunch about how he deals with Satan and evil in his second volume on the powers.[3] I said, "You really do describe Satan and evil in such a way that it could include what I have encountered in deliverance ministry. And yet your contribution as a whole marginalizes it. Your work seems to avoid deliverance ministry and focuses instead on the 'powers' in the structural, corporate, sociopolitical sense." He acknowledged that to be the case. But he also said he cannot deny the other reality.

He then told a story about the ministry of a widely known psychotherapist in New York City. Her ministry includes body healing and, on occasion, confrontation of evil powers. She attended the 1987 conference at AMBS because of her interest in the subject, and also contributed significantly to it. The story revolves around her effort to help a client in a hard case.

She had invited Wink to come and support her as she somewhat experimentally used a ritual of exorcism to free a client that had not responded to counseling after years of her best efforts. (Those with experience in this ministry generally agree that exorcism is not to

---

2. The papers presented at the conference were published as *Essays on Spiritual Bondage and Deliverance*, Occasional Papers, no. 11, ed. Willard M. Swartley (Elkhart, IN: Institute of Mennonite Studies, 1988).

3. Walter Wink, *Naming the Powers: The Language of Power in the New Testament* (Philadelphia: Fortress Press, 1984).

be undertaken by a person working alone.) She had come to feel that this case needed to be addressed in a different way. So she planned for a different type of session, with the client's willing participation, outside of her regular schedule, in the evening hours.

She followed an exorcistic ritual, probably an Episcopalian liturgy. After the exorcistic rite, all three celebrated the Eucharist. She also used the ritual of anointing with oil. The exorcistic ritual included strong words of denunciation of evil spirits. Wink told me, "What I saw happen that night was marvelous and very moving. She told me later that after that evening event, the counseling progressed to closure within months. The ritual of exorcism brought the healing that many years of counseling did not achieve." This story suggests that counseling and deliverance are not equally suitable for all cases.

My earliest encounter with this ministry was in 1976 at Eastern Mennonite College (now University), when I was asked to meet with the dean and a local psychiatrist to reflect theologically on the role of exorcism in relation to psychiatric intervention. I recall my comment at that time, made rather glibly: "The psychiatrist and the deliverance minister both work at the same issues. They have different vocabularies, they have different strategies, but one takes longer than the other. You can guess which one goes faster."

Over the years, I have changed my mind. In some cases, particularly where issues of sexual abuse are involved, that may be true. But on other issues, it's a different matter, a completely different world. It is not just a matter of different language and choice of procedures. I give two examples.

Dean Hochstetler and I did not have a choice the night a man much bigger than I am came into the church's fellowship hall in a wild frenzy, ready to harm us. This man charged in like an enraged beast. (Usually one engages in discernment first, but there was no time for discernment that night). This man had called his pastor that day and said he was coming to the church to murder him. Immediately the pastor called Dean, and Dean called me. Together we were to bind back the evil spirit afflicting this man. The man had driven to the church in his pickup. He had gotten out, walked halfway toward the church entrance, with gun in hand, then turned around, went back to his vehicle, drove away from the church, went home, and then called the pastor, saying, "I need spiritual help." That is why we were called together that night.

During the day and especially as I drove to Goshen that evening, I was struggling, crying, and babbling to God, "I'm a nonresistant Christian. What do I do when confronted with violence? I don't want to go. I want to stay home. Why do I go to this thing?" I was carrying on in this way, yet at the same time binding the powers of evil in the name of Jesus. What kept coming to my mind/spirit during this struggle was Jesus' teaching, "Love your enemies," and I wondered how this was relevant. What did it mean in this context?

When the man entered the building, only commands in the name of Jesus to do no violence would settle him for a time. Before long, this man almost twice my size came lunging toward me, his fist aimed at my head. At that instant the pneumatic word snapped from my mouth, "Jesus said, 'Love your enemies.'" Immediately, the man collapsed to the floor. If it had not been for that word, I'm not sure I would be here to tell the story. I didn't know why I was given that word when I was wrestling with God. But it was God's word—Jesus' word—for the occasion.

Yes, this man came to murder his pastor in the church. Why would he do that? What was going on within him? Over time, I have learned that one cannot really plan for how this kind of deliverance ministry will develop. You simply have to prepare yourself to trust in God. And you must rely on the Spirit for the words at the crucial time. Normally, I am slow to start speaking. But at that moment, when that man's fist was coming toward my head, the words just popped out. And this big man collapsed. I had not touched him.

Later in the session, we learned that when this man was twelve years old, someone had murdered his father. From that day on, he had nurtured a strong desire to murder the person who murdered his father. That desire to kill became a power over him that he could not control. So it is not just a question of which set of languages and procedures we would use; we were confronted with a power that had to be controlled by scripture's authoritative word, spoken under pneumatic guidance.

Another situation that calls for deliverance ministry has to do with breaking vows made in witchcraft. Often these covenants are made in secret, sometimes even as a blood pact. My brother-in-law had no experience with this sort of thing and leaned on me for coaching.

Shirley was a social worker living in a small town.[4] She was a wonderful person. No one would have guessed that she was part of a satanic witchcraft coven. Members were required to meet once a year in a mountain area to reaffirm their vows and practice a form of ritual sacrifice. She would not describe specifically what happened but said only, "You would be horrified to know." She was not a churchgoer, but she attended a funeral in my brother-in-law's church to support a grieving client. She was so impressed with the faith of the community that she approached my brother-in-law to ask if he would be willing to help her out of her vows, which were causing headaches, fear, and voices in her head that were telling her what to do.

After consulting with me by phone and much prayer, my brother-in-law gathered a small group from church who would work with him, and he consented to do what he could, by God's power and grace. The battle grew heavy in the second session, when the demons threatened to kill her. Finally in session three, the demons under command in the name of Jesus left. The Lord Jesus triumphed, and the woman was freed. To the coven members who threatened to curse anyone who would not come to the annual ritual, she wrote a letter of confidence and joy, expressing her desire that they too come to realize God's great power and love. What a testimony!

Not long ago, my brother-in-law stopped at our house to visit and he said, "Do you remember Shirley?"

I said, "Yes. How is she doing?"

"Well, she had stopped coming to church because her husband objected. But now, years later, her daughter is engaged to the pastor of another church in town, and she is going there. I met her last week. She gave me a big hug and said, 'If you hadn't helped me, I don't know where I'd be in life.'"

I do not believe this woman could have found freedom except through exorcistic command and her renunciation of demonic power. For some people, the nature of the case calls for the deliverance approach, to lead them to healing and wholeness.

There are at least three different positions on the matter of discernment. First, some hold that what people in Bible times regarded as demonic oppression or possession is essentially mental illness,

4. Names and other details have been changed to protect privacy.

and our understanding and treatment of these disorders is different from that of the ancients.[5]

Second, some hold that mental illness and demonization are different realities. In each case, one must decide whether the person has mental illness or demonization and then proceed with the appropriate treatment.

Third, some hold that mental illness and demonization have overlapping symptoms in some cases. Certain symptoms do not fit the criteria defined in the Diagnostic and Statistical Manual of Mental Disorders, fourth edition (DSM-IV), and may indicate the presence of demonization.[6] In such cases, effective treatment requires both types of help, psychological or psychiatric and deliverance. My experience and understanding of scripture leads me to believe the last viewpoint is more correct. Discernment is important in each situation.

Finally, the most important point is the early Christian confession: Jesus Christ is Savior and Lord! All deliverance is God's work through Christ Jesus, guided by the Spirit. Our lives are secure in the power, love, and grace of the Triune God.

---

5. For an articulation of this view, see S. Vernon McCasland, *By the Finger of God: Demon Possession and Exorcism in Early Christianity in the Light of Modern Views of Mental Illness* (New York: Macmillan, 1951).

6. For articles that sort out these issues, see T. Craig Isaacs, "The Possessive States Disorder: The Diagnosis of Demonic Possession," *Pastoral Psychology* 35, no. 4 (Summer 1987): 263–73; and Ruth Detweiler Lesher, "Psychiatry/Psychology: A Response [to Gerald Kauffman]," in *Essays on Spiritual Bondage and Deliverance*, ed. Swartley, 163–73.

Chapter 14

The Daughters of Zion and deliverance ministries

My story

Sheiler Stokes

Believers sometimes ask, "Why do bad things happen to good people?" Many people who attend church services on a regular basis live in misery. Many go home from worship to abusive relationships, addictive lifestyles, bouts of depression, and feelings of hopelessness. Many live with hurt, anger, and resentment. Given such realities, it is small wonder that we are silent when opportunities arise to share Jesus with others. When Christians have not been delivered from their bondages, how can we communicate convincingly why others should become members of the household of faith?

In the late 1980s, I was invited to an evening church service with my best friend and her sister. They had recently lost their mother to lung cancer and were having a difficult time adjusting. Their mom had never smoked, nor had she worked in a highly polluted environment. When they invited me to join them, it never occurred to me to ask what type of service it would be. I did notice that the name of the church included the word *deliverance*, but I had no idea what that meant. The service was not designed for those who had no understanding of deliverance, and no instruction was offered for those who were first-time visitors. All that I remember, even to this day, is that people were engaged in the service of deliverance. The entire ordeal was overwhelming and engulfed me in fear. I thought my girlfriends had really lost it!

The next time I was confronted with the ministry of deliverance, my girlfriend had answered her call. It was sometime in 1995 or 1996. I was informed that her sister was studying under a well-known deliverance minister. These friends believed that God had called them to minister to the needs of those sometimes classified as undesirables—prostitutes, drug dealers and drug users, people with other forms of addiction, those suffering from mental disorders, those who were abused, as well as perpetrators of abuse. They also aimed to minister to people facing long bouts of grief, those with little sense of self-worth, and second-, third-, and fourth-generation welfare recipients.

In 1997, I answered my call. Another dear friend invited me to join the Daughters of Zion, an ecumenical group of women in ministry, whose mission is to conduct seminars and workshops that empower women. We met monthly about 140 miles from my home. We were taught how to become intercessors. We engaged in group activities. Each month we prayed and fasted during a designated period of time, for a specific cause. Most of the members had been in ministry for a long time and passed along a wealth of knowledge. They shared their personal experiences as well as the experiences of many of the women they had encountered during their ministry. These meetings were enriching experiences. I remember wishing that we lived closer to one another, so we could have weekly meetings instead of monthly ones.

We were taught that some people are called from birth to become Armor Bearers, while others must be trained. We received in-depth instruction on how to become Armor Bearers. All are trained, because anyone may be called to minister. Because of the type of ministry we engage in, we have to be able to cover for one another. When ministers spiritually empty themselves in an effort to help others, they need constant prayer support. The devil comes to steal, kill, destroy, and attack those who are working to help bring God's children out of bondage. As Armor Bearers, we are trained to serve and protect the anointing of those conducting the deliverance ministry.

Armor Bearer training connects us spiritually. When I work with a minister for a while, I learn to flow with that person, heart and soul. It is the Armor Bearer's responsibility to protect the anointing that God has put in place for deliverance, by not allowing others to interfere or distract the person engaged in this ministry. We also make available items the ministers might need, such as cough drops, water, tissues, and towels.

When deliverance is taking place, it is the responsibility of the Armor Bearer to pray constantly. We are taught how to dress for a deliverance service. We must be comfortable and able to follow the deliverance minister, in case someone takes off running or falls to the floor.

Workshops and seminars conducted by the Daughters of Zion are annual events. Attenders can participate in a variety of sessions, selecting those appropriate to their level of understanding or need. Guest speakers often prepare participants for the more spiritually involved sessions.

Once we were educated about familiar spirits by a pastor who explained that, through witchcraft, division and addiction had infested her family. Her grandmother had been married and divorced three times, her mother had been married and divorced five times, and she had been divorced twice and married three times. She had allowed the spirit of addiction to come into her home during her first and second marriages by permitting the use of drugs and alcohol there. We learned that spirits look for the weakest vessel in a home, usually a child. When a spirit has entered a person and gotten comfortable, it invites its companions.

After her second marriage came to a bitter and violent end, she began to pray that God would send her a godly man. Her prayers were answered, and she met and married a pastor. However, this union did not automatically bring about a cure. Even though she had accepted Jesus Christ as her Lord and Savior, took instruction classes, and was intent on being a good wife and mother, misery seemed to follow her. On Sunday, she would sit in the front row of the church and sing, praise, and worship God. But as soon as she returned home, she would curse her husband, climb into bed, and remain there in a state of chronic depression. Although she was a beautiful woman, for days at a time she would not change clothes, comb her hair, or brush her teeth. During this period, her youngest child displayed behavioral problems. He had been kicked out of nursery school. Now at the age of twelve, he had become dishonest, disrespectful, and overtly disobedient. He was scheduled to appear in court, but he did not seem to care about what might happen to him.

Her husband explained that many people have what is known as a spirit of bondage—often transferred from one family member to another. She was then able to identify why she was in such misery and how the things she had done in life may have caused the transfer of evil spirits to her son. She and her husband agreed to submit her son to deliverance. Her husband took control, and through praying, reading scriptures, and commanding boldly that certain spirits leave, the child's deliverance began. The spirits began to talk back, sounding rough and cruel. She could not believe that such harsh words could be coming through the vocal cords of her little boy. After many, many hours, deliverance was obtained, and the child was transformed from a cruel and evil-sounding person to a loving little boy.

As the pastor told her story, people in the audience turned to one another and commented, "I had no idea that things I did in my bedroom behind closed doors could open up an opportunity for demonic spirits to enter my children!" Today, she and her husband are co-pastors and have an amazing deliverance ministry. They travel around the world setting people free from various bondages.

During the evening sessions of the Daughters of Zion seminars and workshops, those with a desire to learn more attend intense and detailed training in the area of deliverance. These sessions are designed for adults; children are not allowed. One such session was led by a woman who co-pastors with her husband in the Washington, DC, area and is also a professor at an esteemed university. She started by informing us, "When I was growing up, there were alcoholics in my family. I was determined not to be an alcoholic but became an addict anyway. Although I did not drink, I became addicted to marijuana. The spirit of addiction was there, and it fell upon me even though I did not want it. I was still functional; I worked in professional positions and earned a Ph.D."

Her teaching in this session covered biblical understandings of generational curses and explained that contemporary experience demonstrates that this phenomenon is still present. She gave one example after another of people in the church who were still broken and miserable. She provided information about the so-called innocent things we do that open the door for demonic spirits, such as reading horoscopes, playing with Ouija boards, going to fortunetellers, and performing acts of witchcraft. She also taught about "the strong man." The strong man is the ruling spirit, and if the strong man is not cast out, deliverance is not complete. For example, if a person is being controlled by anger, it is not enough to cast out the spirit of anger if the ruling spirit is bitterness. In such a case, the person conducting the deliverance must not stop until the spirit of bitterness has been cast out.

Only after a person is sufficiently educated can she or he become a participant in the deliverance service. Deliverance ministry is serious and complex, and my training so far has been minimal. My next step is to train extensively under someone who has been called and is engaged in such a deliverance ministry on a full-time basis. In recent years, I have become acquainted with several different styles and am now evaluating which style would be best suited for the people I am likely to serve.

As clergy, we often encounter people who do not know how to handle adversity, who leave church week after week to reenter a world of misery. How can they witness to others when they are not where they should be in their Christian life? Salvation is not the end but the beginning of the Christian walk. Many who have been saved have not yet been delivered from what oppresses them.

I am excited about the possibility that seminaries may train ministers for deliverance ministries. God is still in the business of freeing people and saving lives—in our time. And those who wish to serve God in a ministry of reconciliation must know how to put God's power to work in the lives of the people they serve. They must know how to remove trespassing demonic spirits from soul and body, so that Jesus the Christ can reign in every area of our lives.

Chapter 15

Demonization and the therapeutic community

My viewpoint

Paul J. Yoder

To suggest that my viewpoint represents the "therapeutic community" as a whole would be presumptuous. The professional mental health community contains widely divergent points of view, just as the Christian church does.

Mental health professionals represent a multitude of fields, degrees, and theoretical orientations. The predominant fields are represented by physicians (psychiatry), psychologists (clinical and counseling), social workers, marriage and family therapists, mental health counselors, nurses, pastoral counselors, biblical counselors, and more. Theoretical orientations include biological, biopsychosocial, psychoanalytic, psychodynamic, cognitive, behavioral, cognitive-behavioral, family systems, interpersonal, and many variations on these themes.

Despite the many approaches and theoretical perspectives related to mental health treatment, the mental health field has largely adopted the medical model. Emotional and behavioral problems are diagnosed as (mental) illnesses on the bases of syndromes—clusters of symptoms, behaviors, and functional impairments. The diagnosis in turn guides the treatment or treatments that are prescribed, which often will include prescription medication and some type of psychotherapy or counseling. To enhance uniformity of diagnosis and provide a framework for ongoing research, these syndromes are described in the *Diagnostic and Statistical Manual of Mental Disorders* (DSM), published by the American Psychiatric Association. The DSM closely parallels the portion of the International Classification of Diseases devoted to "nervous and mental disorders." The DSM has undergone a number of revisions over the years. The current version is the Text Revision of the fourth edition, the DSM-IV-TR.

What I offer is one perspective from one corner of this multifaceted professional community. I am a psychologist with a Ph.D. in clinical psychology. I am licensed as a Health Service Provider in Psychology (HSPP) in the state of Indiana. My orientation by training is behavioral and cognitive-behavioral, but over the years I have come to appreciate other perspectives as well. I have worked in the mental health field for more than twenty years, doing primarily outpatient psychotherapy and psychological testing and evaluation. I have worked in hospital, community mental health center, and private practice settings.

Three positions

How do we understand and treat individuals who are experiencing emotional distress and impairment in their day-to-day functioning, particularly those who present with symptoms that are outside the realm of "normal" human behavior and experience? These would include behaviors typically viewed as bizarre, disorganized, and/or "out of touch with reality." They could include reports of auditory or visual hallucinations (seeing or hearing things that others present would not see or hear); talking with someone who is not there; behaving in markedly different ways within a short time span, displaying changes in voice tone, volume, language complexity, etc., and subsequently denying any memory of the behavior or conversation; or gross misinterpretations of the actions and intentions of others, with subsequent reactions or responses that appear nonsensical to others. For purposes of this discussion, there appear to be three primary positions with regard to this question. These can be characterized as follows.

The first and clearly dominant viewpoint within the mental health community is that these phenomena are the result of a serious mental illness that includes psychotic symptoms in the defining cluster of symptoms. These illnesses involve problems in the neurochemical systems in the brain. Among the illnesses that include psychotic symptoms are schizophrenia; schizoaffective disorder; severe mood disorders, including major depression and bipolar (manic-depressive) disorder with psychotic features; drug (or drug withdrawal) induced psychotic illnesses; and dementias (of various types) with psychotic features. These illnesses have a characteristic onset, course, and duration. They occur with varying degrees of severity and respond to currently available treatment with varying degrees of success. Generally, they require medications to improve neurochemical brain functioning, which will reduce or eliminate the psychotic symptoms and related dysfunction and distress.

Psychotherapy alone is generally not viewed as an effective treatment for illnesses that include psychotic features, but some types of psychotherapy and social support may, in conjunction with medication, help reduce the degree of impairment caused by the illness and assist sufferers in learning how to live with and manage their illness, much as a diabetic may learn to live with and manage diabetes. To complicate matters, the symptoms of many of these illnesses wax and wane and vary in intensity over time, in ways that are not always predictable. People who hear voices that others do not hear do not necessarily hear those voices all the time or even every day. Generally, however, symptoms worsen with increases in psychosocial stressors or losses. Additionally, and importantly, treatment does not involve focusing on or exploring the individuals' hallucinations or apparent delusional beliefs, because doing so exacerbates the level of distress and is not therapeutic.

A second viewpoint held by a minority of mental health professionals, and represented by the International Society for the Study of Dissociation, is that, in addition to all the illnesses in the categories described above, there is another group of illnesses known as dissociative disorders. These disorders normally are the result of early and severe recurring trauma. They present with "psychotic-like" symptoms but require a distinctly different approach to treatment, which emphasizes psychotherapy rather than treatment with medications (although medications can also be helpful).

From this perspective, the symptoms develop initially as coping strategies that constitute an adaptive response to overwhelming trauma (and hence are "normal" rather than "abnormal"; "healthy" rather than caused by "illness"). The coping strategies ultimately become dysfunctional, because the individual has "split" his or her experiences into smaller (more manageable) pieces, with different ego states having amnesia for the experiences, beliefs, and actions of other ego states. Auditory hallucinations result when one or more or the "subconscious" ego states attempt to communicate with or "control" the behavior of the ego state currently "out" (conscious) and in control of the voluntary nervous system. In its most severe form, this condition is Dissociative Identity Disorder (DID), previously known as Multiple Personality Disorder (MPD).

People with DID often report auditory hallucinations, become disoriented at times, seem to have difficulty learning from experience, and often deny or report no memory for behaviors displayed moments earlier. They may also speak in different voices, exhibit different mannerisms, claim different preferences at different times, display differing abilities, and even show different allergic reactions and response patterns on physiological measures and medical tests. Treatment focuses on increasing self-awareness and breaking down internal dissociative barriers through learning to listen to and communicate with the other (dissociated) parts of the self. In this treatment paradigm, there are no "good" or "evil" ego states. As internal barriers to self-awareness and memories decrease (psychodynamically, this would be the equivalent of the subconscious or repressed memories becoming conscious), the degree of integrated functioning increases, often to the point that the sense of separateness disappears (and with it the auditory hallucinations), but all "ego states" remain a part of the whole person.

A third viewpoint, held primarily by those in the Christian community involved in deliverance ministry, and by very few in the professional community, is that these distressing, psychotic-like experiences are caused by supernatural intrusions of unseen evil spirits that are tormenting or infesting the suffering individual. The auditory hallucinations are demons speaking to the sufferer. Visual hallucinations are images being shown to the afflicted person by the demon or demons. Additionally, the demonic presence sometimes speaks through the sufferer with a voice that is distinctly different from the speaker's normal voice and often with a quality that is "out of this world." The demon may claim or report knowledge that the speaker seemingly has no way of knowing, that is later confirmed as accurate. Demons are also reported to cause frightening supernatural phenomena that can be—and occasionally are—witnessed by others. These add to the sufferer's anxiety, distress, and suffering. "Treatment" from this viewpoint is not antipsychotic medication, or psychotherapy to promote integrated functioning, but confrontation of the demonic forces and deliverance through a Christian ministry process that involves clearly defined steps.

Given these three perspectives, the question becomes, is there a single phenomenon that is being described in different ways and called different things? Or could there be two, three—or even more—similar but distinct phenomena, each requiring a different approach to enable the sufferer to achieve healing? Most mental health professionals belong to groups that license practitioners—psychiatrists, psychologists, etc. Because of the common threads in their training, they will generally agree on the criteria for diagnosing or categorizing mental illnesses that include psychotic symptoms, and most would agree that these are biologically based illnesses that in many cases can be treated successfully only with medications. Most would attribute the gains in the treatment of these illnesses over the last half-century to good scientific research that has produced literally hundreds of new medications and treatment strategies that enable millions of people who would have been institutionalized a hundred years ago to live safely and productively in our communities.

In light of these dramatic gains, the majority of mental health professionals would suggest that there is a single phenomenon (mental illness) with a variety of manifestations (diagnoses), caused by impaired brain functioning and best understood and treated from a scientific (medical) perspective. Treatment can include medication and various types of psychotherapy, but the more severe illnesses involving psychotic symptoms almost always require medication as part of the treatment for maximum improvement. Additionally, professionals holding the dominant viewpoint often report that they have "never seen" anyone with a dissociative disorder. Not uncommonly, they will report that they "do not believe in" dissociative disorders, despite the inclusion of these disorders in the DSM-IV-TR. At least some professionals holding the dominant viewpoint would dismiss dissociative disorders as the creation of misguided therapists who become fascinated with their patients' psychoses, and of psychotic patients who want to please their therapists.

Professionals holding the second viewpoint generally would not disagree with the overall "scientific" perspective of the majority position, but they would suggest that the broader mental health community often overlooks and fails to effectively treat an important subset of mentally ill individuals, because the symptoms overlap with those of better known illnesses that normally do require medications for effective treatment. Persons with this viewpoint often report that the clients they treat have been misdiagnosed and ineffectively and inappropriately treated for years by those in the professional community holding the dominant viewpoint. Professionals holding this second viewpoint, in essence, would suggest there are two distinctly different but overlapping phenomena that can reliably be differentiated, and that are effectively treated by related but different therapeutic strategies.

The majority of mental health professionals holding both of the first two viewpoints would dismiss the third viewpoint as religious superstition. The third viewpoint is the one traditionally held by Christians involved in deliverance ministries. Historically, such individuals have been critical of those in the mental health professions, because of both anecdotal reports and their own experiences of individuals finding freedom from suffering through deliverance from demonic affliction after years of ineffective treatment by mental health professionals who failed to recognize the spiritual dimension causing the apparent mental illness. Typically, individuals working in deliverance ministry have had little or no training in the mental health field.

During the late 1980s and early 1990s, a significant minority of people diagnosed with Dissociative Identity Disorder by mental health professionals holding the second viewpoint began to report memories of Satanic Ritual Abuse (SRA), which typically included satanic worship, torturous rituals designed to create dissociated ego states, and invoking demonic "possession" to secretly perpetuate and pass on to the next generation these religious beliefs and practices. The majority of professionals working with these clients came to view SRA as "Sadistic" Ritual Abuse, and they continued to dismiss supernatural involvement, seeing "demonic" manifestations simply as traumatized alter personality states to be understood, nurtured, and ultimately integrated.

However, some Christian mental health professionals familiar with deliverance ministries, and open to the possibility of supernatural or demonic activity, noted that dissociative disorder symptoms not only overlapped with the symptoms of other psychotic mental illnesses, but they also overlapped with "possession states," because they involve "trance" phenomena, in which individuals appear to "switch" from one personality or ego state to another, each having different memories, beliefs, and ways of behaving. These "personalities" also speak with different voice tones, and angry "persecutor" alters, which are common in DID, can sound similar to the "demonic" speech reported to occur during deliverance sessions.

Out of these observations emerged a third, but relatively rare, position in the professional community, the viewpoint that there are three distinct phenomena with overlapping presentations and degrees of distress. In brief, this position suggests that (1) psychotic mental illnesses can be reliably diagnosed and are best treated with medication and supportive psychotherapy within a professional/medical framework; (2) dissociative disorders can be reliably diagnosed and are best treated with psychotherapy and supplemental medications within a professional/medical framework; and (3) demonic oppression can also cause emotional distress and psychotic and dissociative-like episodes and behavior, can be reliably identified, and is best "treated" through deliverance ministry within a faith-based/church community. Additionally, this viewpoint would suggest that these are not mutually exclusive phenomena. That is, a given individual could have a psychotic illness and a dissociative disorder and be demonically oppressed.

In *Uncovering the Mystery of MPD,*[1] James Friesen provides some suggested guidelines for "Discerning Alter Personalities from Demons." He recommends deliverance ministry for dealing with demons, and psychotherapy for treating and integrating alter personalities.

These positions all share the concern for alleviating suffering. They also share a concern that those who intervene on the basis of other positions may do more harm than good. One problem is that professionals tend to specialize, so those who work with individuals with schizophrenia rarely also work with persons with dissociative disorders—and vice versa. In addition, most deliverance work is done by people who lack mental health training or credentials.

In my more than twenty years of working in the mental health field, I have worked with individuals diagnosed with dissociative disorders who recovered completely through treatment with psychotherapy; some who came to understand themselves better and made significant progress but continued to experience dissociative symptoms; and some who seemed to make almost no progress despite hard work in psychotherapy and the use of medications prescribed

1. *Uncovering the Mystery of MPD,* by James G. Friesen (San Bernardino: Here's Life Publishers, 1991).

by my physician colleagues. I have also worked with individuals with psychotic illnesses, including schizophrenia. Again, some have made remarkable changes with a combination of medication and supportive therapy, and others have made only moderate or minimal improvement. Finally, I have worked with individuals (with and without dissociative disorder diagnoses and with and without SRA memories) reporting demonic infestation or oppression, who appeared to benefit significantly from deliverance ministry and support provided by the faith community. Unfortunately, I have also worked with people who continued to suffer despite efforts from each of the above approaches to their problems.

Conclusion

My experiences lead me to the conclusion that there are three distinct but overlapping phenomena. My experience also suggests that these are not either/or, mutually exclusive options—that is, it is possible to have one, two, or all three phenomena present in a given case.

In an ideal world, mental health professionals and the church community alike would have a thorough understanding of the signs and characteristics of each phenomenon and initiate or refer people for the appropriate treatment. However, this is not an ideal world, and professional standards dictate practicing in accordance with established norms. As a result, mental health professionals who engage in deliverance ministry risk charges of malpractice and loss of the license that enables them to continue their professional practice.

As a licensed professional, I am cautious about suggesting to people that they appear to be demonized and recommending that they seek deliverance. However, I do support individuals exploring a faith-based intervention that is congruent with their spiritual beliefs, especially when I know those in the faith community will not disparage professional mental health treatment or dismiss the possibility that there could be a mental illness present that deliverance will not resolve. The stakes are high for those who are suffering whom we seek to serve. I encourage us all to listen carefully to people's experiences of suffering and distress, to be open to alternative understandings and intervention strategies, and to support and encourage people who are suffering to persist in their quest for healing and wholeness.

Preparing for the challenge

Chapter 16

Preparing pastors to face the challenge

Deliverance ministry and pastoral care

Loren L. Johns and Arthur McPhee

In the following pages, we will sketch in outline some of the key implications of the essays in this book for the task of educating and preparing pastors for pastoral ministry. Given the limits of what we can say in these few pages, we can do little more than identify a few theses, with little argumentation or evidence to support them.

Thesis 1. *Jesus is Lord, and Jesus saves.* Although these words sound commonplace, this confession is powerful and lies at the heart of any Christian confrontation of evil. That Jesus is Lord is much more than an idea: our hope and joy lie in the reality that God saves people from evil through the lordship of Jesus, helping them overcome the devil and experience healing and joy in life. Today's church has a weak theology of salvation in part because it has an inadequate theology of evil. The church can address these inadequacies by emphasizing Jesus' victory over Satan through the *Christus Victor* understanding of the atonement in preaching and teaching. We can also seek protection from evil through regular prayer, including the Lord's Prayer. We can emphasize the exorcistic power of commitment to Christ in believers baptism, and we can encourage testimonies from those helped by the power of Christ to overcome sin and temptation.

Thesis 2. *Privileging a modernist or Enlightenment worldview that denies evil and understands demon oppression in only psychological terms is inappropriate, narrowminded, and culturally imperialistic.* North Americans cannot deny the reality of evil powers in daily life. Even if North American Christians do not experience or identify demon possession as regularly or as visibly as do Christians in some other continents, we should not exclude the experiences of those brothers and sisters in our theology. Learning from the witness and wisdom of Christians from other parts of the world is important in many areas of life and theology, particularly in the areas of spiritual oppression and deliverance ministries. It is not necessary to solve or express an opinion about metaphysical, ontological, or worldview issues in order to respond fittingly in life-giving ways as a pastor to demon oppression. Jesus did not ignore the reality of Satan's activity in the world; neither should we.

Thesis 3. *The problem of evil and the practice of deliverance ministry should be a part of the full scope of seminary education.* That is, these subjects should be studied biblically, theologically, historically, anthropologically, and as a matter of pastoral theology. For instance, pastors should know that Jesus' exorcism of demons was not new to Early Judaism.[1] They should know about the important role exorcism had in the appeal of Christianity in the Roman Empire in the first centuries after Christ.[2] They should know about such things as the origins and practice of the "Rituale Romanum," the formal Rite of Exorcism (established in 1614 by Pope Paul V), as well as the more recent and controversial "De Exorcismus et Supplicationibus Quibusdam." This edict was approved by Pope John Paul II on October 1, 1998, though it was criticized by Cardinal Ratzinger (now Pope Benedict XVI).[3] Exorcism is not some strange or new thing practiced by some fringe Evangelical or Pentecostal groups: it has been part of the tradition of the church since the time of Jesus.

Thesis 4. *Not every pastor should expect to be a deliverance minister.* But whether or not they have this gift of the Spirit, all pastors should be aware of related spiritual, psychological, and pas-

---

1. Besides the Septuagint traditions (Tobit) and Josephus (*Jewish Antiquities*), we have ample evidence from the Old Testament Pseudepigrapha (*Ahiqar*) and the Dead Sea Scrolls. Note, for instance, Tobit 6:7-8 (cf. 4Q196 frg. 13); Tobit 8:3; Josephus, *Jewish Antiquities* 8.45–47; and the Genesis Apocryphon according to 1QapGen 20:12-29; 4Q510 5; and 4Q560.

2. For instance, exorcism became part of the baptismal rite as early as the second century. See §7 of Letter 16 of Leo the Great to the Bishops of Sicily, where he cites the Apostolic Rule as requiring exorcism as part of the baptismal rite (*The Nicene and Post-Nicene Fathers* 3.12.1.1.16.7). Freedom from the oppression of demons was one of the things that made Christianity attractive to pagans. See Alan Kreider, *The Change of Conversion and the Origin of Christendom* (Harrisburg, PA: Trinity Press International, 1999). Renunciation of the devil remains central to Roman Catholic and many Protestant baptismal rites. Renunciation of the devil is even more prominent in the Eastern Orthodox Church. A prayer of exorcism was part of the Roman Catholic baptismal rite until the Vatican II reforms.

3. When Pope John Paul II revised the 1614 rite, Cardinal Ratzinger opposed the move, preferring the 1614 rite and desiring to see it restored to use.

toral issues. They should also be knowledgeable about the gifts and resources in their area, on which they may draw when necessary. They should pray in specific instances for the Lord's deliverance and highlight the possible connection between sin and illness when anointing the sick. And they should recognize in their theology, preaching, and teaching the connection between Jesus' preaching of the kingdom and his deliverance activity.

Thesis 5. *An Anabaptist-Mennonite view of the church would suggest that ministries of exorcism and the pastoral care of demon-oppressed people should be exercised in the context of the congregation rather than by unconnected and unaccountable ministers.* Spiritual discernment is a gift of God's Spirit. That does not mean that it is essentially individualistic; often God's healing and deliverance of Christians happen through the exercise of multiple gifts of the Spirit. Both evil and salvation (or healing) are complex issues that require the presence and power of God as well as the full breadth of God's gifts.

Thesis 6. *It is neither necessary nor possible to figure out what portion of a person's healing derives from a supernatural encounter (for example, through exorcism) and what portion arises from so-called natural processes (psychological counseling, for example).* In the same way, it would be a mistake to identify pastoral care exclusively with one process or the other.

Thesis 7. *Pastors should avoid the all-or-nothing temptation.* Just as pastors should avoid denying the reality of evil, they should steer clear of the temptation to attribute all the sins of the flesh to the work of the devil or to seek personal or spiritual maturity through some miraculous and decisive exorcism. There is a spiritual danger in denying the reality of evil; there is also a spiritual danger in crediting to the devil all suffering or temptation or sins of the flesh.[4] All Christians should avoid evil (James 4:7), including experimentation with evil (Matt. 10:16; Rom. 16:19; 1 Cor. 14:20), but they should also be slow to designate as evil those things that they do not understand in a scientific way (acupuncture or reflexology, for example).

Thesis 8. *As with all pastoral care ministries, deliverance ministries carry the danger of egoism: pastors engaged in deliverance ministries may take themselves too seriously or think more of*

---

4. On the latter temptation, see the helpful perspectives of Paul M. Miller in *The Devil Did* Not *Make Me Do It* (Scottdale, PA: Herald Press, 1977).

themselves than they ought to think. Deliverance ministers should have some kind of accountability or reference group that includes theologians, biblical scholars, psychotherapists, and others who can engage in discernment together (see thesis 5 above). An Anabaptist orientation to deliverance ministry emphasizes the congregational context for such a ministry. Deliverance ministries should be grounded in a congregational or multidisciplinary context, in which a wide range of the gifts of the Spirit can operate. This statement does not mean that small groups or a whole congregation need to engage in a process of collective discernment in areas that require sensitive and confidential handling. However, it does mean that the ministry of exorcism should be accountable to the church, just as all ministries should be.

Chapter 17

Where from here?

J. Nelson Kraybill

Social activists in the Western church today practice what might be called *macroexorcism*—naming and confronting the powers of evil on a systemic and political level. Other Christians practice what might be called *microexorcism*—confronting the powers of evil on a personal level. A full expression of the gospel of Jesus Christ requires the church to embrace both, and practitioners of the two kinds of exorcism need each other.

Essays in this volume unsettle me, because they reach into what for me is the unfamiliar territory of the personal demonic. Exorcism has not been part of my own ministry—at least not in the stereotypical mode depicted in novels and cinema. I am not entirely unacquainted with exorcism, however, being a student of Revelation. I have struggled for years to make sense of this personification of evil: "The great dragon was thrown down, that ancient serpent, who is called the Devil and Satan, the deceiver of the whole world—he was thrown down to earth, and his angels were thrown down with him" (Rev. 12:9).

This surely is some kind of exorcism. But the serpent in John's Apocalypse likely represents *systemic* evil in the first-century Roman world. John of Patmos saw the Devil as the power behind a vast empire bewitched by demented rulers, such as Nero and Domitian. I share the majority opinion of Bible scholars today that the first beast of Revelation (13:1-10) represents the Roman Empire as a whole, and the harlot of chapter 17 represents the city of Rome itself. The evidence of imperial demonization must have seemed compelling to John: the military system of the Roman Empire had destroyed Jerusalem, the economic system enslaved millions, and the political system blasphemously had a "divine" emperor at its apex.

I resonate with this reading of Revelation, because it provides a spiritual framework for unmasking the global powers today. Today's imperial beasts generate, for example, the current war in Iraq or the slavery of national debt in the two-thirds world. Having been weaned on progressive peace and justice movements of the 1970s and 1980s, I readily embrace the idea that the fall of Babylon in Revelation 18 represents God's eventual judgment on structures of economic, military, and ideological oppression. The last book of the Bible is a vast drama of *macroexorcism* in which empire-wide evil is named, confronted, and defeated by the blood of the Lamb. Even as a pacifist, I do not rue the day when the "ancient serpent, who is the Devil and Satan," will be bound for a thousand years and thrown into the lake of fire and sulphur (Revelation 20).

Reading and applying accounts of microexorcism in the synoptic Gospels, however, requires a greater leap of understanding for me. I suspect the same is true for many academic theologians and others of my generation in North America. My experience and worldview make it more likely that I will show up at a prayer vigil in front of a military base than at a prayer meeting for the salvation of individuals in my neighborhood. This is odd, because the actual practice of Jesus and of the early church placed at least as much emphasis on individual freedom from the powers of evil as it did on structural and political deliverance.

Systemic evil in the Old and New Testaments

I have drawn much inspiration from such progressive political and theological currents as Liberation Theology or the civil rights struggle. Both movements have sought, in effect, to exorcise economic or racial injustice from entire societies. Both stand in the tradition of Old Testament writers who expected God to act against systemic evil—sometimes personified as a chaos monster called Yam, Behemoth, Leviathan, or Rahab. The psalmist depicts God holding divine council to confront the gods who led nations to "judge unjustly and show partiality to the wicked" (Ps. 82:2). The book of Daniel portrays spiritual warfare on an international level, with Michael (patron angel of the Jewish nation) joining battle against the "prince of Persia" and the "prince of Greece" (Dan. 10:20).

In a similar vein, the New Testament alludes to dark spiritual forces to be avoided or exorcized on a macro level. Jesus rejected the devil's offer for him to wield conventional political power (Luke 4:5-8). The author of the Fourth Gospel presents the ministry of Jesus as a kind of macroexorcism. As the passion and crucifixion approach, Jesus declares, "Now the ruler of this world will be driven out" (John

12:31). The author of Ephesians notes that believers once were "following the course of this world, following the ruler of the power of the air" (Eph. 2:2). Similarly, 1 John 5:19 declares that "the whole world lies under the power of the evil one."

Such biblical images of structural evil are useful when we seek to make sense of warped military, economic, and political systems in the twenty-first century. I find myself using language of spiritual deliverance when praying for an end to the arms trade, or an end to the cycle of terrorism and counter-terrorism, or an end to the grinding poverty of millions who do not benefit from a globalized economy. At a gathering to support immigrants, or at a prison where capital punishment is inflicted, I have joined in public prayers that amount to exorcism.

Why not personal exorcism?

So why have I never been present at a personal exorcism? Why has my spiritual imagination made relatively little room for the personal role of Satan as adversary in my own life? I have pondered this question since my first month as seminary president in 1997, when Mennonite deliverance minister Dean Hochstetler showed up at my office and handed me the first of his many "case study" narratives of bondage and deliverance.

Hochstetler's case studies are raw and vivid (while protecting the anonymity of the sufferer). There is no lingering on lurid details, just a succinct, matter-of-fact description of low self-esteem, sexual abuse, depression, or occult practice embedded in family systems. The accounts sometimes include subhuman voices emanating from the sufferers, contorted faces, or victims being hurled to the ground. Always there is prayer in the name of Jesus. Often there is long travail, persistent confrontation, and eventual freedom from bondage.

Hochstetler himself projects an assertive pastoral presence that sometimes makes me squirm. I would not want to be on the opposing side when he takes up spiritual battle. He passionately desires to see ministers in the church accept the reality of spiritual warfare on a personal level. He believes most clergy are woefully unprepared to deal with the powerful grip of Satan on the lives of some individuals. His heart breaks for people in many congregations who are in spiritual bondage, people who do not have a minister adequately prepared to name and confront the powers in Jesus' name.

The kind of microexorcism that Hochstetler practices has ample precedent in the Gospels. Jesus' first act, after launching his public ministry at the synagogue in Nazareth, was to expel a demon from a man at Capernaum (Luke 4:31-37). The disciples had similar experiences, and returned from their first preaching mission marveling that "even the demons submit to us!" (Luke 10:17). After I began to pay attention to the amount of personal spiritual deliverance in the synoptic Gospels, I felt compelled to incorporate some understanding of such ministry into my own worldview.

Our worldview matters

Despite the fact that microexorcism appears throughout the synoptic Gospels and Acts, modern readers of the New Testament are likely to push the phenomenon to the margins by ascribing it to an outdated worldview. Having been schooled by the Enlightenment, we no longer conceive of a three-tiered universe (heaven above, hell below, earth in the middle) or a personal devil carrying a pitchfork. We are scientific people, looking for cause-and-effect explanations in a Newtonian world that no longer has room for divine intervention to circumvent the laws of physics or the theories of personality.

While the eighteenth-century Enlightenment indeed was a watershed in Western perceptions of spiritual reality, our society today is more open to the numinous. By all accounts, spiritual movements such as Wicca and Satanism are on the rise. Hollywood produces a steady stream of movies with powerful spiritual warfare content, from Star Wars to Harry Potter. Bookstore shelves sag under the weight of recent volumes on the occult, New Age, horoscopes, and ancient Eastern religions. We live in a profoundly spiritual society, in which the language and practices of the powers—good and evil—are burgeoning.

Is this a lamentable reversion to medieval ignorance, or a widening of spiritual bandwidth that creates opportunity for the church? I think it is the latter. Of course we do not celebrate the resurgence of magic, curses, and dark powers. But perhaps our society is alert to a spiritual dimension that academic theologians and post-Enlightenment pastors ignore at our peril. Some of us took up spiritual language and practice to "engage the powers" of empire, racism, and political or military domination.[1] Now, in the same way, we must recognize that dark forces operate on a personal level and require similar confrontation and spiritual struggle.

Importance of a vibrant eschatology

Sustained spiritual and political struggle against forces of empire and political oppression requires followers of Jesus to have a vibrant eschatology, a theology of God's end plan for the world. The same is true for those who engage in personal exorcism.

Archbishop Oscar Romero, confronting the powers of empire and a corrupt government in El Salvador, was assassinated while celebrating the Eucharist at a hospital chapel in San Salvador on February 17, 1980. His final homily included these words:

> The expectation of a new earth ... should not deaden, but rather enliven us.... When we have spread human dignity, unity and freedom ... throughout the earth in the Spirit of the Lord and in accord with his command, we will find that, when Christ surrenders the eternal and universal kingdom to the Father, human nature will be free of all stain, illuminated and transformed.... The kingdom is already mysteriously present on our earth; when the Lord comes, he will perfect his creation. This hope comforts us as Christians.... This body broken and this blood shed for human beings encourage us to give our body and blood up to suffering and pain, as Christ did—not for self, but to bring justice and peace to our people.[2]

While I am not aware that Archbishop Romero used exorcism language to confront the *militares* of El Salvador, his ministry had a macro impact. This great spiritual warrior, aware that he was in a life-and-death struggle with political and economic powers, grounded his hope in the kingdom of God that he already saw breaking into the world.

---

1. See especially Walter Wink, *Engaging the Powers: Discernment and Resistance in a World of Domination* (Minneapolis: Fortress Press, 1992).

2. Oscar Romero, "In Death Is Our Life," in *A Martyr's Message of Hope: Six Homilies by Archbishop Oscar Romero,* trans. and ed. Felipe Ortega et al. (Kansas City, MO: Celebration Books, 1981), 162–66.

When asked about his authority to exorcise, Jesus replied, "If it is by the finger of God that I cast out the demons, then the kingdom of God has come to you" (Luke 11:20). Casting out demons in the synoptic Gospels is so closely related to proclamation of the reign of God that it appears to be one of the signs of the end times breaking into the present.

Casting out demons is more than mere therapeutic technique, and is something other than magic. Exorcism on a macro or micro level is reclaiming for God that which was created through Christ (Col. 1:16) but which has wittingly or unwittingly become part of creation-in-rebellion. Viewed in this cosmic perspective, the resurrection of Jesus is the pivotal moment of history when the ultimate exorcism—defeat of death itself—gave humankind hope that God will redeem all of creation.

For Christians, who ground our faith in the resurrection of Jesus, it is imperative to view all forms of exorcism as God's work in which we are humble ministers. There should be confidence and boldness in confronting the powers but no swagger or personal aggrandizement. If we believe that God raised Jesus from the dead, it does not require a great step of faith to believe that God can cleanse a nation of war lust or free a deeply troubled individual from bondage to malevolent forces that lead to physical and spiritual death.

The early church can provide a model

The church in the twenty-first century may benefit from seeing how believers in the first centuries of the Christian era confronted the powers. We should not make too much of the distinction between personal and systemic evil. There are many examples from the early church of deliverance that bridged personal and structural dimensions of evil. Justin Martyr, a bishop executed at Rome in the mid-second century, ascribed to demonic influence the harsh treatment of Christians by Roman officials: "The evil demons, who hate us, and who keep such men as these subject to themselves, and serving them in the capacity of judges, incite them, as rulers actuated by evil spirits, to put us to death."[3] Justin elsewhere described individual salvation

3. Justin, *2 Apol.* 1. *The Apostolic Fathers, with Justin Martyr and Irenaeus*, ed. Alexander Roberts and James Donaldson; Ante-Nicene Fathers, vol. 1 (Edinburgh: T & T Clark, 1925), 188; Early Church Fathers 1.1.6.2.0.1.

through Christ as deliverance from demons—with ethical, economic, and political implications:

> We who formerly delighted in fornication, but now embrace chastity alone; we who formerly used magical arts, dedicate ourselves to the good and unbegotten God; we who valued above all things the acquisition of wealth and possessions, now bring what we have into a common stock, and communicate to every one in need; we who hated and destroyed one another, and on account of their different manners would not live with [people] of a different tribe, now, since the coming of Christ, live familiarly with them, and pray for our enemies.[4]

That kind of exorcism strikes me as something urgently needed in our violent and unjust world.

Perpetua of Carthage, martyred in AD 203, gives another glimpse of spiritual warfare in the early church. This aristocratic young woman found a new identity in Christ that freed her both from the pagan Roman imperial ideology and from the patriarchy of a society that demanded that she bow to the spiritual directives of her father or husband. Awaiting execution, Perpetua recorded a vision she received:

> I saw a ladder of tremendous height made of bronze, reaching all the way to the heavens.... At the foot of the ladder lay a dragon of enormous size, and it would attack those who tried to climb up and try to terrify them from doing so.... "He will not harm me," I said, "in the name of Jesus Christ." Slowly, as though he were afraid of me, the dragon stuck his head out from underneath the ladder. Then, using it as my first step, I trod on his head and went up.[5]

What an image of spiritual deliverance in the face of structural evil! In the name of Jesus, Perpetua steps on the head of imperial power and boosts herself toward freedom in the presence of God.

Supporting Perpetua in this spiritual battle was a whole Christian community who prayed and encouraged. Deacons visited and

---

4. Justin, *1 Apol.* 14. *Apostolic Fathers,* 167.

5. Joyce E. Salisbury, *Perpetua's Passion: The Death and Memory of a Young Roman Woman* (New York: Routledge, 1997), 99.

baptized her while she was under house arrest. Her soul mate while awaiting execution was her female slave, who also had confessed Christ. At the arena itself, a group of Christian martyrs prayed and exhorted one another as they awaited their turn with the beasts.

The role of community in deliverance ministry

Paul Yoder observes that freedom from emotional and spiritual oppression happens in relationship to community, and it is not difficult to see this dynamic in the New Testament.[6] Jesus sent out seventy disciples *in pairs* when he commissioned them to proclaim the kingdom. During this mission, the seventy seemed surprised to discover that their ministry included exorcism (Luke 10:17). These first missionaries did not go out as solo religious entrepreneurs but as dyads seeking to build community. They lodged in households, speaking first the words that still resonate with social activists in the church today: "Peace to this house!" (Luke 10:5). It was through ministry pairs, based in households (extended families), that peace-proclaiming came to include freeing individuals from demon possession in the name of Jesus (cf. Matt. 10:8).

In his pastoral counsel for the church at Corinth, Paul tells believers there to gather as a community to confront sexual immorality in the life of a church member. "When you are assembled, and my spirit is present with the power of our Lord Jesus, you are to hand this man over to Satan for the destruction of the flesh, so that his spirit may be saved in the day of the Lord" (1 Cor. 5:4-5). It is beyond the scope of this article to resolve issues around handing a man "over to Satan," but Paul envisions something redemptive rather than punitive. A kind of exorcism is happening here, and it takes place in community.

Despite Paul's counsel to the church at Corinth, I shudder to think of entire congregations gathering to conduct exorcism for one individual. Such public exposure of one person's spiritual life carries enormous risk of manipulation and emotional damage. When Paul told the church at Corinth to confront evil when they were "assembled," he probably was addressing a living-room sized congregation, not an auditorium filled with hundreds of people—and certainly not a television audience.

---

6. See Paul J. Yoder, "Demonization and the Therapeutic Community," chapter 15 in this volume.

Those who engage in exorcism, whether on a personal or a systemic level, must be accountable to the wider faith community. When Jesus sent out the seventy, they "returned with joy" to report to the Lord and to one another what had transpired (Luke 10:17). There is accountability in this narrative, with Jesus providing the communal interpretation of what individual missionaries had experienced. The commissioning and debriefing we see in Luke 10 is suggestive of how the faith community today can provide accountability for exorcists who confront the powers of evil.

Exorcism seems fraught with theological and spiritual hazards, and the church should embrace it with caution. When practicing macroexorcism against the powers of social or political injustice, for example, Christians run the risk of appearing to align ourselves with a given political party. It would be a mistake to convey the idea that partisan politics will usher in the kingdom of God. When practicing microexorcism against the personal demonic, Christians may be tempted to use the suggestion of demonic influence as a way to intimidate opponents or gain a platform in the church. Exorcism, whether personal or systemic, is a high-octane spiritual practice that can burn out of control and do great damage. Such direct encounter with the powers requires spiritual maturity, constant prayer, and the humility to take counsel from fellow believers.

How literal are the demons?

How literally should we take the biblical language of demons and spirits? Some of what the New Testament calls demon possession, we may recognize as illness that will respond to medication or therapy. The church can support such clinical responses with pastoral care and with prayer for healing. We should recognize deliverance from oppressive circumstances as coming from God, even if nothing like a classic exorcism has taken place.

By definition, language about the spiritual world takes us into mystery, into something beyond the strictly measurable and tangible. Establishing whether demons "literally" exist seems less important to me than finding meaningful ways to respond to malignant patterns of human behavior that issue in suffering. There are profound disorders of the soul that wreak havoc, and it is useful to give those persistent and destructive forces a name. I cannot look at the death grip of addictions, for example, or at the devastation of sexual abuse in a family system, without believing that a predatory spiritual presence is seeking to destroy. Land mines that end lives and disable innocent people around the world must be of demonic design. I am ready to accept the biblical label of "demons" as a rubric for addressing such insidious undercurrents in human experience.

Keeping the focus on God

People and structures of this world can align themselves with the will of a loving God, or they can align themselves with creation-in-rebellion. As Christians, our primary focus should remain on the redeeming God, whom we worship and obey. We must not become so preoccupied with evil that we function as if Satan is a second god vying with the God of our Lord Jesus Christ for supremacy. Christians are monotheists, and we do not believe there is a good God and an evil god.

Revelation 12 depicts Satan as a member of the heavenly court who is expelled from God's presence when he rebels. Evil is nothing more or less than God's created spiritual and physical order in rebellion. Satan and his henchmen personify the awful reality of what happens when the creature no longer obeys the Creator. Such rebellion and subsequent enslavement to evil happens all around us on an individual and systemic level. The church today needs to awaken to the reality of evil and confront the powers in Jesus' name. We should recover the early church practice of including some form of exorcism in catechetical instruction. We need deliverance from the powers of greed, promiscuity, nationalism, violence, and individualism so pervasive in the Western world.

I will be most hopeful about Christian deliverance ministry when the church addresses both the systemic/political aspects of spiritual bondage and the individual dimensions of captivity to sin and demonic oppression. When the same Christian community cautiously practices macro and micro deliverance in the name of Jesus, the kingdom of God truly has come near, and the two levels of exorcism are most likely to keep each other in balance.

Appendixes

Appendix 1 Dean Hochstetler's resources for reflection and ministry[1]

Section A Occult practices and the church today

Occult means dark, sinister, and hidden. It has other meanings as well, but here it refers to the realm of satanic activity.

The first occult account in the Bible is found in Genesis 30:37-43 where tree branches are used to alter gene structure in animals. Occultism, sorcery, witchcraft, and allied themes are sprinkled throughout the biblical record. The last time it is recorded is in Revelation 22:15 where it is referred to as magic arts.

The passage in Deuteronomy 18:9-14 outlines the major headings of "detestable practices." King James text says "abominable." Isaiah 47:9-15 provides another outline of these dark practices that vary in form from one society to another.

Biblical classifications and current forms

I. The occult involves child sacrifices. Abortion is in vogue now. The god of convenience and pleasure is being served which in this case results in murder.

II. Divination means the discovery of things hidden and secret by the aid of the spirit world.

   A. Divining rods are used to find sites such as wells, tiles, pipes, or whatever else you think or verbalize. Pendulums can be employed to determine the sex of an unborn child or over maps to find minerals, water, oil, and other objects. It works most of the time. I have seen seminary students involved with pendulums.

   B. Fortunetelling, palm reading, crystal balls, tea leaf readers, interpreting omens and the like are a few of the forms that still flourish.

   C. Dr. Abraham's black box can be used to worm animals, kill aphids in hay fields, and many other uses. A prominent Mennonite pastor in Virginia used this approach to heal the sick two generations ago. I have had many phone calls concerning this practice.

   D. Iridology or iris diagnosis is done by dividing the iris of a person's eye into 12–360 segments and by what the practitioner "sees" therein, a diagnosis of bodily ailments is made and then vitamins, minerals, or herbs are prescribed for cure. This practice flourishes

1. The materials printed here are fruits of Dean Hochstetler's years of deliverance ministry; they reflect his views and are stated in his own words.

in northern and central Indiana, southern Michigan, western Ohio, Pennsylvania, and many other areas.

E. Horoscopes are used to plant crops at proper times, determine dates to catch fish, to plan business affairs, arrange marriage partners, putting the roof on a building in the right sign so the shingles will stay "down," and to order lifestyles for many people today. If horoscopes are left out of newspapers, the editors will likely receive an avalanche of phone calls. Many "New Age" practices have a "fortunetelling" component. This is only a brief list of the many current forms.

III. Casting of spells uses magic. (This is not harmless sleight of hand tricks such as getting golf balls from your nose or handkerchiefs out of your sleeves.) The issue is the kind of magic that has a demonic component.

A. Love magic is used to get desirable sex partners.
B. Hate magic is powerful. Voodoo falls into this category of magic.
C. Persecution magic is used to afflict people.
D. Defense magic is used to ward off spells and curses.
E. Apport manic is the ability to bring objects into view and make them disappear. Manipulating objects without touch (telekinesis) is a form of apport magic.
F. Another name for healing magic is called powwow.
    1. Eggs, strings, hot coals, formulas, and putting a child around a table leg can be used for bodily healing. This takes various forms depending on the community.
    2. Various strokings, while repeating formulas, are used on occasion.
    3. Reciting the verse in Ezekiel 16:6 and adding the name of the person needing help is read into the verse. It is used especially for treating leukemia or to stop bleeding.
    4. Other Bible verses may be taken out of context in conjunction with formulas.
    5. Wart treatments may involve the use of coins, beans, bacon rinds, and much more. Formulas are used here as well. Spanish-speaking communities have "curanderos." Germans have people who can practice "Brauche." Healing magic has many forms not listed here.
    6. Letters of protection may be used against fire, storms, misfortune, sickness, and much more. There are many of these letters in our communities. They appear in our newspapers as "prayers to the blessed virgin" or something similar.
    7. Energy based manipulations for healing based on the supposed fourteen meridian lines of the body have many forms. Chi,

yin-yang adjustments, acupuncture, yoga, and transcendental meditations are a few among a plethora of similar practices that are Chinese or Hindu in origin. Therapeutic touch is taught to nursing students. Healing magic has many forms and is found in some form in all societies. For more information, consult *New Age Medicine* by Dr. Paul Risser, M.D., I.V.P. 1987, pages 44–47. Unfortunately, this book is out of print. There are two other helpful books currently in print: *Can You Trust Your Doctor?* by Weldon and Ankerberg, publisher Wolgmuth and Hyatt, 1991, and *Encyclopedia of New Age Beliefs,* same authors, publisher Harvest House, 1996.

8. Computers are used in connection with a wire to the practitioner, one to the client, and another one to the plate containing vitamins, minerals, or herbs. Pushing on the client's fingertips produces blips on the computer and by this method, diagnosis is made and then the contents on the plate are differentiated and prescribed. Here the practice gets respectability by its "scientific" hook up, that is, the computer.
9. Applied kinesiology or muscle testing determines ailments and prescribes cures. This is not to be confused with kinesiology that is a scientific study of the muscles on the skeletal frame of the body.

A very informative but now out-of-print hook, *Long Lost Friend* by Johann Georg Hohman, on how to practice magic healing, divining rod use, and much more, had a German publication in 1820. Bussard's Knob Press, Dover, Pennsylvania, in 1969, published the English translation.

This book was and still is "revered" by many Pennsylvania Dutch and considered more valuable than the Bible by some of them. It is a take-off of the *Fifth and Sixth Books of Moses* that were authored by a Catholic monk, Albertus Magus, who died in Germany in 1280. These two spurious books are still in print and filled with many sorcery formulas. They have nothing to do with the Bible or Moses.

IV. With death magic, people are actually killed by casting spells, curses, and formulas. I have counseled many persons who were involved in Satan worship or similar practices and have told me of people they have killed with the power of demonic magic. This, too, takes many forms.

V. Spiritism consists of securing direct help of satanic powers to affect the environment, afflict people, animals, and things. It is even used in bodily healing. Many societies have spiritism mixed into their religious practices and worship.

In God's eyes

Occult practices violate the second commandment. False gods are served which curses family systems (Deut. 5:9.) These detestable practices are strictly forbidden to God's people in the Old and New Testament. According to the Old Testament, if you were involved, it was death by stoning (Leviticus 20). In the New Testament, it is exclusion from the kingdom (Revelation 21:8 and 22:15). Galatians 5:19 alludes to occult practices also and yet the pulpits of our churches (Mennonites included) are strangely silent on these issues. Christian halls of learning are remarkably silent on these occult issues. If you even raise the issue, you are likely to be scoffed and laughed at. Christian Missionary Alliance Seminary at Nyack, New York, teaches the reality of the demonic realm and what to do about it to their students. Should not we do the same? Deuteronomy 18:12 is the Old Testament passage that justifies war. Canaan was filled with sorcery. Israel became involved, too, because they did not drive out all the inhabitants as they were instructed.

Occult involvements are a prime reason for the "deadwood spiritually" that exists in the church. People's lives are often burdened by these practices, the etiology of which is either personal or ancestral and they may not be aware of it due to ignorance. For this reason, these "sins" are never confessed. I am old enough to remember the days of strict church discipline, but I never heard of anyone that was disciplined for using sorcery.

Acts 19:19 tells us of believers who still needed to destroy their former books of sorcery. How does this apply to us? Think about Ouija boards that are a cross between fortunetelling and spiritism or the Harry Potter books that can be used to begin witchcraft practice. Do our divining rods need to be destroyed? Hard rock music glorifies the satanic and dulls the mind. Does this kind of music have a place among us? I have watched several churches burn such occultic items after being informed of their content and danger.

Reincarnation beliefs are invariably mixed with occult practices. It is a counterfeit of the resurrection. There are many "past life" therapists.

All forms of occult practices can be categorized in four different forms that are outlined in Deuteronomy 18:9-14. A far more complete list can be found in the writings of Dr. Kurt Koch, especially *Occult ABC.* Kregel Publishing Company, Grand Rapids, Michigan, publishes them.

Eyes Opened to Satan's Subtlety, written by a French Mennonite, Emile Kremer, from Colmar, France, is very helpful in addressing occult practices and their consequences. It is a private publication available from Harvey Christian Publishers, 3107 Highway 321, Hampton, Tennessee 37658. The phone number is (423)768-2297 and the price is around $8.00. He died in 1987. Dr. Kurt Koch refers to him in his publications.

Emile Kremer was one of the few men who successfully withstood Hitler. The reason was Emile knew how to handle the evil spirit world that motivated Hitler. Hitler and all his cabinet members of Nazi Germany were members of a Satan worshiping coven. This is documented in a book *Occultism in Government* by Alan Street published privately in 1977. (Refer to chapter 4, pages 18–43.) The U.S. government has not been free of such influences. It is documented in the same book.

Occult practices are still issues in the church today

A Mennonite pastor recently told me of a Sunday school class of mature adults in which a person raised the subject of the evils of using divining rods. It became a heated discussion. Many people in the class said, "How else do you find a well?" The gifts of the Holy Spirit listed in 1 Corinthians 12 include the gift of knowledge and also discernment. Should we not use them as a benefit for all of us? Why resort to sorcery??

I recall so vividly a church that had a well over 100 feet deep that had poor water quality. A charter church member using a divining rod had found the well site. The elders of the church held a prayer meeting asking the Lord where to put a new well. The inspiration came to one of them to dig twelve feet south of a certain oak tree. They dug at this location and found all the good water they could use at an unheard-of depth of twelve feet. There are no other comparable wells in that community. Occult practices are never one hundred percent accurate nor can they be scientifically investigated. James Randies' challenge to prove it is all a hoax is safe. It cannot be done!

Reasons why sorcery is still among us

Occult practices, although not effective in all cases, are accurate enough that people believe in them. It is for this reason that people get involved. The rationale is, "It works, therefore it is good." There is great failure to see that the deception of Satan as recorded in Genesis 3 is still current. A mix of rat poison in your sugar that you might eat will kill you even if you are ignorant of the poison. Occultism is a counterfeit of Holy Spirit gifts to the church. Satan is a master counterfeiter. There are no nineteen dollar bills. Only a fool would try to make some. A counterfeit needs to be measured or compared with a genuine article to determine its solidity. The gifts of the Holy Spirit are reality; therefore, Satan counterfeits them.

Effects of occult involvements physically and spiritually in people's lives

Exodus 20:3-5, Deuteronomy 5:7-9, Numbers 14:18, Exodus 34:6-7, Daniel 9, and Nehemiah 9 contain scripture verses about confession and repentance. They are still needed today both personally and corporately. Occult practices (sorcery) are sin.

A. not all effects are in the same person
B. spiritual blindness—offended at the suggestion that occultism is sin

C. lack of assurance of salvation
D. wild Pentecostalism, atheism, and legalism
E. inability to appropriate gifts of the Holy Spirit—closed to his person
F. ancestral burdens; four times the rate of normal population of crippled, mentally retarded, and deformed children born; this is my general observation as well as the opinion given to me verbally by Dr. Kurt Koch
G. fifty-five percent of the mentally ill have ancestry
H. tendencies to immorality—lust, bestiality, homosexuality in some cases
I. some types of epilepsy
J. thoughts and acts of suicide
K. marital problems—problems of the female reproductive system in particular
L. constant sickness and incurable disease
M. extreme bed wetting into teenage years; could be a medical problem but often has occult ties
N. sleep walking
O. freak accidents
P. compulsive behavior and actions
Q. severe behavioral and emotional problems
R. gossip, strife, and dissension
S. inability to hear others
T. unable to forgive others
U. haunted places—these may have their origin in one or more of the following items:
    1. curse—spell cast on the premises by a sorcerer
    2. sorcery performed there
    3. sorcerer dies there—resident demonic spirit remains
    4. demonized person lives there
    5. murder on the premises—suicide
    6. person lives there who has a heavy occult ancestry and the dark spirits have followed them
    7. objects present that are designed or used in heathen, occultic, or satanic worship
V. inherited problems
W. possibility of demonic invasion of the person
X. violent death bed scenes; Emile Kremer quotes Johann Blumhardt on this horror in his book. I affirm the same.

This is an exemplary list even though much more could be said. The writings of Emile Kremer and Dr. Kurt Koch have much to say about this subject as I do, but my space is limited. However, I must make a comment as I wish to share an observation relevant to letter "J" on suicides. There was a period of twenty-five years that I investigated all the suicides I had found in the Mennonite-Amish groups although I am certain I missed some of them. In every case I investigated, I found occult practices involving pow-wow healings, using divining rods, or both in the person's own life or near ancestry. Remember King Saul's death was a suicide. He had gone to see the spirit medium (1 Samuel 28 and 1 Chronicles 10:13.) He also had disobeyed Samuel's instruction in 1 Samuel 15.

Exercise Christian authority

Genuine Christians appropriating their union with Christ can bring occult practitioners' work to a halt. Avail yourself of the authority delegated to the believer. "In him" is a direct result of that oneness. Let us by faith appropriate what is ours (Romans 6, Ephesians 1:1 up to 2:7) using your authority to bring these practices to a standstill (Ephesians 3:10). Pray verbally in the presence of the act in Jesus' name against the dark spirits that motivate the practice. Pay attention to Matthew 12:29. Therefore, bind and loose. It brings God glory.

Conclusion

Acts 16 makes it clear that attacking the strongholds of darkness is one method of evangelism. The demon was cast out. Paul and Silas were jailed because of all that took place. The whole community heard the gospel. Acts 13:8-12 and Acts 19:13-20 are similar accounts. Acts 26:18 tells us to open their eyes, to turn them from darkness to light, and from Satan's dark powers to God so that people around may find salvation, forgiveness of sins, and surrender their lives to the service of the Lord Jesus Christ.

North American Christian churches will need a far better understanding of what occultism consists of than they currently have. People burdened by occult practices are often not aware of it, making evangelization more difficult. The church should recognize its archenemy and know how to address the issue in the power and authority of Jesus' name.

Mission strategists are recognizing the reality of the dark spirit world and the VICTORY OF JESUS over them in many parts of he world. Let us demonstrate to those in our own communities the glory of God, the praise of Jesus, and the release for the oppressed.

Appendix 1 Dean Hochstetler's resources for reflection and ministry[1]

Section B Seven levels of a person's makeup and dangers of occult activity

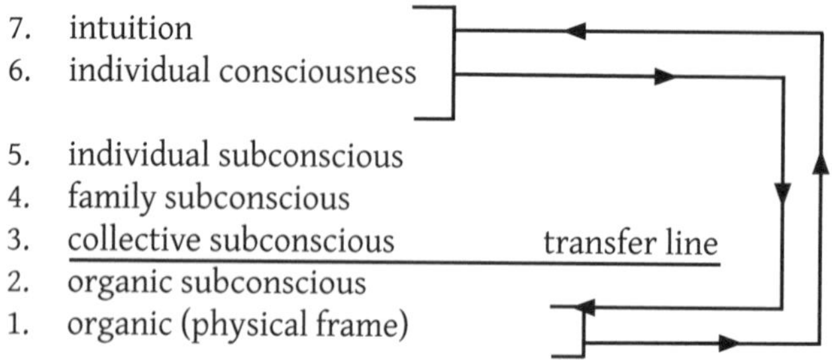

Level 7 is where one communicates with God, prays, hears the Holy Spirit's voice. Level 6 is the realm of decision making, reasoning, judgment as to life's issues. Levels 7 and 6 are where decisions about saving faith in Jesus are made. Level 5 is the realm of our subconscious activity. Level 4 is the storehouse of family traits. Level 3 is where all the traits that make us part of the human race are stored. Level 2 is the realm of, for example, heartbeat, liver functions, and digestive processes, over which we have little control. Level 1 is our meat and bones, for example. Levels 2 and 1 are where we get physically sick.

Occult practices damage levels 7 and 6. In case of magic healings (which are most devastating to the human makeup)—powwow, to try for (English terms), "Brauche" (German), "la obra de ojo fuerte" (Spanish)—it is a direct attack on the human makeup in totality. If physical healing is received (levels 2 and 1), then the problems will be shifted into the psychic levels (levels 7 and 6). If mental problems are healed magically (levels 7 and 6), then the shift is the other way—physical problems in levels 2 and 1.

These "healings" are not genuine, only counterfeits, as Satan cannot produce genuine things. He does nothing "for free." Therefore, the healing is a "trade off." These physical healings are in reality a shift into the spiritual and psychic realm of the person. Therefore, problems will now appear in the person's life as well as in their descendants. Demonic healings always damage saving faith in Jesus. Divine healings always strengthen faith.

Therefore, magic healings of whatever form, New Age energy manipulations, iridology, therapeutic touch, crystals, acupuncture, and martial arts

1. The materials printed here are fruits of Dean Hochstetler's years of deliverance ministry; they reflect his views and are stated in his own words.

are dangerous as well. Martial arts have occult origins and power. All occult practices are included here.

This diagram shows why occult practices, especially healings of demonic origin, are detrimental to Christian faith. People who are involved in occult practices come to Christ with difficulty at times, even after there is confession of these involvements. Some never do, until these curses are broken.

Those who do come to Christ for salvation, and do not confess and repent of these practices, and do not renounce Satan and his works and ways from one's life, generally will never live victorious Christian lives until this whole realm is recognized and addressed in Jesus' name.

On occasion, when magic healings are confessed, the illness or problem that was healed will return. Christian prayer, anointing, and commanding Satan to go to the abyss will restore the person from the ailment.

Appendix 1 Dean Hochstetler's resources for reflection and ministry[1]

Section C Freedom and victory in Jesus

"If the Son shall set you free; you're free indeed" (John 8:32-36).

I. Absolute honesty with God and counselor is necessary. You cannot deceive God!

II. Confess all known sin. Be specific and itemize. Personal sins bring guilt which needs removal (Hebrews 9:11-14 and 10:19-22).

A. Pride, rebellion against God or other authority need to be confessed.

B. Make lists of resentment, hatred, and bitterness against anyone living or dead.

C. Make a list of sexual partners outside of marriage and break the soul ties (Genesis 2:24).

D. Spell out all occult involvements for people (Deuteronomy 18:9-14 and Isaiah 47:9-15). Occult means dark, secret, and hidden practices by aid of the demonic spirit world. The use of occult practices is designed to bind people (allegiance) to satanic forces in life or to afflict the environment. The average pastor cannot define occult practices in terms that his parishioners can understand, nor has he ever preached on these texts. Often people do not understand what they have been involved in. Occultism is increasing at an alarming rate. Water divining (smelling), pendulum use, magic healings (powwow), iris diagnosis, applied kinesiology, therapeutic touch, acupuncture, crystal use, satanic worship, and Ouija boards are still among us! The counselor needs to inform the client what occult practices include and their consequences (Deuteronomy 5:9 and 2 Corinthians 11:14). Occultism has a plethora of forms.

E. Ancestral sins, inherited curses, and burdens need to be brought to the cross.

F. 80 percent of demonization is ancestrally rooted and needs confession of "the whole core of evil." Hence there is the need to confess ancestral, occult, and other evil practices that are rooted in the ancestry. A person is not "guilty" for what the ancestors have done, but can often be burdened by the consequences and curses of their evil deeds (Deuteronomy 5:8-9; Deuteronomy 23:2 and chapters 27 and 28; Matthew 23:29-36).

---

1. The materials printed here are fruits of Dean Hochstetler's years of deliverance ministry; they reflect his views and are stated in his own words.

III. Forgive (Matthew 18:15-22) everyone that has ever harmed you or caused you to suffer.
IV. Matthew 18:23-35: fail to do so and you will be tortured.
V. Admit and confess deception and worship of false gods.
VI. Pronounce absolution (John 20:23). This is tremendously effective for the person's emotional welfare. A person who has confessed sin needs to hear that he or she is forgiven.
VII. Check for the presence of demonic entities that are rooted personally or ancestrally. There may be need to "bind and loose" (Matthew 12:29; 16:19; 18:18). This comes last unless one is impeded by the demons as work toward freedom is progressing. If the person is a believer in Jesus and the person has a demon problem, ALL legal ground (the garbage of life) for the evil presence must be broken before the demons can be cast out in the name of Jesus. In unbelievers, there is no duality of allegiance. Demons need to be cast or crowded out, if they are attached to the person. Some demons are exceedingly tenacious and time is needed (see Luke 8:29). You stay at it until it is done. It does not necessarily all happen in one session; sometimes, yes. Not all troubled persons are demonized, but some are; therefore, the need to check to see if there are attachments (1 John 4). Confession of all known sin, guilt, and receiving the full value of the cross of Jesus (John 19:30) often forces the wicked spirits to leave. (This consists of an understanding of the value of the blood and broken body of Jesus.) Then there is no need to check it out. Emotional pain needs healing; get the person to the healer who is Jesus and get out of the way (Theophostic approach). This is not an absolute. It is a tool to use when needed and appropriate.
VIII. Renunciation of Satan, his host, works, and ways from one's life, and a conscious transfer from Satan's darkness to the kingdom of the Lord Jesus Christ and his light is important. Full commitment of one's life to Jesus is necessary.
IX. Pastoral care is of absolute importance until sound faith in Jesus is established (Luke 8:35). Every severely demonized person is shattered emotionally and the emotional structure needs to be rebuilt. Solid faith in the Lord Jesus is absolute. Help in other areas of life may be needed. It doesn't have to be a pastor but a competent caregiver. Daily care may be necessary for a while. Biblical truth must be established in the person's life. "In him" (Jesus), must be appropriated and understood. The value of the cross of Jesus, his shed blood, death, burial, resurrection, ascension, and seating above the principalities and powers (demonic world) must be grasped. Help the person to appropriate authority in Christ. The "in him" position of Romans 6 and Ephesians 1 up to 2:7 state or imply this principle about thirty-five times.

Courage. These eight principles have stood the test of time and many situations. Do not bypass them. They are the basis for the formerly afflicted person to live a victorious Christian life.

Revelation 12:9 and Revelation 12:11 are still true. The devil is overcome by the blood of the Lamb and the word of our testimony.

This is an outline of areas to be addressed with a troubled person. This paper does not address all the specifics which may be used. The sequence of use depends on the person's situation, the counselor, and the Holy Spirit's leading.

I am indebted to the contributions of others working in deliverance ministry, and I continue to learn from them. This is a field of work that has no experts. Christ in us (Holy Spirit) and the Bible are our guide and hope of glory.

Appendix 1 Dean Hochstetler's deliverance ministry resources[1]

Section D A pre-ministry questionnaire

Below are areas that through various types of experience have been found to open the door to demonic oppression. For each of the items listed, indicate (fill in the box) any involvement (participation, observation, lip service, reading or any interest) by yourself (S), parents (P), grandparents (GP), great-grandparents (GG), spouse (SP), or other relatives, friends, schoolmates, teachers, or neighbors (O; identify who). Note: Definitions for terms in this questionnaire are at the end of the document.

False religions[2]	S	P	GP	GG	SP	O
American Indian rites						
Bahai						
Buddhism						
Children of God						
Christian Science						
Confucianism						
Hare Krishna						
Hinduism (Bhagavad-Gita)						
Islam (Qur'an)						
Jehovah's Witnesses						
Mormonism						
New Age						
Rosicrucianism						
Satanism						
Scientology						
Spiritism						
Swedenborgianism						
Taoism						
The Way International						
Unification Church (Moonies)						
Unity (The Daily Word)						
Others not listed						
Any negative influences from places of worship associated with these religions[3]						

False teachings and philosophies	S	P	GP	GG	SP	O
Humanism:						
Materialism						
The Human Manifesto						
William James teaching						

1. The materials printed here are fruits of Dean Hochstetler's years of deliverance ministry; they reflect his views and are stated in his own words. They are included for purposes of illustration. Copyright © 2006 Dean Hochstetler, 1752 Waterfall Drive, Nappanee, IN 46550. Used by permission; all rights reserved.

2. False religions claim there are other gods besides Jesus and other ways of salvation not founded on the person of Jesus Christ. Have you ever denied that Jesus is the only way, truth, and life? Have you denied his divinity? His virgin birth? His bodily resurrection? His second coming? Have you denied the Trinity?

3. For example, Mormon Tabernacle, Indian burial grounds, etc.

The power of positive thinking						
Reincarnation: Have you studied or made contact with:						
Déjà vu						
Edgar Cayce books						
Elisabeth Kübler-Ross (later books)						
Jeane Dixon's writings						
Other reincarnation teachings						
Other false teachings:						
Atheism						
Deism						
EST (Forum)						
Eckankar						
Marxism						
Nihilism[4]						
Silva Mind Control						
Theosophy						
Monism (All Is One)						
Pantheism (God in Everything)						

Occult direction or guidance[5]	**S**	**P**	**GP**	**GG**	**SP**	**O**
Astrology (horoscope, Zodiac signs)						
Automatic writing						
Biofeedback						
Biorhythms						
Charms						
Crystal balls						
Handwriting analysis						
Life readings						
Mirror mantics						
Numerology						
Occult jewelry						
Ouija board						
Palm reading						
Pendulum[6]						
People/saints who have died						
Psychics, mediums						
Channelers						
Séances						
Tarot cards						
Tea leaves						
Water witching, divining, smelling						

Occult and psychic power and control[7]	**S**	**P**	**GP**	**GG**	**SP**	**O**
Acupuncture						

4. Writings by Immanuel Kant, Albert Camus, Jean-Paul Sartre, Friedrich Nietsche.

5. It is dangerous to seek direction or guidance for our lives outside of Jesus and the word of God. Have you seriously or just for fun searched for direction or guidance from any of the sources listed here?

6. Used for fortunes or to determine sex of unborn children.

7. It is dangerous to seek direction or guidance for our lives outside of Jesus and the word of God. Have you seriously or just for fun searched for direction or guidance from any of the sources listed here?

Apport magic[8]						
Astral or soul travel						
Black mass						
Clairvoyance						
Color diagnosis/therapy[9]						
Conversations with spirits or spirit guides[10]						
Crystal healing						
Curses or spells						
Excursion of the soul						
Healing fanaticism						
Healing magic:						
Codgering						
Root work						
Measuring the soul						
Strokings						
Use of fetishes						
Use of eggs and strings						
Use of hot coals						
Use of formulas[11]						
Powwowing						
Brauche (German)						
La obra de ojo fuerte (Spanish)						
Hexes						
Iridology or iris diagnosis						
Levitation						
Magic (black, white, death)						
Parapsychology (study of the occult)						
Predictive dreams						
Psychic healing						
Psychokinesis						
Sensitivity training						
Soul force						
Speaking in tongues						
Spiritist church or lodge						
Spiritistic healing or visions						
Tabletipping						
Wart treatment (not medical)						
Witchraft (white or black)						
Mind control[12]						
Hypnotism (even medical or dental)						
Mental telepathy						
Attempts to influence or control others by mental suggestions						
Metaphysics						
Psychic harassment of others						
Martial arts involvement						
Judo						
Karate						

8. Materialization and dematerialization, not sleight of hand.
9. Magical healing diagnosis using colored strings.
10. Demons.
11. For example, Ezekiel 16:6, to stop bleeding.
12. Have you ever been involved with or studied any of the mind sciences, such as those listed here?

Kung Fu						
Taekwon Do						
False meditation study or participation						
Transcendental meditation						
Yoga						
Others not listed here						

Superstitions[13]	S	P	GP	GG	SP	O
Breaking a mirror						
Birds flying against a window						
Death/tragedies/accidents come in threes						
Fear of black cats						
Fear of walking under ladders						
Finger crossing						
Friday the 13th						
Hex signs						
Knocking on wood						
Lucky numbers						
Lucky pieces[14]						
Opening an umbrella indoors						
Throwing salt over shoulder						
Superstitious routines or rituals[15]						
Wishing on an object (falling star, etc.)						
Other						

Detrimental influences[16]	S	P	GP	GG	SP	O
Mind-altering drugs						
Cocaine						
Crack						
Heroin						
LSD						
Marijuana						
Others (please list)						
Amphetamines						
Barbiturates						
Diet pills						
Over-the-counter drugs						
Prescription drugs						
Alcohol[17]						
Other addictions						
Anorexia						
Bulimia						
Caffeine						
Chronic or compulsive daydreaming						
In bondage to food						

13. Superstition is another way of giving power to someone or something other than Jesus Christ. Even if you think you do not believe them but have merely given lip service to them, you can unconsciously weaken your faith in Jesus. Have you practiced any of the superstitions listed here?

14. For example, kitchen witch, four-leaf clover, rabbit's foot, St. Christopher medal.

15. Following the same steps each time to make certain things happen or not happen.

16. Have you used, abused, or dealt with any of othe items on this list?

17. Have you ever been dependent on alcohol or been drunk?

Nicotine						
Have you ever been deeply involved in:						
New Country & Western music						
Non-Christian rock music						
Soap operas						
Violent and/or occult books/movies[18]						
Friday the 13th						
Halloween						
Hellraiser						
Nightmare on Elm Street						
Poltergeist						
Rambo						
Stephen King novels						
The Exorcist						
Harry Potter books/movies						
Other books or movies of this nature						
Have you ever listened to or told ghost stories?						
Has science fiction had an influence in your life?[19]						
Have you ever played video games, such as:						
Occult-based games						
8-ball						
Dungeons and Dragons						
Ka-Bala						
Halloween activities						
Others not listed here						

Negative personal involvement	**S**	**P**	**GP**	**GG**	**SP**	**O**
Mental abuse to you						
Have you had an abortion or been involved with someone who has?						
Physical abuse to you						
Accidental or tragic deaths						
Bad dreams (nightmares)						
Death wish (for anyone, even yourself)						
Hearing voices						
Illegitimate birth						
Miscarriage or still birth						
Deep rebellion, anger, resentment, or unforgiveness toward:						
God						
Establishment						
Abusive persons						
Children						
Deceased (dead) persons						
Self						
Spouse						
Authority						
Parents						
Other						
Commitment to secret societies						

18. Have you read books or seen movies that portray or glorify violence or the occult, such as those listed here?

19. Sometimes portrays mind-control or forces other than God to control people and/or events.

Masonic order						
Eastern Star						
Sororities/fraternities						
Racial organizations[20]						
The Order of the Arrow						
Suicidal thoughts or attempts						
Blood pacts						
Vows[21]						
Personal experience in war or similar violence						
Other						

Habitual sins[22]	S	P	GP	GG	SP	O
Excessive anxiety						
Excessive worry						
Gambling						
Gossip						
Greed						
Lying						
Profanity						
Stealing						
Drunkenness						

Sexual sins[23]	S	P	GP	GG	SP	O
Have you ever been sexually violated or abused or molested (no penetration)?						
Have you ever sexually abused someone else (child or adult)?						
Have you been exposed to pornography in any of the following forms?						
Live shows						
Magazines						
Novels						
Photographs						
Pornographic films						
TV shows/videos						
Have you had a problem with:						
Childhood experimentation (with relatives or friends)						
Incest						
Lust						
Masturbation						
Sex fantasies						
Voyeurism						
Have you allowed yourself to be involved in any of the following sexual sins?						
Adultery						

20. For example, KKK, Black Panthers.

21. See definitions below.

22. By experience, we have found that many people have a particularly vulnerable area of sin in their lives with which they struggle continuously. Have you ever struggled with any of the sins listed here in a compulsive way?

23. Though sexual sins are by far the most difficult to expose, total freedom and cleansing await those who do.

Heavy petting						
Fornication						
Have you been troubled with any of the following sexual deviations?						
Bestiality (sex with animals)						
Exhibitionism						
Fetishes						
Homosexuality/lesbianism						
Necrophilia						
Pedophilia						
Sadism/masochism						
Transvestism						
Other						
Soul ties						

Emotional and psychological troubles[24]	S	P	GP	GG	SP	O
Abandonment (emotional/physical)						
Adopted						
Worry						
Fear of:						
Being sick						
Rejection						
Confrontation						
Man						
Places						
Disapproval						
Judgment (from God or man)						
Condemnation						
Accusation						
Reproof						
Failure						
Heights						
Close places						
Darkness						
Hugs/touching						
Authority						
Others not listed						
Anxiety						
Nervous habits						
Tenseness						
Restlessness						
Insomnia						
Sleep walking						
Epilepsy (that can't be medically explained)						
Extreme sensitivity						
Excitable						
Headaches						
Mental illness						
Retardation						
Senility						
Schizophrenia						
Bipolar (manic-depression)						
Depression						

24. Are any of these found on a regular basis?

Dissociative disorders						
Paranoia						
Hallucinations						
Jealousy						
Envy						
Suspicious						
Distrust						
Persecution						
Confusion						
Frustration						
Incoherence						
Forgetfulness						
Doubt						
Unbelief						
Skepticism						
Indecision						
Procrastination						
Indifference						
Compromise						
Self-deception						
Intellectualism						
Rationalization						
Egotism						
Hysteria						
Lying						
Deceit						
Vanity						
Self-righteousness						
Haughtiness						
Importance						
Arrogance						
Dramatic						
Pretension						
Argumentative						
Covetousness						
Stealing						
Kleptomania						
Greed						
Discontent						
Perfectionist						
Critical						
Intolerance						
Competitive						
Impatient						
Agitation						
Grief						
Sorrow						
Crying						
Sadness						
Heartbreak						
Cruelty						
Unusual fatigue						
Laziness						
Infirmity (any disease or sickness)						
Physical handicaps (inherited or accidental)						

Hyperactive						
Coarse jesting						
Gossip						
Mockery						
Belittling						
Idleness						
Loss of time						
Self-pity						
Self-reward						
Guilt						
Shame						
Unworthiness						
Easily embarrassed						
Prostitution						
Cross-dressing						
Narcissism (excessive love of oneself)						
Apathetic						
Depressed						
Boastful						
Homesick						
Insignificant						
Withdrawn						
Secretive						
Loneliness						
Manipulative						
Controlling						
False responsibility						
False compassion						
Bitterness						
Hatred						
Violence						
Revenge						
Murder						
Stubbornness						
Hot temper						
Rebellion						
Disobedience						
Anti-submissive						
Bickering						
Dominating						
Destructive						
Sadism						
Fault-finding						
Insecure						
Inferior						
Timidity						
Pouting						
Daydreams						
Passive						
Stoic						
Sleepiness						
Listlessness						
Despair						
Gloom						
Escape from feelings						

Runs from responsibilities						
Hypochondriac						

How were you raised?	S	P	GP	GG	SP	O
With mom and stepdad?						
In a two-parent home with your own mom and dad?						
Did your parents have joint custody?						
Did one parent have custody, the other visitation rights?						
Were you ever placed in a foster home?						
Were you raised with foster children in your home?						
Were you raised in an orphanage?						

Pre-ministry requirements

Pray that the Holy Spirit will reveal to you any of the following. *Write these down.* You must be absolutely truthful before God and me. You cannot deceive God. This also helps us to discern the problem(s). Ask that the Holy Spirit would bring these back to your memory if you feel you have forgotten. By filling out the questionnaire, you should be able to answer these questions. Use the definitions pages for help as well.

1. Be completely honest with God.
2. List *all* known *unconfessed* sin; be specific.
3. List all occult involvements that are marked on the questionnaire (see definitions on last pages); personally and ancestry if known.
4. List all hurt and pain in your life that is not healed.
5. List resentment (unforgiveness) against anyone, living or dead.
6. List ancestral hurts and pains of your family system, if known.
7. List personal sexual history and be specific. List each involvement outside of marriage vows. Sexual activity outside of marriage causes *soul ties.* To break these ties, list names, places, or faces.
8. List ancestral sexual history, if known.
9. List suicides in family system.
10. List abortions or miscarriages—self or family.

Personal information

Religious background

Denominational preference:
What church do you currently attend?
Church address:
Pastor's name:
Pastor's phone:
May we contact your pastor for information and help? Circle one: Yes No When?
Church attendance per month (circle one): 1 2 3 4 5 6 7 8 9 10+
Church attended in childhood:
Have you been baptized? Circle one: Yes No When?
If married, what is the religious background of your spouse?
Spouse's church attendance:
Church name and address:
Church attendance per month (circle one): 1 2 3 4 5 6 7 8 9 10+
Do you consider yourself a Christian? Circle one: Yes No Uncertain

Do you believe in God? Circle one: Yes No Uncertain
Write a short paragraph on how you came to know Jesus Christ as your Lord and Savior:
Have you come to a place in your spiritual life where you can say that you know for certain that if you were to die tonight you would go to heaven? Circle one: Yes No Uncertain
If you have received Christ as your Savior, what changes have taken place in your life since you became saved?
Do you read the Bible? Circle one: Never Occasionally Often
Do you have family devotions? Circle one: Never Occasionally Often
Describe your family devotions.
Explain any recent changes in your spiritual life.

Basic problem identification

Briefly answer the following questions.
What is the problem that brings you here?
What have you done about the problem already?
What do you seek from this counseling?
What circumstances led to your coming here at this point in time?
Is there any other information that you think we should know?

Personality information

Have you had any psychotherapy or counseling before? Circle one: Yes No
Counselor/therapist name:
Dates of treatment:
Medication prescribed:
Outcome and diagnosis:

Circle any of the following words that you believe best describe you:

Active	Leader	Persistent	Serious	Easy-going	Sensitive	Moody
Ambitious	Excitable	Imaginative	Hard-boiled	Submissive	Impulsive	Introvert
Often blue	Likeable	Self-confident	Nervous	Impatient	Shy	Lonely
Extrovert	Quiet	Self-conscious	Hardworking	Good-natured	Calm	Other:

Have you had any psychotherapy or counseling before?	Yes	No	When?
Have you ever felt people were watching you?	Yes	No	When?
Do people's faces ever seem distorted?	Yes	No	When?
Do you ever have difficulty distinguishing faces?	Yes	No	When?
Are you sometimes unable to judge distance?	Yes	No	When?
Have you ever had hallucinations?	Yes	No	When?
Are you ever afraid of being in vehicles?	Yes	No	When?
Is your hearing exceptionally good?	Yes	No	When?

Approximately how many hours of sleep each night?
Each night when do you: Go to bed Fall asleep Wake up Get out of bed
Describe recent changes in sleep habits:

Health information

Rate your health. Circle one: Very good Good Average Declining Other
Height: Approximate weight (in lbs.) Recent weight changes:
List all important present or past illnesses, injuries, or handicaps:
Do the above limit you in any way? Yes No Please describe:
Date of last medical examination: Report:
Your physician: Address:
Do you drink alcoholic beverages? Yes No When? How much?
Are you presently taking medication? Yes No When? How much?
Have you used drugs for other than medical purposes? Yes No When?
What? Amounts/dosage?

Have you ever had a severe emotional upset? Yes No Outcome?
Are you willing to sign a release of information form so that your counselor may write for social, psychiatric, or medical reports? Yes No

Definitions of items in questionnaire

Abortion—An induced expulsion of a fetus that results in its death.
Abuse—Mistreatment of a human being or animal. May be directed at children or adults. Physical, mental, verbal, sexual, or even spiritual abuse.
Acupuncture—Occult theory of positive/negative forces (yin-yang) or energies to bring body, mind, and spirit into "alignment."
Adultery—Sexual intercourse with someone other than one's spouse, or (for a single person) with a married partner.
Albert Camus—Existential novelist who also adopted nihilistic (see "Nihilism" below) attitudes which are obviously seen in his novels.
Alcohol—The liquid that is the intoxicating element in fermented and distilled liquor. In various forms from beer to hard liquor. Physically and psychologically addictive.
American Indian Rites—Any rituals, chants, dances, etc., performed by American Indians based on their animistic religions.
Amphetamines—A compound or one of its derivatives used especially as a stimulant of the nervous system. "Speed."
Amulet, Charm, Fetish, Good-luck Symbol, Talisman—A magically charged object frequently inscribed with magic formulas or biblical scriptures, having protective powers (demonic) against sickness, other ills, and calamities.
Anorexia—Severe eating disorder wherein the person refrains from or severely limits intake of food. Characterized by rapid weight loss, disruption of menstrual cycle, psychological distortions of physical self-image. Often due to sexual molestation.
Apport Magic—The transference of objects through closed rooms or sealed containers by means of the penetration of matter. Supernatural appearances and disappearances of material images in connection with the activities of a Spiritistic Medium.
Astral or Soul Travel—The practice of sending your soul on an out-of-body journey to distant places to discover hidden things. This is a common practice among more advanced New Age and Eastern religion practitioners and Spiritistic Mediums.
Astrology—An ancient art or pseudoscience "which claims to forecast events on earth, human character and man's fate by observation of the fixed stars and of the sun, moon and planets."
Atheism—The rejection of belief in God.
Automatic Writing—Writing letters, words, or sentences either in a waking state or in a trance, which are considered to be messages from the spirit world. Practices of Hinduism, Buddhism, and others.
Baha'i—Fragmented from Islam. Belief that Moses, Jesus, and Muhammad (founder of Baha'i) were equal prophets. Denies Trinity. Jesus considered only one of nine manifestations of the divine being, not our atonement for sins. Salvation by works only.
Barbiturate—A drug used as a sedative or to induce sleep.
Bestiality—Sexual contact with animals.
Biofeedback—A technique of seeking to control certain emotional states, such as anxiety or depression, by training oneself, with the aid of electronic devices, to modify involuntary functions, such as heartbeat.
Biorhythms—Psychological/scientific study of the cycle of one's physical, emotional, and intellectual levels; often used to make decisions about one's daily activities.
Black Mass—A satanic religious ceremony which honors Satan and denigrates Christ.
Black Panthers—A militant black organization which was very strong in the 1960s and 1970s. Advocated the use of violence to achieve objectives.
Black Witchcraft—Occult and satanic power used for evil purposes, involving spells, incantations, hexes, rituals, voodoo, etc.

Blood Pact—A pledge to Satan signed with blood from the person making the promise.
Buddhism—Originally an Indian religion founded by the Buddha (enlightened one). Belief in Buddha, dharma (doctrine) and sangha (order), karma, and reincarnation. Goal is to achieve astral awareness of self and total being. Follows the Eight-fold Path to overcome negative influences of the world. **Zen Buddhism** is a modem branch which emphasizes meditation to reach intuitive levels of being. Students follow a Zen master. Buddha said, "Work out your own salvation with diligence."
Bulimia—Eating disorder characterized by purging oneself of food by vomiting or using laxatives.
Channeling (Speaking in a trance)—Under the control of demonic power, a Spiritistic medium loses consciousness and deceptively imitates communication with the dead.
Charms—In magic, an incantation or object believed to have special supernatural power.
Children of God—The Family of Love. Established by David Berg. Claims to promote liberty in Christ, such as sexual freedom, substantial alcohol consumption, and other immoralities. Berg is exalted and worshiped. Promotes revolution, hatred of parents and authority, free sex, anti-Semitism, belief in universal salvation, involvement in occultism/spiritism. Teaches Jesus was immoral.
Christian Science—Founded by Mary Baker Eddy based on the teachings of P. P. Quimby. Considers sickness to be an error and truth will cast it out. God is a principle. Claims no power in the blood of Jesus, denies the Trinity and the deity of Christ. Emphasis on the Mind which does all healing and is all. Considers evil, Satan, and death to be errors and lies. Strongly rejects the use of medical expertise and treatments.
Clairvoyance (Second Sight)—The ability to discern objects or information not present to the normal senses.
Cocaine—A drug that is obtained from the leaves of a South American shrub (coca) and can result in severe psychological dependence. Is sometimes used as a local anesthetic.
Color Diagnosis—Colors are symbolic of various meanings. Black: evil, devil, sorrow, darkness; Blue: pornography, sadness, water; Green: nature, soothing, restful, cleansing; Red: blood, sex, energy; White: purity, innocence, sincerity; Yellow: power, glory, wealth, perfection; Orange: adaptability, desanctification; Purple: progress, ambition, power.
Confucianism—A Chinese philosophy organized by Confucius, with a religious base of animism and ancestor worship. Emphasizes ethical choices and man's basic goodness, thus humanitarianism and self-respect are advocated. No discussion of God or heaven.
Crack—A form of cocaine in concentrated form which looks like a white stone. Is smoked in a pipe and is often immediately addictive.
Crystal Ball—A sphere of glass (or crystal) used by a medium to see future events or symbols.
Crystals—Stones cut to display the color spectrum. New Agers believe them to be a source of energy and healing, and they are worn as jewelry or placed in windows for those purposes.
Curses or Spells—Curses or the casting/breaking of spells. Curses may be incurred as a result of our sins or the sins of our forefathers (Deuteronomy 27–28). Spells are produced by occult practitioners by the release of demonic power through hypnosis, magnetism, mesmerism, or some other form of magic resulting in extrasensory influence. Spells stir up love or hate, persecute or defend against enemies, kill humans or animals, and heal or inflict diseases.
Death Wish—A conscious or subconscious desire for someone or oneself to die or be severely injured or hurt.
Deism—A system based on the beliefs that: (1) God created the universe but left it to run on its own; (2) the universe runs on a cause-and-effect basis; (3) man has no essential relation to God; (4) man can determine what God is like by studying the universe.
Déjà Vu—Sensation of having been somewhere before, having already done what one is doing, or knowing someone or something beforehand when it is physically impossible. Used as "evidence" for reincarnation theory. Is usually scientifically explainable.
Diet Pills—Over-the-counter or prescribed medications that reduce the appetite in order for the user to lose weight. Usually high in caffeine, producing nervousness. May be addictive.
Divining Rod—A forked object (hazel tree twig, wire, etc.) used to locate water (water witch-

ing or water smelling), minerals, or other objects.
Dungeons and Dragons—A game where the player assumes the personality of an evil spirit.
ESP—Extrasensory perception. Knowledge or impressions that come from sources beyond one's senses, usually occult sources. *Telepathic* if information comes from other people; *precognitive* if the information is known before the event happens.
EST—Erhard Seminars Training. Founded by Werner Erhard. A conglomeration of mystical and pseudopsychological techniques designed to master and rebuild individuals to adopt Erhard's worldview—that everything is relative and subjective (similar to existentialism, but even more self-centered). Reincarnation and that one is his own god are core beliefs. Also, one determines his own environment and destiny.
Eastern Religions—Any involvement in Hinduism, Confucianism, Buddhism, Taoism, Shintoism, Islam.
Eastern Star—A fraternal organization similar to the Masonic order, but for women only. Rebekah's Lodge is another example. Also heavily involved in esoteric and non-Christian teachings. Very exclusive and racist. Also includes Rainbow Girls.
Eckankar—A pantheistic, New Age religion which uses various meditations in its practices.
Edgar Cayce—A minister involved in "channeling" who provided "cures" for many sick persons. There are many books by and about him.
8-Ball—A "toy" used to divine answers to questions which need only a "yes" or "no" answer.
Elisabeth Kübler-Ross—New Age writer who focuses on concepts of death and dying, particularly on descriptions by those who have had near-death experiences. Her early works on death and dying, regarding the steps of denial, anger, bargaining, and acceptance are sound and useful, however. She has a spirit guide named Salem.
Excursion of the Soul—Soul travel.
Exhibitionism—Sexual gratification from exposing one's genitals or other private parts to adults or children who are involuntary observers.
Fantasies—Imaginings. Inappropriate sexual fantasies would include imagining sex with someone other than one's spouse, imagining watching others involved in a sexual activity, etc.
Fetishes—Objects which become sexually stimulating, using the object as a sexual symbol or association with sexual activity. The object may become part of a series of acts that lead to sexual activity.
Fornication—Premarital sexual intercourse.
Fortunetelling or Divination—The art of forecasting future events and reading human character.
Fraternities/Sororities—Social, honorary, or professional organizations usually identified with colleges. Extensive use of vows, pledges, and secret knowledge and practices.
Friedrich Nietzsche—German writer and nihilistic (see "Nihilism" below) philosopher.
Handwriting Analysis—Study of one's handwriting to detect forgeries, to determine character or aptitude, or to diagnose diseases.
Hare Krishna—Claim Krishna as their personal god. Believe in karma and reincarnation and use mantras (repeated syllables used in meditation). Claim Bhagavad-Gita as scripture. Their aim is to achieve Krishna-consciousness which liberates them from the incarnation cycle. Salvation comes by absolute devotion to Krishna. Men have shaved heads except for one lock of hair. Practice vegetarianism.
Healing Fanaticism—Involvement in "faith healing" cults or with "faith healers" who are involved in sensationalism.
Healing Magic—See Magic: Healing.
Heroin—An addictive narcotic substance made from morphine, a derivative of opium.
Hexes—Spells or curses used in witchcraft, usually to harass or influence a person or persons.
Hinduism—Eastern religion (India). Various sects with beliefs ranging from monism (all is one), pantheism (all is divine), animism (God is all objects), polytheism (many gods), henotheism (worship one god over other gods), monotheism (one god only). Atonement through

karmic reincarnation. Salvation through works and/or self-realization. Bhagavad-Gita and Upanishads among their Vedas (scriptures of wisdom or knowledge).

Homosexuality—Sexual interest in a person of one's own sex. Tends to be used as a term to indicate male-male sexual relationship.

Horoscope—A diagram used by astrologers for divination showing the positions of planets and stars with the signs of the Zodiac; daily fortune interpreted by astrologer.

Humanism—Human reason and scientific innovation are the final authority for life, replacing God. Believe all is matter and energy arranged by chance.

Humanist Manifesto I* and *II—Written in 1933 and 1973, respectively. Says, "No deity will save us; we must save ourselves," and that this is "the complete realization of the human personality."

Hypnosis—An induced state which resembles sleep and in which the subject (person) is responsive to suggestions of the inducer. (Dr. Paul Tournier, a Christian expert, says every form of hypnosis is an invasion into the personality of the person.)

Hypnotism—Being hypnotized by anyone (individually or in a group) for any purpose.

Immanuel Kant—German philosopher who labeled his position as transcendental or critical idealism, a form of existentialism (belief that being is revealed to a person through his presence and participation in a changing and potentially dangerous world). Belief is that one can't know spiritual but only the physical aspects of life. He was a student of Immanuel Swedenborg, an occult practitioner of the mid-1700s. See page 631 of *Handbook of Cults* for more information.

Incest—Sexual intercourse between closely related family members.

Indian Burial Grounds—Areas considered sacred by Indians because the dead of their tribes were placed there. Supposedly protected by spirits.

Iridology or Iris Diagnosis—Receiving treatment for an ailment, from a person not having formal medical training, which is based on the recognition or distinction of diseases by observation of the iris or rainbow membrane of your eye.

Islam—A major world religion based on the messages of Muhammad. A believer is called a Muslim. Allah is their only God and there is no Trinity. Jesus is considered a prophet of Allah, and was not crucified. Belief in works and fate, but no grace. Fasting is a means of atonement. The Qur'an, their scripture, is a collection of revelations from Allah to Muhammad. No way for forgiveness, only revenge. Based on 7th century Arabian culture and moon worship, but is elevated to a worldwide religion status.

Jean-Paul Sartre—A French philosopher who was an existentialist/nihilist and who said, "Man makes himself who he is."

Jeane Dixon—Reading her predictions or belief in her ability to foretell the future.

Jehovah's Witnesses—Founded by Charles Russell in the late 1800s in Pennsylvania. Use their own translation of the Bible (The New World Translation). Deny the doctrine of the Trinity, especially denying the person of the Holy Spirit. See Christ as a created being, who before his incarnation as Jesus was known as Michael. Teach that Christ offers partial atonement for sins, but man must work out the rest. Believe the second coming of Christ has already happened. Deny hell and punishment.

Judo—A Japanese martial art derived from jujitsu that emphasizes quick movements and leverage to throw an opponent and is meant to be defensive rather than offensive. Steeped in Eastern mysticism.

KKK (Ku Klux Klan)—A racist organization which declares itself as a white, Christian organization. Practices violence and persecution of blacks and other minorities (also other groups such as Catholics and Jews).

Ka-Bala, Kabbalah—The perpetuation of ancient and secret religious doctrines from Judaism; a metaphysical system with connections to magic and occult practices. Secret knowledge is given to initiates. Has been available as a game.

Karate—The Japanese art of self-defense in which an attacker is disabled by crippling kicks and punches. Steeped in Eastern mysticism.

Kung Fu—A Chinese art of self-defense resembling karate. Steeped in Eastern mysticism.

LSD—Lysergic acid diethylamide, a crystalline compound that causes psychotic symptoms similar to those of schizophrenia.
Lesbianism—Female-female homosexuality.
Levitation—People or objects are raised up and appear to float in the air or sail through the air, as if held or thrown by an invisible hand.
Life Readings—A projected horoscope of one's life; also, a session with a psychic or channeler to learn of past lives (reincarnation) and future events.
Lust of the Eyes—Wanting what one sees, particularly as it applies to sexual lust (e.g., imagining someone undressed while seeing him/her dressed).
Magic: Black, White, Neutral, Healing—Divinely forbidden arts of bringing about results beyond human power (counterfeits of divine healings or miracles) by recourse to superhuman spirit agencies (Satan and demons). See Deuteronomy 18:9-13 on casting spells.
Marijuana—An intoxicating drug obtained from the hemp plant and smoked in cigarettes.
Marxism—Doctrines originated by Marx and Engels, declared to be a form of materialism. Now mostly social and economic in its theories.
Masochism—The infliction of pain to oneself.
Masonic Order—A fraternal organization (Free Masons) which is characterized by esoteric and non-Christian teachings, particularly at its uppermost levels. Exclusive and tends to be racist. Includes the order of DeMolay for boys.
Masturbation—Manual stimulation of the genital organs exclusive of sexual intercourse.
Materialism—A philosophy or doctrine that whatever exists is either matter or entirely dependent on matter for its existence.
Meditation—An altered state of consciousness obtained via breathing techniques, chanting words or phrases (mantra), or use of yoga or other Eastern religious techniques.
Mental Telepathy—Communication from one mind to another through occult or supernatural channels.
Metaphysics—The part of philosophy concerned with the study of the ultimate causes and the underlying nature of things or knowledge. It attempts to explore the realm of the extrasensory, beyond the world of natural experience.
Monism—belief that all is one.
Mind Sciences—General collection of pseudosciences which allege that the mind is the ultimate source of reality. Any of the teachings which stress the mind-over-matter concept.
Mirror-Mantics—With the help of a magic mirror, crystal ball, rock crystals, or other reflecting object (including the surface of water), a mirror-magician tries to discover things unknown to the person asking him or her questions. Also used for healing and magical persecution. A good example is in the story of Snow White ("Mirror, mirror, on the wall ...").
Mormonism—Church of Jesus Christ of Latter-Day Saints. Established by Joseph Smith Jr. Claims to possess priesthoods of Aaron and Melchizedek and establishes a hierarchy within the church. Teaches more than one god and more than one holy spirit. Remission of sins based on baptism in their church. Denies the virgin birth as taught in scriptures. Salvation by works, baptism, and obedience. Limits the effectiveness of Jesus' blood. Denies his death on the cross, but teaches he died on a stake. Believes that the *Book of Mormon* is equal to the Holy Bible.
Necrophilia—Sexual activity with a corpse.
New Age—A hodgepodge of religious systems brought together which includes some beliefs from Buddhism, Taoism, and Hinduism. neo-paganism, mysticism, Spiritism, Judeo-Christianity. Emphasis on reincarnation, meditation, channeling, astral travel, vegetarianism, monism, and pantheism, etc. Rejects concept of evil, rather interprets as positive/negative energy necessary for balance (yin-yang theory). Jesus was a Christ-spirit and not the only human to be one.
Nicotine—A poisonous substance found in tobacco. Addictive to the user.
Nihilism—Philosophy which denies the reality of existence; therefore, nothing has meaning. Traditional beliefs and values are unfounded; existence is senseless and useless.
Numerology—The study of the occult significance of numbers.

philosophical, and charismatic elements. Reverend Moon's writings are considered the final authority. Sees Jesus as imperfect and Moon as greater than Jesus. Uses brainwashing techniques and arranged marriages.
Unity—Unity Church Universal. A gnostic cult and pantheistic metaphysical system which emphasizes mental healing and reincarnation. Sin, disease, and death can be overcome by right thinking and living. Sees the Bible as one source among many which contain truth. God is a principle or force, not a person, within each person. Denies Jesus as Christ and instead claims all men have the Christ spirit within them.
Vows—A solemn promise one is bound to, i.e., "vow that I will never ..." or "vow that I will not ..."
Voyeurism—The seeking of sexual stimulation by watching something sexually arousing. ("Peeping Tom").
Wart Treatment—Ritualistic in nature, i.e., putting a hair of the afflicted person in a hole made in a tree.
Water Witching or Water Divining or Water Smelling—Locating water using a divining rod or other occult methods.
White Witchcraft—Occult use of power supposedly for good purposes, such as healing, prosperity, fertility, etc.
William James—American psychologist and philosopher who believed in radical empiricism and pragmatism (truth is based on personal experience).
Yoga—A form of meditation from India which emphasizes self-control over one's body and spirit. Usually done in a "Buddha" position (crossed legs).
Zen Meditation—Stresses self-discipline and use of meditation in order to attain direct intuitive insight. Sometimes uses "tantra" which is a sexual mystic experience.
Zodiac Signs—Twelve astrological signs based on a belt of constellations. Person's birth date determines his or her sun sign of the Zodiac (the main sign used).
Zoroastrianism—Persian in origin. Has similarities to Christianity in that it teaches monotheism, the coming of a savior, resurrection of the body, judgment, and eternal life. However, they believe that the spirit of evil is as powerful as their god and cannot be defeated. Their god is not a personal one. Worship is ritual only. Salvation by works. Believe good outweighs bad and that is heaven. There is a lack of righteousness in their god. Practice involves superstition and occultism.

CHRIST IS VICTOR

RELEASE

The undersigned has requested that ______________ and or those persons associated with ____ (him/her) provide Christian care to the undersigned. Not being professionally trained counselors or paid for counseling, but desiring to help the undersigned who has requested help, __________ and those associated with ____ (him/her) will agree to give Christian care within the scope of ___ (his/her) or their ability.

The undersigned hereby releases and forever discharges any claims, causes of action, demands on rights with respect to any care received, or any alleged mis-counseling or advice provided to the undersigned, and the undersigned agrees to hold harmless and to defend ______________ and those associated with ____ (him/her) from the same.

1.		2.
Client name printed	Date	Client name printed
Client signature	Witness	Client signature
Age of Client	Parent/Spouse of Client	Age of Client
Address of Client		Address of Client
Phone Number of Client		Phone Number of Client

This document was developed over time by David Payne of Fort Wayne, In. and Dean Hochstetler, 13684 N. S. R. 19, Nappanee, In. 46550; after June 15, address will be 1752 Waterfall Drive, Nappanee, In. 46550. It has been revised twice in which Ben & Angela Snyder participated.

This document is to be used and duplicated for ministry purposes and not for publication along with someone else's documentary. For publication purposes ask permission. Obviously you need to change names on the release form. I am not responsible for how, where or with whom you use this questionnaire or the results of it's use.

Dean Hochstetler

Parts of an earlier version of this questionnaire were developed by David Payne and Dean Hochstetler. According to Dean, "Persons doing deliverance ministry may copy the materials in Appendix 1D for use in their work, but not for resale or publication. The inventory should be used only by persons who have received training to do deliverance ministry. In the absence of such training, do not photocopy the questionnaire for use in counseling or attempts to do deliverance ministry."

Appendix 2 A prayer for protection[1]

Willard Swartley

Lord God Almighty,
we praise your holy name,
we give you thanks for your great love and power.
You alone are the Sovereign One,
Creator and Ruler of heaven and earth.

Lord Jesus Christ,
You are the Savior of the world;
by your cross and resurrection you have set us free.
Deliver us, Lord, from every evil; grant us peace and wholeness of life.

Lord Jesus,
we rejoice in your victory over Satan and sin;
we rejoice that you share your victory with us.

Lord Jesus,
in your name and with your authority,
we bind and rebuke every evil spirit.
We claim your power, Christ Jesus,
over all demonic oppression.

Lord Jesus,
we bless you that you have overcome the world.
We praise you, Lord, that you have set us free.

Come, Holy Spirit,
fill us with your divine power and love.

May your holy angels, O God,
Protect and keep us now and always.

We pray in Jesus' name. AMEN

1. Adapted from Willard Swartley's prayer for deliverance healing.

Appendix 3 Exorcism 101: What can we learn from the way Jesus cast out demons?[1]

Clinton E. Arnold

The Gerasene demoniac account (Matt. 8:28-34; Mark 5:1-20; Luke 8:26-39) is so alien to our experience that New Testament scholar E. P. Sanders compared it to the strange apocryphal legends about Jesus—such as his turning clay birds into real ones. Although evangelicals would not go that far, we are in a quandary about how to make sense of the passage. Should we negotiate with demons the way Jesus did? If no pigs are available, should we consider casting demons into a tank of goldfish?

Many scholars grapple with questions the text presents: Where did this event happen—Gerasa, Gadara, or somewhere else? How many demoniacs were there? (Matthew says there were two; Luke and Mark say one.) These questions, while important, do not help us draw out implications for our beliefs and practices today.

Part of the difficulty is that we are still not sure if we believe in the reality of demons. Liberal biblical scholarship has often suggested that the text reflects a worldview that has no relevance today, that the demonic was the first century's way of describing modern psychological diagnoses (personalities in dissociative disorder or a projection of the inner self) or political categories (the demons are symbols of an oppressive power structure).

Evangelicals typically affirm the reality of demons but often see the function of the story as magnifying the authority of Jesus. Little attention is given to what we can learn from Jesus about dealing with demons.

Here are some lessons we can learn if we assume the reality of demons as created, personal spirit beings, and see the Gospels as containing lessons on discipleship from Jesus:

- Many demons can inhabit a person simultaneously. A Roman legion normally consisted of 6,000 men.
- Demons can manifest their presence by speaking through a person and, at times, taking control of a person's body. They can even increase a person's normal physical strength.
- Demons can inflict self-injury and injury to others.
- Demons can be transferred from one host to another. They can enter animals and control their bodily movements.
- Demons resist leaving their host. They may plead for their own well-being.

---

1. Clinton E. Arnold is chairman of the department of New Testament at Talbot School of Theology, Biola University, and author of *Three Crucial Questions on Spiritual Warfare.*

There are also some important lessons that we learn in Jesus' response to the demonized man:

- Jesus speaks directly to the evil spirit and asks the demon its name. We can pray and ask God to deliver someone from evil, but it may be necessary to address a spirit directly in the way that Jesus did.
- If the spirits resisted even Jesus before they departed, it should come as no surprise if demons resist our commands.
- Jesus issues a command to the demons based on his own authority. In contrast to exorcists of his day, who used elaborate rituals and incantations, Jesus simply utters the command, "Come out of the man!" Based on our union with Jesus Christ, our being filled with the same Spirit by which he cast out evil spirits (Matt. 12:28; Luke 11:20), and our right to exercise authority in his name over this realm, we can issue a firm and direct command to an intruding spirit with the expectation that it will leave.

Many aspects of the story of the Gerasene demoniac strike us as different from our experience. But could that be our unique problem in North America at this time in history? Christians from other parts of the world—including Africa and Asia—have witnessed these phenomena and engage in struggles with spirits.

Church history contains many accounts of Christians engaging in similar battles. In fact, in his exposition of this passage, the illustrious fourth-century Christian leader John Chrysostom noted, "These things anyone may see happening now also!"

Has the naturalistic worldview that permeates our culture impaired our perception of spiritual reality and hindered our ability to minister to people who are deeply afflicted?

Bibliography for deliverance ministries[1]

Willard M. Swartley

Biblical/theological

Alexander, William Menzies. *Demonic Possession in the New Testament: Its Historical, Medical and Theological Aspects.* Grand Rapids, MI: Baker Books, 1980. First published 1902 by T. & T. Clark.

Arnold, Clinton E. *Ephesians: Power and Magic. The Concept of Power in Ephesians in Light of Its Historical Setting.* Society for New Testament Studies monograph series, no. 63. Cambridge: University of Cambridge Press, 1989.

———. *Powers of Darkness: Principalities and Powers in Paul's Letters.* Downers Grove, IL: InterVarsity Press, 1992.

———. *Three Crucial Questions about Spiritual Warfare.* Grand Rapids, MI: Baker Books, 1997.

Barker, M. J. "Possession and the Occult: A Psychiatrist's View." *Churchman* 94, no. 3 (1980): 246–53.

Bender, Philip D. "The Holy War Trajectory in the Synoptic Gospels and the Pauline Writings." Master's thesis, Associated Mennonite Biblical Seminary, 1987.

Berkhof, Hendrik. *Christ and the Powers.* Translated by John H. Yoder. Scottdale, PA: Herald Press, 1962.

Betz, Hans Dieter, ed. *The Greek Magical Papyri in Translation, Including the Demotic Spells.* Chicago: University of Chicago Press, 1986. Shows the extent to which magical formulae were used to ward off demons in the Hellenistic world.

Böcher, Otto. *Das Neue Testament und die dämonischen Mächte* (Stuttgarten Bibel-Studien 58). Stuttgart: Katholisches Bibelwerk, 1972. Excellent treatment of the New Testament data, including both active and passive resistance to demon power. Accents Jesus' vic-

1. Entries that are not readily accessible or whose relevance is not immediately apparent are annotated.

tory over the demons and the Christian's consequent resources for victory.

Boersma, Hans. *Violence, Hospitality, and the Cross: Reappropriating the Atonement Tradition.* Grand Rapids, MI: Baker Academic, 2004. Takes God's battle against evil as key to understanding the atonement.

Borg, Marcus J. *Jesus, a New Vision: Spirit, Culture, and the Life of Discipleship* (San Francisco: Harper & Row, 1987).

Boyd, Gregory A. *God at War: The Bible and Spiritual Conflict.* Downers Grove, IL: InterVarsity Press, 1997.

———. *Is God to Blame? Moving beyond Pat Answers to the Problem of Evil.* Downers Grove, IL: InterVarsity Press, 2003.

———. *Satan and the Problem of Evil: Constructing a Trinitarian Warfare Theodicy.* Downers Grove, IL: InterVarsity Press, 2001.

Burkholder, Lawrence. "The Theological Foundations of Deliverance Ministry." *Conrad Grebel Review* 19, no, 1 (Winter 2001): 38–68. See also "Response to Lawrence Burkholder," by Dana Keener, 74–78.

Caird, G. B. *Principalities and Powers: A Study in Pauline Theology.* Oxford: Clarendon Press, 1956.

Campenhausen, H. von. "Zur Auslegung von Röm. 13: Die dämonische Deutung des exousia-Begriffs." In *Festschrift für Alfred Bertholet zum 80. Geburtstag,* edited by Walter Baumgartner, Otto Eissfeldt, Karl Elliger, and Leonhard Rost, 97–113. Tübingen: J. C. B. Mohr (P. Siebeck), 1950.

Carr, Wesley. *Angels and Principalities: The Background, Meaning and Development of the Pauline Phrase* hai archai kai hai exousiai. Society for New Testament Studies Monograph Series, no. 42. Cambridge: Cambridge University Press, 1981.

Churchman 94, no. 3 (1980). This issue of this British Anglican journal contains four studies on demons and exorcism from different disciplines of analysis. See entries under Dow, Graham; Dunn, James D. G., and Graham H. Twelftree; Langley, Myrtle S.; and Barker, M. J.

Cosby, Gordon. "A Prayer of a Chance: Taking Evil Seriously, pt. 1: Interview by Jim Wallis." *Sojourners* 15, no. 6 (June 1986), 14–19. Shows the reality of demonic evil in the structural and personal dimensions of people's lives; a practical, pastoral perspective.

Dalton, William J. *Christ's Proclamation to the Spirits: A Study of 1 Peter 3:18–4:6.* Analecta Biblica, no. 23. Rome: Pontifical Biblical Institute, 1965.

Dawn, Marva J. "The Biblical Concept of 'the Principalities and Powers': John Yoder Points to Jacques Ellul." In *The Wisdom of the Cross: Essays in Honor of John Howard Yoder,* edited by Stanley Hauerwas,

Chris K. Huebner, Harry J. Huebner, Mark Thiessen Nation, 168–86. Grand Rapids, MI: Eerdmans, 1999.

———. *Powers, Weakness, and the Tabernacling of God.* Grand Rapids, MI: Eerdmans, 2001.

———. See Ellul, Jacques, and Marva J. Dawn.

Day, Peggy Lynne. *An Adversary in Heaven: Sātān in the Hebrew Bible.* Harvard Semitic Monographs, no. 43. Atlanta: Scholars Press, 1988.

Dibelius, Martin. *Die Geisterwelt im Glauben des Paulus.* Göttingen: Vandenhoeck and Ruprecht, 1909.

Dickason, C. Fred. *Angels: Elect and Evil.* Chicago: Moody Press, 1975.

———. *Demon Possession and the Christian.* Chicago: Moody Press, 1987. Comprehensive treatment of Bible texts and practice.

Dow, Graham. "The Case for the Existence of Demons." *Churchman* 94, no. 3 (1980): 199–208.

Dunn, James D. G. and Graham H. Twelftree. "Demon-Possession and Exorcism in the New Testament." *Churchman* 94, no. 3 (1980): 210–25.

Ellul, Jacques, and Marva J. Dawn. "Chronicle of the Problems of Civilization." In *Sources and Trajectories: Eight Early Articles by Jacques Ellul That Set the Stage,* translated by Marva J. Dawn, 13–28. Grand Rapids, MI: Eerdmans, 1997.

Entz, Loren. "Challenges to Abou's Jesus." *Evangelical Missions Quarterly* 22, no. 1 (January 1986): 46–50. A story testifying to Christ's power over demonic power.

Evans, Craig A. "Inaugurating the Kingdom of God and Defeating the Kingdom of Satan." *Bulletin for Biblical Research* 15, no. 1 (2005): 49–75.

Ferguson, Everett. *Demonology of the Early Christian World.* New York: E. Mellen Press, 1984.

Finger, Thomas N. *Christian Theology: An Eschatological Approach,* vol. 1. Nashville: Thomas Nelson, 1985. Significant in showing the relation of Jesus' ministry and atoning death-resurrection to the demonic in (291–98).

———. *Christian Theology: An Eschatological Approach,* vol. 2. Scottdale, PA: Herald Press, 1989. Significant in showing the relation of sin to the demonic (see chapter 7).

———, and Willard M. Swartley. "Bondage and Deliverance: Biblical and Theological Perspectives." In *Essays on Spiritual Bondage and Deliverance,* edited by Willard M. Swartley, 10–45. Elkhart, IN: Institute of Mennonite Studies, 1988. See also "Response to Thomas Finger and Willard Swartley," by Josephine Massynbaerde Ford, 39–45.

Foerster, W. "δαίμων, δαιμόνιον. In *Theological Dictionary of the New Testament*, edited by Gerhard Kittel and Gerhard Friedrich, translated and edited by Geoffrey W. Bromiley, 2: 1–20. Grand Rapids, MI: Eerdmans, 1964.

Ford, Josephine M. "The Social and Political Implications of the Miraculous in Acts." In *Faces of Renewal: Studies in Honor of Stanley M. Horton Presented on His 70th Birthday*, edited by Paul Elbert. Peabody, MA: Hendrickson Publishers, 1988. Sees Luke's redactional purpose including the use of signs to vindicate Christian faith against rival claims; each manifestation of the Holy Spirit is contrasted to "the false use of supernatural power."

Forsyth, Neil. *The Old Enemy: Satan and the Combat Myth*. Princeton, NJ: Princeton University Press, 1987.

Fretheim, Terence E. "Theological Reflections on the Wrath of God in the Old Testament." *Horizons in Biblical Theology* 24, no. 2 (December 2002): 1–26.

Gager, John G. *Curse Tablets and Binding Spells from the Ancient World*. New York: Oxford University Press, 1992.

Garrett, Susan R. *The Demise of the Devil: Magic and the Demonic in Luke's Writings*. Minneapolis: Fortress Press, 1989.

———. *The Temptations of Jesus in Mark's Gospel*. Grand Rapids, MI: Eerdmans, 1998. Examines all the incidents of "testing" and discusses the issue of the relation between God and Satan in temptation.

Gerlach, Horst. *Of Sin, Bondage, and Deliverance: Application of the Biblical Principle of Cause and Effect*, 2nd ed. Marienheide: Verlag 7000, 1994.

Girard, René. "How Can Satan Cast Out Satan?" In *Biblische Theologie und gesellschaftlicher Wandel: Für Norbert Lohfink SJ*, edited by Georg Braulik, Walter Gross, and Sean E. McEvenue, 125–41. Freiberg: Herder, 1993.

———. *I See Satan Fall Like Lightning*. Maryknoll, NY: Orbis Books, 2001.

Graham, Gordon. *Evil and Christian Ethics*. New Studies in Christian Ethics. Cambridge: Cambridge University Press, 2001. Addresses intersection between moral philosophy and angels and demons.

Gumprecht, Jane D. *New Age Health Care: Holy or Holistic?* Orange, CA: Promise Publishing, 1988.

Hanson, Anthony Tyrrell. *The Wrath of the Lamb*. London: SPCK, 1957.

Harms-Wiebe, Raymond Peter. "A Pauline Power Encounter Response to Umbanda." *Mission Focus* 15, no. 1 (March 1987): 6–10. Important case analysis from mission experience.

Holland, Scott. "The Gospel of Peace and the Violence of God." *Cross Currents* 51, no. 4 (Winter 2002): 470–83. Reprinted in *Seeking Cul-*

tures of Peace: A Peace Church Conversation, edited by Fernando Enns, Scott Holland, and Ann K. Riggs, 132–46. Telford, PA: Cascadia Publishing House, 2004.

Horrobin, Peter J. *Healing through Deliverance: The Biblical Basis*. Chichester, England: Sovereign World, 1991.

Huebner, Harry. "Christian Pacifism and the Character of God." In *The Church as Theological Community: Essays in Honour of David Schroeder*, edited by Harry Huebner, 256–58. Winnipeg: CMBC Publications, 1990.

Hunsinger, George. "The Politics of the Nonviolent God: Reflections on René Girard and Karl Barth." *Scottish Journal of Theology* 51, no. 1 (1998): 61–85.

Kallas, James G. *Jesus and the Power of Satan*. Philadelphia: Westminster Press, 1968.

———. *Revelation: God and Satan in the Apocalypse*. Minneapolis: Augsburg Publishing House, 1973.

———. *The Satanward View: A Study in Pauline Theology*. Philadelphia: Westminster Press, 1966.

———. *The Significance of the Synoptic Miracles*. Greenwich, CT: Seabury Press, 1961.

Kamp, Timothy James. "The Biblical Forms and Elements of Power Encounter." Master's thesis, Columbia Graduate School of Bible and Missions, 1985. Copy in the Associated Mennonite Biblical Seminary library. Presents the broader biblical theological background of the divine encounter with evil, in which exorcism is but one expression.

Keim, Paul. "Is God Nonviolent?" *Conrad Grebel Review* 21, no. 1 (Winter 2003): 25–32.

Kelly, Henry Ansgar. *The Devil at Baptism: Ritual, Theology and Drama*. Ithaca, NY: Cornell University Press, 1985. Provides important documentation of the early and medieval church's understanding of the relation between baptism and exorcism.

Kelsey, Morton T. *Discernment: A Study in Ecstasy and Evil*. New York: Paulist Press, 1978. Chapter 3 deals with the reality of a spiritual world, both angelic and demonic.

Klauck, Hans-Josef. *Magic and Paganism in Early Christianity: The World of the Acts of the Apostles*. Edinburgh: T. & T. Clark, 2000.

Koch, Kurt E. *Demonology: Past and Present*. Grand Rapids, MI: Kregel Publications, 1973.

———. *Occult Bondage and Deliverance: Advice for Counselling the Sick, the Troubled, and the Occultly Oppressed.* Grand Rapids, MI: Kregel Publications, 1971.

Kroker, Valdemar. "Spiritism in Brazil."*Mission Focus* 15, no. 1 (March 1987): 1–6. Important case analysis from mission experience.

Langley, Myrtle S. "Spirit-Possession, Exorcism and Social Context: An Anthropological Perspective with Theological Implications." *Churchman* 94, no. 3 (1980): 225–45.

Langton, Edward. *Essentials of Demonology: A Study of Jewish and Christian Doctrine, Its Origin and Development.* London: Epworth Press, 1949. Most thorough, clear, and reliable in description and correlation between time periods. Most thorough treatment available on the Old Testament.

———. *Good and Evil Spirits: A Study of the Jewish and Christian Doctrine, Its Origin and Development.* London: SPCK, 1942. Another exhaustive study of Jewish and Christian thought.

Lee, Jung Young. "Interpreting the Demonic Powers in Pauline Thought." *Novum Testamentum* 12, no. 1 (1970): 54–69.

Leivestad, Ragnar. *Christ the Conqueror: Ideas of Conflict and Victory in the New Testament*. London: SPCK, 1954.

Lhermitte, Jean. *Diabolical Possession: True and False.* London: Burns & Oats, 1963.

Lind, Millard C. *Yahweh Is a Warrior: The Theology of Warfare in Ancient Israel.* Scottdale, PA: Herald Press, 1980.

Longenecker, Bruce W. "'Until Christ Is Formed in You': Suprahuman Forces and Moral Character in Galatians." *Catholic Biblical Quarterly* 61 (January 1999): 92–108.

Madsen, Catherine. "Notes on God's Violence." *Cross Currents* 51, no. 2 (Summer 2001): 229–56.

Mbon, Friday M. "Deliverance in the Complaint Psalms: Religious Claim or Religious Experience?" *Studies in Biblical Theology* 12, no. 1 (April 1982): 3–15.

McCasland, S. Vernon. *By the Finger of God: Demon Possession and Exorcism in Early Christianity in the Light of Modern Views of Mental Illness.* New York: Macmillan, 1951. Holds that what was understood as demon possession in the first century, modern people would rightly classify and treat as mental illness.

McClain, George. *Claiming All Things for God: Prayer, Discernment, and Ritual for Social Change*. Nashville: Abingdon Press, 1998.

McDonald, Patricia M. *God and Violence: Biblical Resources for Living in a Small World.* Scottdale, PA: Herald Press, 2004.

McGill, Arthur. "Suffering: A Test of Theological Method." In *Disguises of the Demonic: Contemporary Perspectives on the Power of Evil*, edited by Alan M. Olson, 116–33. New York: Association Press, 1975.
———. *Suffering: A Test of Theological Method*. Philadelphia: Westminster Press, 1982.
Mettinger, Tryggve. "Fighting the Powers of Chaos and Hell—Towards the Biblical Portrait of God." *Studia Theologica* 39 (1985): 21–38.
Mission Focus 15, no. 1 (March 1987). Issue includes two important case analyses from mission experience. See entries under Kroker, Valdemar; and Harms-Wiebe, Raymond Peter.
Moreau, A. Scott, Tokunboh Adeyemo, David G. Burnett, Bryant L. Myers, and Hwa Yung, eds. *Deliver Us from Evil: An Uneasy Frontier in Christian Mission*. Monrovia, CA: World Vision International, 2002. Contains twenty-one essays assessing the demonic and exorcism biblically, historically, and theologically; narrative stories; and reflections that relate deliverance ministry to other forms of healing, such as medicine, worship, and folk religions.
Morrison, Clinton D. *The Powers That Be: Earthly Rulers and Demonic Powers in Romans 13:1-7*. Studies in Biblical Theology, no. 29. Naperville, IL: A. R. Allenson, 1960.
O'Brien, Peter T. "Principalities and Powers: Opponents of the Church." In *Biblical Interpretation and the Church: The Problem of Contextualization*, edited by D. A. Carson, 110–50. Nashville: Thomas Nelson, 1984.
Prince, Derek. *War in Heaven: God's Epic Battle with Evil*. Grand Rapids, MI: Chosen Books, 2003.
Schlier, Heinrich. *Principalities and Powers in the New Testament*. Quaestiones disputatae, no. 3. Freiberg: Herder, 1961.
Sears, Robert T. "A Catholic View of Exorcism and Deliverance." In *Essays on Spiritual Bondage and Deliverance*, edited by Willard M. Swartley, 100–114. See also "Response to Robert T. Sears," by Harold E. Bauman, 115–17.
Smith, Jonathan Z. "Towards Interpreting Demonic Powers in Hellenistic and Roman Antiquity." In *Aufstieg und Niedergang der römischen Welt* II 16.1., edited by W. Haase, 425–39. Berlin: Walter de Gruyter, 1978. Description of Hellenistic worldviews, showing levels of intermediaries (charts); includes no theological analysis or comparison to New Testament.
Stevens, Bruce A. "Why Must the Son of Man Suffer: The Divine Warrior in the Gospel of Mark." *Biblische Zeitschrift* 31, no. 1 (1987): 101–110. Shows how the ancient Near Eastern and Old Testament

views of divine warrior climax through transformation in the Son of Man who gives his life a ransom for many.

Suenens, Léon-Joseph. *Renewal and the Powers of Darkness.* Malines Document, no. 4, translated by Olga Prendergast. Ann Arbor, MI: Servant Books, 1983.

Surin, Kenneth. *Theology and the Problem of Evil.* Oxford: Basil Blackwell, 1986.

Swartley, Willard M. "Biblical Faith Confronting Opposing Spiritual Realities." *Direction* 29, no. 2 (Fall 2000): 100–113. See other articles presenting different points of view on spiritual warfare.

———. "Binding the Strong Man: Matthew 12:22-30." *The Mennonite* (18 November 2003), 16–17.

———. "God's Moral Character as the Basis for Human Ethics." In *Covenant of Peace: The Missing Piece in New Testament Theology and Ethics,* 377–98. Grand Rapids, MI: Eerdmans, 2006.

———. *Israel's Scripture Traditions and the Synoptic Gospels: Story Shaping Story.* Peabody, MA: Hendrickson Publishers, 1994. Chapters 3 and 4 treat Jesus' ministry in the Synoptics in relation to exodus and "conquest" traditions, show the transformative aspects of the "warfare" traditions, and examine Jesus' exorcist ministry.

———. "Jesus Christ: Victor over Evil." In *Transforming the Powers: Peace, Justice, and the Domination System,* edited by Ray C. Gingerich and Ted Grimsrud, 96–112. Minneapolis: Fortress Press, 2006.

———. "Paul: Victor over Evil." In *Transforming the Powers: Peace, Justice, and the Domination System,* edited by Ray C. Gingerich and Ted Grimsrud, 222–93. Minneapolis: Fortress Press, 2006.

———. "Resistance and Nonresistance: When and How?" In *Transforming the Powers: Peace, Justice, and the Domination System,* edited by Ray C. Gingerich and Ted Grimsrud, 143–56. Minneapolis: Fortress Press, 2006.

———. ed. *Essays on Spiritual Bondage and Deliverance.* Occasional Papers, no. 11. Elkhart, IN: Institute of Mennonite Studies, 1988.

Twelftree, Graham H. *Christ Triumphant: Exorcism Then and Now.* London: Hodder and Stoughton, 1985.

———. *Jesus the Exorcist: A Contribution to the Study of the Historical Jesus.* Peabody, MA: Hendrickson Publishers, 1993.

———. "The Place of Exorcism in Contemporary Ministry." *St. Mark's Review* 127 (September 1986): 25–39.

Van Dam, Willem Cornelis, with J. ter. Vrugt-Lentz. *Dämonen and Besessene: Die Dämonen in Geschichte und Gegenwart und ihre Austreibung.*

Aschaffenburg: P. Pattloch Verlag, 1970. A comprehensive and careful study.

Van der Loos, Hendrik. *The Miracles of Jesus.* Leiden: E. J. Brill, 1965, 339–78. Good treatment of exorcisms in context of Jesus' miracles as a whole. For similar studies, see "Review" of four books in *Religious Studies Review* 12 (January 1986).

Vogler, Werner. "Dämonen and Exorzismen im Neuen Testament." In *Theologische Versuche* 15, edited by Joachim Rogge and Gottfried Schille, 9–20. Berlin: Evangelische Verlagsanstalt, 1985. Basic overview of New Testament data, concentrating mostly on the Synoptics.

Warner, Timothy. "An Evangelical Position on Bondage and Deliverance." In *Essays on Spiritual Bondage and Deliverance*, edited by Willard M. Swartley, 77–88. See also "Response to Timothy M. Warner," by Gayle Gerber Koontz, 89–99.

———. "Teaching Power Encounter." *Evangelical Missions Quarterly* 22, no. 1 (January 1986): 66–71.

Webber, Robert E. *Celebrating Our Faith: Evangelism through Worship.* San Francisco: Harper & Row, 1986.

Wink, Walter. *Engaging the Powers: Discernment and Resistance in a World of Domination.* Minneapolis: Fortress Press, 1992.

———. *Naming the Powers: The Language of Power in the New Testament.* Philadelphia: Fortress Press, 1984.

———. *Unmasking the Powers: The Invisible Forces That Determine Human Existence.* Philadelphia: Fortress Press, 1986. This volume develops the interrelationship between both spiritual and psychic realities and personal (inner and outer) and corporate systemic "possession." Uses Jungian categories for analysis.

Wright, Nigel. *A Theology of the Dark Side: Putting the Power of Evil in its Place.* Downers Grove, IL: InterVarsity Press, 2003. A revised edition of his earlier British publication, *The Fair Face of Evil.* Combines numerous levels of analysis: worldviews, the problem of evil, discernment, procedures in deliverance ministry, the powers, and other related issues.

Yoder Neufeld, Thomas. "Resistance and Nonresistance: The Two Legs of a Biblical Peace Stance." *Conrad Grebel Review* 21, no. 1 (Winter 2003): 56–81.

Historical

Amorth, Gabriele. *An Exorcist Tells His Story.* Translated by Nicoletta V. MacKenzie. San Francisco: Ignatius Press, 1999. Looks at topic theologically, considering Christ's triumphs (and Satan's?) among the saints historically. Introduces the rite and manner of exorcism from the Roman Catholic perspective, and ends with directive to the Catholic church.

Athanasius. *The Incarnation of the Word of God: Being the Treatise of St Athanasius: De incarnatione Verbi Dei.* Translated by a religious of CSMV. Introduction by C. S. Lewis. New York: Macmillan, 1947. Refers to Christ's victory over the demons as key point in his apologetic, 60–70.

Augustine, Saint, Bishop of Hippo. "The Divination of Demons." Translated by Ruth Wentworth Brown. In *Treatises on Marriage and Other Subjects*, edited by Roy J. Deferrari, 417–40. New York: Fathers of the Church, 1955. Essay is a rebuttal of rational arguments that demons cannot know and predict future events. The essay seems to have been occasioned by widespread reports that demons foretold the destruction of the temple of Serapis to one of the idol worshipers. Augustine contends that demons can foretell those acts they intend to perform. He defends the superiority of prophecy (foretelling the future, including downfall of demons) given by God.

Aulén, Gustaf. *Christus Victor: An Historical Study of the Three Main Types of the Idea of Atonement.* New York: Macmillan, 1961. Holds that the classic view, that of the early church, was Christ's victory over Satan and evil.

Brown, Peter. "Sorcery, Demons and the Rise of Christianity: From Late Antiquity into the Middle Ages." In *Religion and Society in the Age of Saint Augustine,* 118–46. New York: Harper & Row, 1972. Careful analysis of sources; holds that power over demons was a significant element in the authority of the early church leaders and in the growth of the Christian community.

Douglas, Mary, ed. *Purity and Danger: An Analysis of Concepts of Pollution and Taboo.* New York: Praeger, 1966. A major study of taboo.

———. *Witchcraft Confessions and Accusations.* ASA Monographs, no. 9. London: Tavistock Publications, 1970. Eighteen essays representing worldwide settings; analyzes power factors sociologically; some essays relate rise of sorcery to misfortune.

Fairbairn, W. R. D. "The Repression and the Return of Bad Objects (with Special Reference to the 'War Neuroses')." In *Essential Papers on Object Relations,* edited by Peter Buckley. New York: New York University Press, 1986. See 102–107, especially 113–18. Chapters 3, 14, and 18 are also helpful. Used significantly in Gerald Kauffman,

"Representations of God and the Devil: A Psychiatric Perspective from Object Relations Theory" (see below).

Kallas, James. *The Real Satan: From Biblical Times to the Present.* Minneapolis: Augsburg Publishing House, 1975.

Mallow, Vernon R. *The Demonic: A Selected Theological Study; An Examination into the Theology of Edwin Lewis, Karl Barth, and Paul Tillich.* Lanham, MD: University Press of America, 1983. Analyzes the works of three theologians to show alternative models of resolving the problem (origin and nature) of evil.

Martin, Dennis. "Resisting the Devil in the Patristic, Medieval, and Reformation Church." In *Essays on Spiritual Bondage and Deliverance*, edited by Willard M. Swartley, 46–71. See also "Response to Dennis Martin," by Thomas Finger, 72–76.

Martin, Malachi. *Hostage to the Devil: The Possession and Exorcism of Five Living Americans.* New York: Bantam Books, 1977.

Nicodemus of the Holy Mountain, ed. *Unseen Warfare: The Spiritual Combat and Path to Paradise of Lorenzo Scupoli.* Crestwood, NY: St. Vladimir's Seminary Press, 1995.

Nugent, Christopher. *Masks of Satan: The Demonic in History.* London: Sheed and Ward, 1983. Traces the "faces" of evil, the demonic (satanic), in history, including Gilles de Rais (executioner of Joan of Arc), Nietzsche, and Hitler.

Oesterreich, T. K. *Possession, Demonical and Other: Among Primitive Races in Antiquity, the Middle Ages, and Modern Times.* Translated by D. Ibberson. Hyde Park, NY: University Books, 1966. Includes many primary source descriptions of "possessions" across time. First published in 1921, it takes a dim view of exorcism and hopes for more scientific knowledge of parapsychic states.

Russell, Jeffrey Burton. *The Devil: Perceptions of Evil from Antiquity to Primitive Christianity.* Ithaca, NY: Cornell University Press, 1977. Basically descriptive with some critical analysis.

———. *The Prince of Darkness: Radical Evil and the Power of Good in History.* Ithaca, NY: Cornell University Press, 1988.

———. *Satan: The Early Christian Tradition.* Ithaca, NY: Cornell University Press, 1981. Basically descriptive with some critical analysis.

"The Sacrament of Holy Baptism according to the Ancient Rite of the Syrian Orthodox Church of Antioch." Translated by Deacon Murad Saliba Barsom; edited and published by Metropolitan Mar Athanasius Yeshue Samuel, Archbishop of the Syrian Orthodox Church in the USA and Canada. Available from 49 Kipp Avenue, Lodi, NJ

07644. Contains strong exorcist language as part of the baptismal liturgy.

Swartley, Willard M. "Exorcism." In *Mennonite Encyclopedia*, vol. 5, edited by Cornelius J. Dyck and Dennis D. Martin, 285–87. Scottdale, PA: Herald Press, 1990.

———. "Satan." In *Mennonite Encyclopedia*, vol. 5, edited by Cornelius J. Dyck and Dennis D. Martin, 791–94. Scottdale, PA: Herald Press, 1990.

Valantasis, Richard. "Daemons and the Perfecting of the Monk's Body: Monastic Anthropology, Daemonology, and Asceticism." *Semeia* 58 (1992): 45–79. Contends that monks in early centuries regarded demons as seeking to entrap or preclude the monks' successful struggle against the passions of the flesh, thus undermining their ability to live dispassionately, and thus know higher living and perfection of the body. Physical suffering, too, was seen as a testing to the perfecting and transformation of the body in its journey toward the angelic celestial sphere.

Woolley, Reginald Maxwell. *Exorcism and the Healing of the Sick*. London: SPCK, 1932. Traces the practice and liturgies of exorcism from New Testament period through the 5th and 6th centuries in Eastern and Western Christianity.

Social sciences/theology

Augsburger, David W. "Possession, Shamanism, and Healing across Cultures: A Theology of the Demonic." In *Pastoral Counseling across Cultures*. Philadelphia: Westminster John Knox Press, 1995. A phenomenological analysis of "possession" across cultures.

Bowen, Murray. *Family Therapy in Clinical Practice*. Northvale, NJ: J. Aronson, 1978.

Dueck, Alvin. *Between Jerusalem and Athens: Ethical Perspectives on Culture, Religion, and Psychotherapy*. Grand Rapids, MI: Baker Books, 1995.

Friesen, James G., *Uncovering the Mystery of MPD*. San Bernardino, CA: Here's Life Publishers, 1991.

———, E. James Wilder, et al. *The Life Model: Living from the Heart Jesus Gave You: The Essentials of Christian Living,* rev. ed. Van Nuys, CA: Shepherd's House, 2000. Available from CARE Packaging (9731 South M-37, Baldwin, MI 49304; http://www.carepkg.org/).

Goodman, Felicitas D. *How About Demons?: Possession and Exorcism in the Modern World*. Bloomington: Indiana University Press, 1988.

Describes the nature of "possession" cross-culturally, both desired and undesired.

Hall, C. Margaret. *The Bowen Family Theory and Its Uses.* Northvale, NJ: J. Aronson, 1991.

Hammer, Ron. "The Systemic Spirit of the Family: Reframing Intergenerational Sin in a Therapeutic Culture." Chapter 5 in this volume.

Hiebert, Paul G. "The Flaw of the Excluded Middle." In *Anthropological Reflections on Missiological Issues,* ed. Paul G. Hiebert, 189–215. Grand Rapids, MI: Baker Books, 1994. See also "Flaw of the Excluded Middle." In *Evangelical Dictionary of World Missions,* ed. A. Scott Moreau. Grand Rapids, MI: Baker Books, 2000.

———. "Spiritual Warfare and Wordview." Paper presented to Council on International Anabaptist Ministries, 2000.

———. "Worldviews and Why They Matter." Chapter 1 in this volume.

Hollenbach, Paul W. "Jesus, Demoniacs, and Public Authorities: A Socio-Historical Study." *Journal of Academy of Religion* 49 (December 1981): 567–88.

Isaacs, T. Craig. "The Possessive States Disorder: The Diagnosis of Demonic Possession." *Pastoral Psychology* 35, no. 4 (Summer 1987): 263–73. Includes a diagnostic description of possession in categories of DSM-III. Used in Ruth Lesher, "Psychiatry/Psychology: A Response [to Kauffman]."

Kauffman, Gerald. "Representations of God and the Devil: A Psychiatric Perspective from Object Relations Theory." In *Essays on Spiritual Bondage and Deliverance,* edited by Willard M. Swartley, 150–62. See also "Psychiatry/Psychology: A Response [to Gerald Kauffman]," by Ruth Detweiler Lesher, 163–73.

Knight, Cheryl, and Jo M. Getzinger. "Care-Giving: The Cornerstone of Healing: A Manual for Supporting and Caring for Satanic Ritual Abuse Survivors," rev. ed. Baldwin, MI: CARE Packaging, 2001. Most thorough analysis and practical guide in this area. This organization has books and tapes on healing for sexual and ritual abuse, and healing more broadly, including: *Prayers and Scriptures for Survivors of Satanic Ritual Abuse and their Caregivers* (9731 South M-37, Baldwin, MI 49304; http://www.carepkg.org/).

Koch, Kurt E. *Christian Counseling and Occultism: The Christian Counseling of Persons Who Are Psychically Vexed or Ailing because of Involvement in Occultism.* Grand Rapids, MI: Kregel Publications, 1972.

Lesher, Ruth Detweiler. "Psychiatry/Psychology: A Response [to Gerald Kauffman]." In *Essays on Spiritual Bondage and Deliverance*, edited by Willard M. Swartley, 163–73.

Linn, Matthew, and Dennis Linn, eds. *Deliverance Prayer: Experiential, Psychological, and Theological Approaches.* New York: Paulist Press, 1981. Ten essays from a variety of authors and contexts sympathetically exploring and offering guidance on deliverance ministry. Important. Includes two appendices: "Exorcism in Catholic Moral Theology" and "Gender Identity Change in a Transsexual: An Exorcism," the latter a scientifically verified case study.

Loewen, Jacob A. *The Bible in Cross-Cultural Perspective.* Pasadena, CA: William Carey Library, 2000. See especially chapters 11–13, 19–20. See review by Willard M. Swartley in *Direction* 30, no. 2 (Fall 2001): 224–27.

———. "Demon Possession and Exorcism in Africa, in the New Testament and in North America." In *Essays on Spiritual Bondage and Deliverance*, edited by Willard M. Swartley, 118–45. See also "Response to Jacob A. Loewen," by Robert L. Ramseyer, 146–49.

McAll, Kenneth. *A Guide to Healing the Family Tree.* London: Santa Barbara, CA: Queenship Pub., 1996.

———. *Healing the Family Tree.* London: Sheldon Press, 1982.

McGoldrick, Monica, Randy Gerson, and Sylvia Shellenberger. *Genograms: Assessment and Intervention.* New York: W. W. Norton, 1999.

Meissner, W. W. *Psychoanalysis and the Religious Experience.* New Haven: Yale University Press, 1984. Some parts very helpful. Used in Gerald Kauffman, "Representations of God and the Devil: A Psychiatric Perspective from Object Relations Theory" (see above).

Parkin, David J., ed. *The Anthropology of Evil.* Oxford: Basil Blackwell, 1985. Fourteen essays; theological analyses, including theodicy. Includes Buddhist, Hindu, and Muslim views.

Pattison, E. Mansell. "Psychosocial Interpretations of Exorcism." *Journal of Operational Psychiatry* 8, no. 2 (1977): 5–19. Reprinted in *Magic, Witchcraft, and Religion: An Anthropological Study of the Supernatural*, edited by Arthur C. Lehmann and James E. Myers. Palo Alto: Mayfield Publishing Co., 1985. A provocative analysis of the relationship between the role of the exorcist and that of the psychiatrist.

———, and R. M. Wintrob. "Possession and Exorcism in Contemporary America." *Journal of Operational Psychiatry* 12 (1981): 13–20.

Peck, M. Scott. *Glimpses of the Devil: A Psychiatrist's Personal Accounts of Possession, Exorcism, and Redemption.* New York: Free Press, 2005. Narrates the influence of his friendship with Malachi Martin (Leprechaun, as he calls him). A fascinating and insightful account of two exorcisms, with chapters devoted to diagnosis, exorcism, and follow-up for each, and commentary on the first. Part 3 of the book offers Peck's perspectives. Especially good for those who doubt the existence of the devil and demonic infestation.

———. *People of the Lie: The Hope for Healing Human Evil*. New York: Simon and Schuster, 1983. A perspective from psychiatric practice and his relatively new Christian commitment. Helpful for case studies and method employed.

Richards, P. Scott, and Allen E. Bergin. *A Spiritual Strategy for Counseling and Psychotherapy*. Washington DC: American Psychological Association, 1997. Scott and Bergin recognize and address the issue of different worldviews as well as theistic considerations, pertinent to counseling and psychotherapy. Although it does not directly address issues of bondage and deliverance, the book provides space for putting spiritual concerns at the heart of the therapy process.

Robinson, Lillian H., ed. *Psychiatry* and *Religion: Overlapping Concerns.* Washington, DC: American Psychiatric Press, 1986. Some helpful essays.

Sargant, William. *The Mind Possessed: The Physiology of Possession, Mysticism, and Faith Healing.* New York: Penguin, 1975. Recommended by John W. Miller to work at the question of the relation between the mental and the spiritual.

Satir, Virginia. *The New Peoplemaking*. Mountain View, CA: Science and Behavior Books, 1988.

Shuster, Marguerite. *Power, Pathology, Paradox: The Dynamics of Evil and Good.* Grand Rapids, MI: Academie Books, 1987. Helpful insights, including deliverance.

Smith, Edward M. *Healing Life's Deepest Hurts: Let the Light of Christ Dispel the Darkness in Your Soul.* Ventura, CA: Regal Books, 2002.

Smucker, Mervin R. and John A. Hostetler. "The Case of Jane: Psychotherapy and Deliverance." In *Essays on Spiritual Bondage and Deliverance,* edited by Willard M. Swartley, 179–91.

Van Gelder, David W. "A Case of Demon Possession." *The Journal of Pastoral Care* 41, no. 2 (June 1987): 151–61. Case study analysis of a possessed sixteen-year-old boy with theological and psychological interpretations.

Virkler, Henry A., and Mary B. Virkler. "Demonic Involvement in Human Life and Illness." *Journal of Psychology and Theology* 5 (Spring 1977): 95–102.

Ward, Colleen A., and Michael H. Beaubrun. "The Psychodynamics of Demon Possession." *Journal for the Scientific Study of Religion* 19 (June 1980): 201–207.

Experiential

Lacendre, Barney, as told to Owen Salway. *The Bushman and the Spirits: Spiritual Warfare on the Canadian Frontier.* Camp Hill, PA: Horizon Books, 1999.

Michaelsen, Johanna. *The Beautiful Side of Evil.* Eugene, OR: Harvest House Publishers, 1982. Recounts her own story of occult practices in psychic healing and other New Age practices, and her deliverance from these.

Miller, Jane. "Jane Miller's Story and Testimony." In *Essays on Spiritual Bondage and Deliverance*, edited by Willard M. Swartley, 174–78. See also the sociological and clinical psychological analysis of this story by Mervin R. Smucker and John A. Hostetler, "The Case of Jane: Psychotherapy and Deliverance," 179–91.

Pastoral care

Yalom, Irving. Plenary Address. 1st Annual Conference on Personal Meaning, International Network on Personal Meaning. Vancouver, BC, August 2000.

Yoder, Amzie. "Pastoral Care and Exorcism." Paper (undated) written for an Associated Mennonite Biblical Seminary independent study under Marlin Miller. Appendix is "Clergy Manual for Christian Healing," developed by "The International Order of St. Luke the Physician."

Practical/pastoral[2]

Anderson, Neil T. *The Bondage Breaker*. Eugene, OR: Harvest House Publishers, 1990.

———. *Breaking through to Spiritual Maturity: Overcoming the Personal and Spiritual Strongholds That Can Keep You from Experiencing True Freedom in Christ* [Ventura, CA:] Gospel Light, 1992.

———. *Living Free in Christ.* Ventura, CA: Regal Books, 1993.

———. *Setting Your Church Free: A Biblical Plan to Help Your Church.* Ventura, CA: Regal Books, 1994.

———. *Victory over Darkness: Realizing the Power of Your Identity in Christ.* Ventura, CA: Regal Books, 1990.

2. A selection of the many books available on this topic.

Bubeck, Mark I. *The Adversary: The Christian Versus Demon Activity.* Chicago: Moody Press, 1975.

———*Overcoming the Adversary: Warfare Praying against Demon Activity.* Chicago: Moody Press, 1984.

Burkholder, Lawrence E. "Generational Sin and Demonic Oppression." Chapter 3 in this volume.

———. "Let My People Go: A Mennonite Theology of Exorcism." Master's thesis, Conrad Gebel College, 1999.

Daniel, Joshua. *Victory over Demons and Fear.* N.p.: The Laymen's Evangelical Fellowship, International, 1995.

Dickason, C. Fred. *Demon Possession and the Christian.* Chicago: Moody Press, 1987.

Foster, K. Neill, with Paul L. King. *Binding and Loosing: Exercising Authority over the Dark Powers.* Camp Hill, PA: Christian Publications, 1998.

Friesen, Randy. "Spiritual Warfare: Equipping Principles for Disciples of Christ." Unpublished paper, 2000.

Horrobin, Peter. *Healing through Deliverance.* Vol. 2, *The Practical Ministry.* Chichester, England: Sovereign World, 1995.

Jacobs, Cindy. *Deliver Us from Evil.* Ventura, CA: Regal, 2001. Discusses the numerous avenues and manifestations of evil spirit influence and dominion, including the Pokemon and Potter phenomena.

Jacobs, Donald R. *Demons: An Examination of Demons at Work in the World Today.* Scottdale, PA: Herald Press, 1972.

Koch, Kurt E. *Demonology, Past and Present.* Grand Rapids, MI: Kregel Publications, 1973.

———. *Occult Bondage and Deliverance: Advice for Counselling the Sick, the Troubled, and the Occultly Oppressed.* Grand Rapids, MI: Kregel Publications, 1971.

Kremer, Emile. *Eyes Opened to Satan's Subtlety: The Origin, Nature and Consequences of Superstition, Divination and Magic, and the Full Redemption through the Cross.* Belfast: Raven, 1969. Connected to French Mennonite circles, Kremer presents a bold statement that casts the net of satanic influences quite wide, to include, for example, acupuncture.

MacMillan, John A. *The Authority of the Believer.* Camp Hill, PA: Camp Hill Publications, 1997. Important teaching.

MacNutt, Francis. *Deliverance from Evil Spirits: A Practical Manual.* Grand Rapids, MI: Chosen Books, 1995. One of the best.

Mallone, George. *Arming for Spiritual Warfare: How Christians Can Prepare to Fight the Enemy.* Downers Grove, IL: InterVarsity Press, 1990.

McManus, Jim. *The Healing Power of the Sacraments.* Notre Dame, IN: Ave Maria Press, 1984. See especially "A Service of Prayer for Healing" (including exorcism), 85–106.

Miller, Paul M. *The Devil Did* Not *Make Me Do It: A Study in Christian Deliverance.* Scottdale, PA: Herald Press, 1977.

Mitchell, David L. "Deliver Us from Evil." *Alliance Life* (2 March 1988), 6–9.

———. *Liberty in Jesus: Evil Spirits and Exorcism in Biblical Perspective.* Toronto: Clements Pub., 2003.

Murphy, Ed. *The Handbook for Spiritual Warfare.* Nashville: Thomas Nelson, 1992.

Murrell, Conrad. *Practical Demonology: Tactics for Demon Warfare,* 3rd ed. Bentley, LA: Saber Publications, 1982.

Olson, Ken. *Exorcism: Fact or Fiction?* Nashville: Thomas Nelson, 1992.

Penn-Lewis, Jessie. *War on the Saints: A Text Book for Believers on the Work of Deceiving Spirits among the Children of God.* Leicester: Overcomer Office, 1912.

Richards, John. *But Deliver Us from Evil: An Introduction to the Demonic Dimension in Pastoral Care.* New York: Seabury Press, 1974.

Twelftree, Graham H. "The Place of Exorcism in Contemporary Ministry." *St. Mark's Review* 127 (September 1986): 25–39. One of the best short pieces available.

Warner, Timothy M. *Spiritual Warfare: Victory over the Powers of this Dark World.* Wheaton, IL: Crossway Books, 1991.

Winslow, Mark H. "Pastoral Care of the Demonized Person." In *Essays on Spiritual Bondage and Deliverance,* edited by Willard M. Swartley, 192–206. See also "Response to Mark Winslow," by Marcus G. Smucker, 207–210.

Other

Christianity Today (3 September 2001): 46–58. Series of articles on exorcism in America, reflecting different views. Concludes with "Exorcism 101," by Clinton E. Arnold (reprinted as Appendix 3 in this volume).

Engelsviken, Tormod. *Spiritual Conflict in Today's Mission.* Lausanne Occasional Paper 29. N.p.: Lausanne Committee for World Evangelization, 2001.

Kraft, Charles H. *Christianity with Power: Your Worldview and Your Experience of the Supernatural.* Ann Arbor, MI: Vine Books, 1989.

———. *Confronting Powerless Christianity: Evangelicals and the Missing Dimension.* Grand Rapids, MI: Chosen Books, 2002.

Norberg, Tilda, with Robert Webber. *Stretch Out Your Hand: Exploring Healing Prayer.* New York: United Church Press, 1990.

Wagner, C. Peter. *Engaging the Enemy: How to Fight and Defeat Territorial Spirits.* Ventura, CA: Gospel Light Publications, 1995. Similar books published in England (Sovereign) under different titles, but much the same content.

Contributors

Harold E. Bauman is a retired Mennonite pastor and leadership trainer living in Goshen, Indiana. He has served for many years as chair of the Bondage and Deliverance Committee of Indiana-Michigan Mennonite Conference, a support-accountability group for Dean Hochstetler and his deliverance ministry. His interest in the topic came through reading C. S. Lewis's *Screwtape Letters*, participating with Dean in deliverance ministry sessions, and carrying out research on how Satan is working as an angel of light in our culture and the church. He is author of two books, *Grief's Slow Work* and *Presence and Power: The Holy Spirit in Your Life and Church.*

Duane Beck is Pastor of Raleigh Mennonite Church (Raleigh, North Carolina). For more than twenty years (1984–2005), he served as pastor of Belmont Mennonite Church (Elkhart, Indiana). Other community and church involvements have included membership on the Elkhart County Community Corrections Advisory Board, and on the boards of the Violence Intervention Project, the Elkhart City Gun Buy-Back Program, the Hermitage Retreat Center, and the Church Life Commission of Indiana-Michigan Mennonite Conference.

Wesley Bontreger has served as Pastor of Yellow Creek Mennonite Church (Goshen, Indiana) since 1986. He earned a Master of Divinity degree from Fuller Theological Seminary (Pasadena, California) in 1984, and a master's degree in marriage and family counseling, also from Fuller, in 1985.

Lawrence E. Burkholder, M.A., M.T.S., is an ordained Mennonite minister. He is currently researching, writing, and counseling in the area of demonic oppressions and deep-level mind healing. Recent publications include "The Theological Foundations of Deliverance Healing" in *Conrad Grebel Review* (2001) and "What's the 'Subtle Energy' in Energy Healing?" in *Perspectives on Science and Christian Faith* (2003).

Ronald E. Hammer, Ph.D., is Pastor of Counseling Ministries at Lake Avenue Church (Pasadena, California), and an Adjunct Professor in Pastoral Counseling at Fuller Theological Seminary (also in Pasadena). He directs a large, church-based counseling center that trains marriage and family therapists. He also has a deliverance ministry. His approach to the hard cases faced in pastoral ministries is as a marriage and family pastoral counselor and educator.

Paul G. Hiebert is Distinguished Professor of Missions and Anthropology, Trinity International University (Deerfield, Illinois). He served in India as a missionary under the Mennonite Brethren Church. He has taught in the Department of Anthropology at the University of Washington, and in Missions and Anthropology at Fuller Theological Seminary (Pasadena, California). He is author of eight books and many articles on anthropology and missions, including *Incarnational Ministry*, coauthored with his daughter Eloise Hiebert Meneses (1996).

Dean Hochstetler and his wife of fifty-three years, Edna (who died on April 25, 2006), are the parents of four sons, one deceased. Dean worked as a welder and machine shop operator. He writes, "The Lord called me into deliverance ministry in 1962. I have tried to be faithful to that call to free the captives Satan has bound. Christ is victor, winning the victory over Satan and his hosts on the cross. I must apply it."

Loren L. Johns is Academic Dean and Associate Professor of New Testament at Associated Mennonite Biblical Seminary (Elkhart, Indiana). He served as a pastor for eight years in Pennsylvania. He is editor of *Apocalypticism and Millennialism: Shaping a Believers Church Eschatology for the Twenty-First Century,* author of *The Lamb Christology of the Apocalypse of John: An Investigation into Its Origins and Rhetorical Force,* and coeditor with Ted Grimsrud of *Peace and Justice Shall Embrace: Power and Theopolitics in the Bible.*

James R. Krabill is Senior Executive for Global Ministries at Mennonite Mission Network (Elkhart, Indiana). For fourteen years, he served as a teacher of Bible and church history among African-initiated churches in West Africa. His publications include *The Hymnody of the*

Harrist Church among the Dida (1995), *Does Your Church "Smell" Like Mission?* (2003), *Is It Insensitive to Share Your Faith?* (2005), and *Evangelical, Ecumenical, and Anabaptist Missiologies in Conversation* (co-edited with Walter Sawatsky and Charles E. Van Engen, 2006).

J. Nelson Kraybill is President of Associated Mennonite Biblical Seminary (Elkhart, Indiana). He is author of *Imperial Cult and Commerce in John's Apocalypse* (1999) and an occasional contributor to various religious publications. He travels widely to preach and teach on contemporary issues of discipleship and mission.

Arthur McPhee is Associate Professor of Intercultural Studies at Associated Mennonite Biblical Seminary (Elkhart, Indiana), where he teaches courses in the history, theology, and practice of the church in mission. He spent twenty-three years as a church planter, pastor, overseer, and itinerant evangelist before beginning his AMBS assignment in 1997. He is editor of the *Journal of the Academy for Evangelism in Theological Education* and author of a recent biography of J. Waskom Pickett, *The Road to Delhi* (2005), detailing the roots of church growth in India and missionary work in the twilight of the British raj.

Mary H. Schertz is Professor of New Testament at Associated Mennonite Biblical Seminary (Elkhart, Indiana). She is Director of the Institute of Mennonite Studies at AMBS and co-editor of *Vision: A Journal for Church and Theology.* She was recently ordained for the teaching ministry by Central District and Indiana-Michigan Mennonite conferences. She co-authored *Seeing the Text: Exegesis for Students of Greek and Hebrew* with Perry Yoder.

Heidi Siemens-Rhodes, Goshen, Indiana, is a freelance writer and parent of young children. She received her Master of Divinity degree from Associated Mennonite Biblical Seminary in 2005. She has published an article in *The Mennonite* and is currently writing parent/caregiver materials for *Gather 'Round*, a curriculum project of the Church of the Brethren, Mennonite Church Canada, and Mennonite Church USA.

Sheiler Stokes completed her Master of Divinity degree at Associated Mennonite Biblical Seminary (Elkhart, Indiana) in 2004. In addition to her current assignment as Pastor of the Bethel African Methodist

Episcopal Church in Hammond, Indiana, she also serves as a counselor and deliverance minister with the Daughters of Zion.

Willard M. Swartley is Professor Emeritus of New Testament at Associated Mennonite Biblical Seminary (Elkhart, Indiana), where he has also served as Academic Dean and Director of Institute of Mennonite Studies. He has been New Testament editor for the *Believers Church Bible Commentary* series, and his most recent publications include *Covenant of Peace: Restoring the Neglected Peace in New Testament Theology and Ethics* (2005) and two articles in *Transforming the Powers* (2006). As New Testament scholar and occasional minister in deliverance, he organized a 1987 conference at AMBS on deliverance ministry that led to the publication (which he edited) of *Essays on Spiritual Bondage and Deliverance* (1988).

Paul J. Yoder is a Clinical Psychologist at Oaklawn Psychiatric Center, Inc. (Goshen, Indiana), where he serves as Team Leader for the Marilyn Avenue outpatient office and provides clinical leadership and supervision to the interdisciplinary team. He received his doctorate in Clinical Psychology in 1984 from Western Michigan University and has worked as a Health Service Provider in Psychology in Indiana since 1986. He has held adjunct appointments at Goshen College (Goshen, Indiana) and the University of Notre Dame, and has worked extensively with individuals experiencing abuse and other forms of trauma, including a number of people who also sought and benefited from deliverance ministry. Currently, his clinical work focuses primarily on providing consultation services through psychological testing and evaluation.

Index of scriptures and other ancient writings

Index of names and subjects